A History of the Gunpowder Plot; the Conspiracy and its Agents

A HISTORY OF
THE GUNPOWDER PLOT

A HISTORY OF
HE GUNPOWDER PLOT

THE CONSPIRACY AND ITS AGENTS

BY

PHILIP SIDNEY

AUTHOR OF 'THE SIDNEYS OF PENSHURST,' ETC.

WITH 16 FACSIMILE ILLUSTRATIONS FROM OLD PRINTS

GUY FAWKES'S HOUSE LAMBETH.   [*From an old print.*

SECOND EDITION REVISED.

LONDON
THE RELIGIOUS TRACT SOCIETY
BOUVERIE STREET AND 65 ST. PAUL'S CHURCHYARD, E.C.
1905

' Please to remember
 The Fifth of November,
The Gunpowder Treason and Plot ;
 I see no reason
 Why the Gunpowder Treason
Should ever be forgot.'

Execution of the Conspirators
In the Gunpowder Plot in the Year 1606.

monograph dealing with the Plot, except the admirable volume of David Jardine, has the story of the conspiracy ever been told with anything like fidelity; and the ignorance of writers concerning the characters and careers of the conspirators themselves is surprising. It is this common ignorance that has helped Jesuits, and other interested persons, in their task of trying to obscure the history of the Plot as much as possible, with the view of inducing the modern world to call into question the accuracy of the facts, and by hook or by crook trying to clear the name and fame of Father Henry Garnet, and other Jesuit priests, from the imputation of the possession of a guilty knowledge of Robert Catesby's proceedings. All these ingenious attempts, however, to question the authenticity of the traditional story have ignominiously failed; and with more original evidence before us to-day than has hitherto been the case, we are able, at last, to form a fairly comprehensive view of the whole of the conspiracy concocted to blow up the Parliament House, and those in it, with gunpowder, on November 5, 1605, and to plunge the country, at the same time, into a state of civil war.

The vexed question as to Father Garnet's complicity in the Plot—about which a furious controversy has raged ever since the time of his

from that formed by Dr. Gardiner, as it does on one other important matter.

PREFACE

I N these pages I relate the oft-told story of the
famous Gunpowder Plot. For spinning
such a well-known yarn, I offer no apology,
because I hold that there is room for another, and
more thoroughly impartial record than has yet
been drawn up. I have based the foundations of
my work entirely upon the original evidence as
represented in the mass of Domestic and Foreign
State Papers, dealing with the reign of James I.,
preserved at the Public Record Office, and at
the British Museum (Additional MSS. 6178).

The result of my investigations has been, in
my humble opinion, not only to verify the
authenticity of the traditional story of the plot,
but to reveal also that the Government knew full
well of the existence of the conspiracy long before
the receipt of the warning letter by Lord Mounteagle—a transaction which can best be described,
in vulgar parlance, as a put-up job.

In no history of England, with perhaps the
exception of that by Dr. S. R. Gardiner,[1] or in no

[1] But, as will be seen below, my opinion as to the vexed
question of Lord Mounteagle's connection with the plot differs

death—is a matter upon which sufficient light has been shed to enable us, at last, to form an accurate opinion of his conduct. That he was no martyr to the secrecy of the confessional is evident, for it can be shown that he was well aware of the proceedings of the conspirators from sources of information frequently given to him outside the confessional box. Father Garnet's personal character, too, has clearly been overrated by Jesuit writers; and it seems almost incredible that an audacious attempt should have been made to have such a man 'beatified' at Rome.

But Father Henry Garnet's policy, bad though it was, does not merit such severe criticism as that which has been correctly bestowed upon the conduct of his colleague, Father Oswald Greenway. This Jesuit not only knew of the plans of the conspirators, both in and out of the confessional, but actually approved of their proceedings to such an extent that when they were engaged in open rebellion, only two days after the failure of the Plot, he rode over several miles across country to say Mass for them, and afterwards went on a mission to get other Romanists in the neighbourhood to join them. This treasonable act on his part is described by himself, in his account of the Plot, in a manner which is so thoroughly characteristic of the policy of the Jesuit writers to suppress the true story of the parts played by Fathers Garnet and Greenway in Robert Catesby's, and in former conspiracies, that I quote it herewith as an example of the danger of trusting to such biassed authorities :—

'Father Oswald[1] went to assist these gentlemen[2] with the Sacraments of the Church, understanding their danger and their need, and this with evident danger to his own person and life ; and all those gentlemen could have borne witness that he publicly told them how he grieved not so much because of their wretched and shameful plight, and the extremity of their peril, as that by their headlong course they had given the Heretics occasion to slander the whole body of Catholics in the Kingdom, and that he flatly refused to stay in their company, lest the Heretics should be able to calumniate himself and the other Fathers of the Society (of Jesus).'

From a perusal of this craftily worded *apologia* a casual reader might conclude that Greenway had, at the risk of his life, visited his unfortunate co-religionists merely out of a sense of duty in order to administer to them the Sacraments[3] of their religion ; and that, after fulfilling his mission, being disgusted with their conduct, he rode away at once. As a matter of fact, Father Greenway went to Huddington, where the conspirators then lay, at Catesby's express invitation, and with Garnet's permission, as was

[1] Tesimond, *alias* Greenway.

[2] Catesby, Digby, Bates, Rookewood, Percy, Grant, the Winters, and the Wrights.

[3] Apparently, he heard some of their confessions, and gave them absolution, as did Father Hart, S.J., on the day following.

proved by the confession of Bates (one of the conspirators), who had carried a written message to that effect. On his arrival, he was greeted gladly with the welcome, 'Here is a gentleman that will live and die with us!' On his departure, he undertook to do his best to summon some influential Romanists living in the neighbourhood, and in Lancashire, to their aid. Eventually, fully conscious of his guilt, he saved his life by escaping to the Continent.

Finally, with reference to the case of Garnet, I should like to call attention to the two following little-known facts which reveal the low estimation in which this Jesuit was held by the majority of English Roman Catholics in the seventeenth century. During the year 1624, a representative of the English Secular Roman Catholic clergy, whilst staying at Rome, was surprised at reading underneath a portrait of Garnet the words 'Propter fidem Catholicam.' He forthwith complained to the Pope, stating that Garnet was not regarded by English Roman Catholics as a martyr, and the inscription was accordingly changed into 'Ab haereticis occisus.' Later on, in the next reign, Panzani, the Papal agent, finding how unpopular the Jesuits were in London, was instructed by Pope Urban VIII. to assure Charles I. that Garnet would not be 'beatified.'

CONTENTS

LIST OF ILLUSTRATIONS

A HISTORY

OF

THE GUNPOWDER PLOT

CHAPTER I

HOW THE PLOT WAS PLANNED

THE death of Queen Elizabeth was hailed with joy by the English Roman Catholics, nearly all of whom looked forward to obtaining thereafter prompt relief from their persecution at the accession of the King of Scots. Over and over again, exasperated beyond measure by the fines and restrictions to which they were subjected under Walsingham and Burghley, they congratulated themselves that the 'Virgin Queen' could not live for ever, and with her death, no matter who might be her successor, would come the dawn of a brighter day.

It was, therefore, with mingled feelings of intense surprise, anger, and dejection that the Roman Catholics gradually found that the heir of Mary Stuart was not prepared to help them, and that under the tyranny of Burghley's son, Robert Cecil, their burdens, instead of being

lightened, were to be made heavier. Goaded
into fury by the cruelty of the new Government,
many of the Romanists were prepared to have
recourse to arms rather than submit to an increase
of the taxation laid upon them.   But the English
Roman Catholics, as a body, strong as they were
numerically, were divided among themselves.
The majority were not inclined to adopt forcible
measures until the last extremity, and looked with
suspicion upon that section of their co-religionists
who permitted themselves to be guided by the
Jesuits, whose coming into England had already
wrought such terrible harm to the Roman cause
during the last twenty years of Elizabeth's
reign.

It was from the Jesuitical party that the
Gunpowder Plotters sprung.   All of these conspirators were acquainted with Father Henry
Garnet, the Superior of the Jesuits in England,
and with the Jesuit Fathers Oldcorne, Greenway,
Baldwin, and Gerard.   To these Jesuits the
conspirators, before the inception of their plot,
were wont to betake themselves for counsel and
direction in matters political and religious ; and
they became identified in due course with the
schemes concocted by Father Robert Parsons
for obtaining aid from Spain.   Such schemes
were heartily disliked by the great mass of the
Roman Catholic laity, and by the secular priests,
who cordially detested the Jesuits and their
pupils.   The power of the Jesuits was, as the

loyal Romanists but too well perceived, a source of weakness to their cause and a source of strength to the King's Protestant advisers, who cleverly made the methods of the Jesuits an excuse for tarring the whole Roman Catholic body with the same brush, and for bringing all its members into disfavour with the Protestant public, insufficiently well-informed to know how to discriminate between the patriotic priests and the Spanish faction.

Most of the plotters had for a long time prior to the year 1605 been 'marked men' in the eyes of the Government.[1] They had been mixed up in more than one doubtful affair under Elizabeth, and had suffered for their temerity. In the rebellion of Lord Essex, Catesby had been wounded, and both he and his friend Tresham were heavily fined. Percy was also actively engaged in this absurd outbreak, as were Thomas Winter and the Wrights. Guy Faukes and Winter had gone to Spain to solicit military aid on behalf of the restoration of their religion in England. Of Grant, Father John Gerard, in his *Narrative of the Gunpowder Plot*, bears witness that he was in the habit of 'paying pursuivants so well for their labour, not with crowns of gold, but with cracked crowns sometimes, and with dry bones instead of drink and other

---

[1] All of them were probably well known by sight to Cecil's spies, with the exception of Faukes. Bates was, perhaps, too insignificant a person to be suspected.

good cheer, that they durst not visit him any more unless they brought store of help with them.' Even Sir Everard Digby, too, had the courage to tell Lord Salisbury in writing that 'If you think fit to deal severely with the Catholics, within brief space there will be massacres, rebellions, and desperate attempts against the King and the State.'

It is extraordinary, therefore, that men, who must have well known with what dire suspicion they were regarded by the British Government, should have ventured to concoct one of the most audacious conspiracies ever known to the ancient or the modern world.[1]

Another extraordinary circumstance inviting comment is the social position of the conspirators. It would be imagined that men engaged in so desperate a business must have been drawn from the lower and poorer grades of society. Not so with the gunpowder conspirators, who were (with one exception) gentlemen by birth, whilst many of their number were possessed of ample fortunes. It was, indeed, pre-eminently an aristocratic company forming that little band of traitors which aimed at the destruction of the three estates of the Realm. Catesby, Tresham, Percy, Rookewood, Digby, and the Winters, were gentlemen

[1] 'And yet I am assured notwithstandinge, that the best sort of Catholics will bear all their losses with patience. But how these tyrannicall proceedings of such base officers may drive particuler men to desperate attempts, that I can not answer for' (Father Garnet to Father Parsons, Oct. 4, 1605).

illustrious lineage; whilst the elder Winter,
ookewood, Tresham, and Digby, were landed
oprietors of large fortune. Several of them,
oreover, were bound by domestic ties of so
easant a nature as to render life and liberty
pecially dear to them ; and the wives, for instance,
Digby and Rookewood were both young and
ndsome. How these men, therefore, should
sk so much by taking part in such a hare-brained
heme, can only be explained by our knowledge
the terrible persecutions which they underwent
the hands of the Government. Otherwise the
otion that courtly country gentlemen, of ancient
ce and ample fortune, could be induced to play
e part of common cut-throats would seem
credible.

That King James himself had incurred
ersonally the hatred of the conspirators is an
nportant factor. They accused him of treachery,
having promised, in Scotland, to grant a
easure of relief to the Romanists, and of having
eliberately broken his solemn word on succeeding
the English throne, notwithstanding that his
ife, Anne of Denmark, greatly favoured their
ppressed religion.[1] That they had been grossly
eceived, is patent from an examination of the list
names of the county families who hurried to

[1] There seems to be no truth in the Jesuit tradition that
e was actually received into the Church of Rome by Father
ercromby, S J. A Carmelite monk, who knew her well, states
t 'she died outside the true Church, although in heart a

the support of the Scottish King as soon as the breath was out of Elizabeth's body. Among these names we note members of the Romanist families of Tichborne, Throgmorton, Arundell, Stourton, Tresham, Towneley, Talbot, and Howard. Bitter in the extreme was their vexation when they found that the fines for recusancy attained a higher figure early in 1605 than they had ever reached before.

Before entering into a discussion concerning the details connected with the construction of the plot, it will be advisable to furnish some account of the characters and careers of the plotters, whose lives are well worth the attention of the biographer. Of the thirteen men who arranged the plot, Robert Catesby was its founder, and I mention the others in chronological order, *i.e.* in accordance with their probable priority in becoming members of the conspiracy. Thus, after Catesby, I shall deal with them in the following sequence, viz. : Thomas Winter, John Wright, Guy Faukes, Thomas Percy, Christopher Wright, Robert Keyes, Thomas Bates, John Grant, Robert Winter, Ambrose Rookewood, Sir Everard Digby, and Francis Tresham. In narrowing down this list to thirteen,[1] I am referring only to those who are known to have actually joined the plot, and to have taken the necessary oath, and not to other persons who

[1] A significant number, especially as the thirteenth conspirator, the last to join, is generally considered to have been the traitor !

were cognisant of its existence and its plans, such as Lord Mounteagle, Father Greenway, and Father Garnet.

As to the actual oath used by the conspirators, the ensuing is the official and generally received version of the text, but whether it is a strictly accurate version I rather venture to question—

'You shall swear by the Blessed Trinity, and by the Sacrament you now propose to receive never to disclose directly or indirectly, by word or circumstance, the matter that shall be proposed to you to keep secret, nor desist from the execution thereof until the rest shall give you leave.'

From the terms of this oath it is plain, as additional evidence reveals, that it was the custom of the plotters to hear Mass and receive the Host on joining the conspiracy. The officiating priests seem always to have been Jesuits, but the best of them, Father John Gerard,[1] was ignorant of the actual existence of the plot. A man of rather more scrupulous character than his colleagues— Garnet, Hart, Baldwin, Oldcorne, or Greenway— it would not (as Sir Everard Digby confessed) have been prudent to inform him of this diabolical measure's being. In common with others of his Order employed on the English Mission, Father Gerard was a man of many pseudonyms, it not

---

[1] This Father Gerard, S.J., must not be confused with the Father John Gerard, S.J., author of *What was the Gunpowder Plot?* (published in 1897).

being safe for a Jesuit priest to travel in England under his own name.   He was known under the various *aliases* of "Brooke,' 'Lee,' and 'Staunton.' Father Edward Oldcorne was generally called 'Mr. Hall,' but he also answered to the names of 'Vincent,' and 'Parker,' when occasion served. Father Garnet was often known as 'Mr. Farmer,' under which name he is mentioned in the corre- spondence of Sir Everard Digby, but he also made use of ' Darcey,' ' Roberts,' ' Meaze,' ' Phillips,' and ' Walley.'   His adoption of the name of 'Farmer' has become famous owing to Shakespeare's refer- ence to him in *Macbeth* (act ii., scene 2).

Porter. ' Here's a knocking, indeed! If a man were porter of Hell-Gate, he should have old turning the key.   Knock, knock, knock! Who's there, i' the name of Beelzebub?—Here's a "far- mer," that hanged himself on the expectation of plenty.—Come in time; have napkins enow about you; here you'll sweat for it.   Knock, knock! Who's there, i' the other devil's name? Faith, here's an "equivocator," that could swear in both the scales against either scale; who committed treason enough for God's sake, yet could not equivocate to Heaven.—O, come in, Equivocator. Knock, knock, knock!   Who's there?—Faith, here's an English tailor come hither, for stealing out of a French hose.'

These references to the 'farmer,' and the 'equivocator,' are so pointed as to direct the reader's attention to Garnet, who in his notorious

use of the Jesuit doctrine of 'mental reservation'—
or, in plainer language, deliberate lying—reduced
equivocation to a fine art.   Moreover, Shakespeare seems to have been at work on *Macbeth*
at about the time of Garnet's trial and execution.
His colleague, Father Oswald Greenway, was
principally known to his friends as 'Tesmond,' or
'Tesimond,' although we find him often called
'Greenwell,' and sometimes 'Beaumont.'

From a review, therefore, of the circumstances
as to how the plot was laid, it will be seen that
the chief conspirators[1] engaged in the Powder
Treason were gentlemen by birth and education,
were bigoted and maltreated members of the
Roman Catholic faith, were nearly all men of
wealth,[2] were on terms of close acquaintance with
the English priests of the Society of Jesus, and
had been (for the most part) engaged in the Essex
rebellion.   They do not seem to have consorted,
so far as we know, with the secular priests, the
Jesuit's rivals, but associated constantly with
Father Garnet and his colleagues.   In the confessions of both Faukes and Winter, no name of
any secular priest is mentioned, but the statement
is recorded that (after the associates had taken 'a
solemne oathe and vowe) they did receave the
Sacrament of Gerrard the Jesuit . . . but he
(Faukes) saith that Gerrard was not acquainted

[1] With the exception of the unfortunate Bates, Catesby's devoted
servant.

[2] Even Catesby, who had spent his own fortune, was heir to
property reversionary on the death of his mother, Lady Catesby.

with their purpose.'[1] But, although no secular
priest is found to have been concerned in the
Gunpowder Treason, only two years before (1603),
an English secular priest, named William Watson,
was one of the principal leaders in the conspiracy
known as the 'Bye Plot.' This William Watson
was greatly disliked by the Jesuits,[2] who hastened
(on hearing of Watson's part in it) to give information to the Government, with the result that
the plotter's plans were frustrated, and Watson,
with others, executed. Information of Watson's
proceedings was given to Cecil by both Garnet
and Gerard, who sought thereby to gain for their
own society a better reputation in the eyes of the
Government, and, at the same time, to deal a
deadly blow at a strong party of their coreligionists
that supported those of the secular clergy,[3] who
resisted the assumption of ecclesiastical authority
in England by the Society of Jesus.[4] The two

[1] It is possible, but not probable, that Gerard was not the
officiating priest, and that Faukes mistook another person for him.

[2] Watson was a man of very unprepossessing appearance. He
squinted, and (according to a Jesuit) to such an extent that 'he
looked nine ways at once.'

[3] There were two secular priests leaders in the 'Bye,' viz. :
Watson and Clarke. Of these, Watson had been completely
deceived by James's false promises to help the Romanists on his
accession to the English throne. He was strongly opposed to the
Jesuits' schemes for demanding the intervention of Spain

[4] 'Poor William Watson was betrayed by the man (Garnet) who,
two years after, would not betray his friend Catesby; and the
virulent opponent (Watson) of the Jesuits expiated his treason on
the scaffold. To put this matter of Watson's fate in its true light,
we must remember that almost at the very time Garnet informed
against Watson, the Jesuits were participating in Wright's and

plots, the 'Bye' and the 'Gunpowder,' are worth comparing with regard to the positions of the Romanists involved in them, for in the first we find none of the pro-Jesuit faction implicated, whilst in the second we find none but pro-Jesuits represented.

Faukes's attempt to induce Philip to invade England' (Father Taunton's *History of the Jesuits in England*).

CHAPTER II

THE name of Guy Faukes has, by reason of the all-important part assigned to him in the conspiracy, become so closely identified with its formation and its direction, that we are apt nowadays to look upon him as the principal plotter, whereas he was really subordinate to another, whose name is not quite so familiar to the man in the street. This, the principal plotter, was Robert Catesby. It was, *ab initio*, Catesby's Conspiracy. It was from his restless brain that the idea of blowing up the House of Peers with gunpowder first emanated.[1]

Having laid his plans, Catesby looked round for confederates, upon whom he could implicitly rely, to help him ; and, on his solicitation, they one after another promised to assist and obey him. He was from beginning to end the captain of the band. He hesitated at nothing to gain his own ends. Promises that he could not fulfil, statements about others that could not be true,

---

[1] I cannot agree with the theory that it was Thomas Winter who put the idea into Catesby's head. All the original evidence tends to prove that Catesby was the founder of the plot.

he made from time to time with the utmost assurance. A lie was not a lie, if told in the interests of the plot. 'Master Catesby,' complained Garnet, 'did me much wrong, and hath confessed that he told them he asked me a question in Queen Elizabeth's time of the powder action, and that I said it was lawful. All which is most untrue. He did it to draw in others.' A man of great courage and resolution, he possessed a wonderful power of making his friends both like and serve him. Utterly unscrupulous, he never repented. He never lost heart, and was always sanguine of success. Even when all was up, and his atrocious plans had utterly failed, he died game, falling in a desperate fight with the officers of the Crown, being determined that he should never be taken alive. He expired from his severe wounds, with his arms clasped round the feet of an image of the Virgin, to whose protection he had commended his sinful soul.

Robert Catesby was, as we have just shown, well fitted to be the promoter of so desperate an enterprise ; and, indeed, he actually laid his plans with consummate skill; but his chances of success, nevertheless, were handicapped by one serious drawback, for the dangerous importance of which he did not make sufficient allowance, and on which I have already commented, namely, that in the ever open eyes of the Government he was a 'marked man.' His movements, as a fact, were watched constantly by spies, and a careful note was made of his associates. Such a man, therefore, was placed in a position of the greatest difficulty when called upon to move about London and the country on errands (in company with notorious recusants) requiring the utmost secrecy.

Born at Lapworth, Warwickshire, in the year 1573, Catesby was the only surviving son of Sir William Catesby by his wife Anne, a daughter of Sir Robert Throckmorton. He was lineally descended from the famous councillor (William Catesby) of King Richard III., whose name lives in the popular couplet—

> 'The catte,[1] the ratte,[2] and Lovell[3] our dogge,
> Ruleth all England under a hogge.'[4]

'Mr. Catesby,' says Father Gerard in his *Narrative of the Gunpowder Plot*, 'was a gentleman of an ancient and great family in England, whose chief estate and dwelling was in Warwickshire, though his ancestors had much living in other shires also. Some of his ancestors had borne great sway in England. But commonly the greatest men are not the best. Some others hath been of great esteem for virtue, as, namely, one knight of his house was commonly known and called in all the country "good Sir William," of whom this memorable thing is recorded: that "when he had lived so

[1] Catesby. He was captured at Bosworth, and beheaded.
[2] Sir Richard Ratcliffe, killed at Bosworth.
[3] Lord Lovel.
[4] Richard III.

long in the fear of God and works of charity, one
time as he was walking in the fields, his good
Angel appeared and showed him the anatomy of
a dead man and willed him to prepare him, for he
should die by such a time.   The good knight,
presently accepting of the message willingly,
recommended himself with a fervent prayer unto
our Blessed Lady in that place, and then went
home and settled all his business both towards
God and the world, and died at his time
appointed."

' Mr. Catesby's estate in his father's time was
great, above three thousand pounds[1] a year,
which now were worth much more ; but Sir
William Catesby, his father, being a Catholic,
and often in prison for his faith, suffered many
losses, and much impaired his estate.   This son
of his, when he came to the living, was very wild,
and as he kept company with the best noblemen
of the land, so he spent much above his rate and
so wasted also good part of his living.   Some
four or five years before Queen Elizabeth died,
he was reclaimed from his wild courses.'

After his failure in the Essex rebellion,[2]
Robert Catesby seems to have become a bigoted
Romanist, and 'grew to be very much respected
by the graver sort of Catholics, and of Priests,

---

[1] Equivalent to nearly thirty thousand pounds of our present
money.
[2] Catesby was for a short time up at Oxford, at Gloucester Hall
(Worcester College).

and of Religious also.' In personal appearance he was, according to Father Gerard, 'above two yards high, and though slender, yet so well-proportioned to his height as any man one should see.' He married, in 1592, Catherine Leigh, of Stoneleigh, Warwickshire, but she died soon after the birth of their second son.[1]

From the date of his release from prison (after being fined three thousand pounds), in 1601, and after his recovery from his wounds incurred when fighting on behalf of Lord Essex, Catesby, compelled to sell his beautiful estate of Castleton to satisfy the fine, lived chiefly with his mother, at Ashby St. Legers,[2] Northamptonshire, till the year 1604, when he and Thomas Winter set about their preparations for the manufacture of the Gunpowder Plot. In asking others to help him, Catesby avowed that he was actuated only by the holiest and noblest motives in the cause of the Catholic religion ; and, at his death, he ' protested solemnly it was only for the honour of the Cross, and the exaltation of that Faith which honoured the Cross, and for the saving of their souls in the same Faith, that had moved him to undertake the business ; and sith he saw it was not God's will it should succeed in that manner they intended, or at that time, he was

[1] The memoir of Catesby in Gillow's *Bibliographical Dictionary of English Catholics* is very inadequate. It ignores his marriage altogether, and the date of his birth.

[2] The house still stands, with an oak-panelled chamber over a gateway called 'the Plot Room.'

willing and ready to give his life for the same
cause' (Gerard).

Such was the resolute Robert Catesby, the
captain of the conspirators, a man of supreme
courage, of winning manners and address, of
great presence of mind in the hour of peril, of
blind devotion to his religion, and of remarkable
personal strength; but cruel and vindictive at
heart, and one who was too sanguine of success to
make sufficient allowance for the serious nature
and number of the impediments which stood in his
way.[1]   He was, as became a chief of such a
company, both an excellent swordsman and a
good rider.   By all the conspirators he seems
to have been regarded with feelings of real
affection, as he was by several of their intimates
who were not actually engaged in the plot.
Sir Everard Digby, at his trial, testified that no
other man but Catesby could have obtained
sufficient influence over him to have induced him
to join such a conspiracy.   Thomas Winter,
Grant, Rookewood, and the Wrights, were all
warmly attached to Catesby, and Rookewood,
during his captivity, spoke of him in much the
same terms as did Digby.   Bates was his servant.
Lord Mounteagle was an old friend.   The
ruffianly Sir Edward Baynham, who was directed
to inform the Pope of the plot (if it succeeded),
acted under Catesby's orders.   Guy Faukes he

[1] One great mistake of his was the low estimate he formed of
the craft and ability of Cecil.

summoned 'out of Flanders.' That Catesby, villain though he was, must still have been a person of a peculiarly fascinating disposition to have wielded so subtle an influence over his fellows cannot be doubted. In point of energy and administrative ability, he stood out head and shoulders above all his confederates, and he alone amongst them was competent to put the conspiracy into working order, and to keep it so long strictly secret from the Government of King James I. Cruel and clever as he was, he ruled those under him with a hand of iron, and never hesitated to commit an act of violence, or concoct a lie, in order to place his subordinates more completely under his sway. He was, in truth, the most unscrupulous and reckless member of all the wicked men who had joined together to attempt a crime that ranks in the annals of history as the most atrocious ever devised by human brains.

THO^s WINTER

Executed in the Year 1606

for the GUNPOWDER PLOT.

Pub. May 1794 by I. Caulfield

CHAPTER III

THOMAS WINTER was a Worcestershire gentleman of good family. He was a relative of several of his fellow-conspirators, namely Catesby, Tresham, Grant, and of course (his elder brother) Robert Winter.[1] He was also a connection by marriage of Lord Mounteagle, to whom the famous letter, revealing the conspiracy, was addressed. He was, so Father Gerard boasts, 'a reasonable good scholar, and able to talk in many matters of learning, but especially in philosophy or histories very well and judicially. He could speak both Latin, Italian, Spanish, and French. He was of mean stature, but strong and comely, and very valiant. He was very devout, and zealous in his faith.'

If this account be true—and there is some reason to doubt it—Winter must have been the most accomplished and capable of all the conspirators, for he was also a soldier as well as a

---

[1] Percy and the Wrights were relations, so that the plot was quite a family affair. Moreover, Catesby's son married one of Percy's daughters.

C

scholar.   Born in 1572, he spent the greater
part of the last decade of Elizabeth's reign on the
Continent, in fighting first in the Netherlands,
curiously enough, against Spain, that very power
to which most of his friends at home looked for
aid.   Before the period of the Essex rebellion,
however, he had changed his politics,[1] and we
find him employed on a secret mission to Madrid,
asking military aid from the Spanish King on
behalf of the English Romanists, so soon as
Elizabeth should die, or even beforehand.   On
this mission he seems to have been sent by the
advice and direction of Lord Mounteagle and
Father Garnet, after they and he had consulted
with Tresham and Catesby.   He was accompanied on his journey by Father Greenway, and
on arriving at Madrid, placed his negotiations
with the Spanish Government under the direction
of Father Cresswell, S.J.   On returning from
this mission, he went across (in 1604) to Brussells,
on a continuation of his errand, to visit the
Constable of Castille, 'whose answer was,' according to Gerard, ' that he had strict command from
his Majesty of Spain to all good offices for the
Catholics; and for his own part, he thought
himself bound in conscience so to do, and that
no good occasion should be omitted.   Thus
much the Constable promised at that time. . . .
But it is an easy matter to satisfy with hopes of

[1] And, I believe, his religion. He was a convert to Roman
Catholicism.

future favours, when he that receives the promises shall not be present to see the performance'!

If Winter failed to obtain the aid sought, his second mission, at any rate, was not absolutely fruitless, for he brought back with him the famous Guy Faukes,[1] with whom he was soon after engaged in planning the great conspiracy.

John Wright, the next of the conspirators on our list, did not possess the remarkable abilities of Catesby and Winter, but he seems to have been well suited to the rough part he played, for he won Catesby's special approval ' for his valour and secrecy in carriage of any business.' Born in December, 1567, Wright was the eldest son of a Yorkshire gentleman. He was a good swordsman, and very fond of using that weapon when a young man, being rude and quick-tempered, though slow of speech. According to Gerard, he became a Romanist about 1600–01, but it is far more likely that he had been received into the Church some five years or more before that date, for as far back as 1596 he had awakened the suspicions of the Government by his close friendship with Catesby. This latter fact is especially interesting, since it shows that the leaders among the conspirators had been practically

---

[1] Guy Faukes, whose reputation as a soldier was well-known, was specially invited to England by Thomas Winter to join in 'a' conspiracy, the real nature of which was not revealed to him till after meeting Catesby. Winter may have been the first to propose hatching 'a' plot, but Catesby nevertheless was the first to invent the Gunpowder Treason.

kept under close supervision by the English Government for nine years before the fatal fifth of November, 1605.   What chance of success, therefore, had a plot, under the direction of such men, escaping detection for any length of time?

Before closing this brief introduction to our account of this pair of conspirators, I may as well mention that, for the sake of simplicity, I have spelled the name 'Winter' as it is now generally written.   Thomas Winter, however, seems almost invariably to have written his name 'Wintour,' as signed by him in letters (still extant) addressed to his confederate Grant, in January and February,[1] 1605; in a letter written in the Tower,[1] November, 25, 1605; and in documents signed by him in the Tower,[1] in December–January, 1605–06. In his confession, preserved at Hatfield, dated November 25, 1605, he (suspiciously) signs himself 'Winter,' a point which has been the subject of much criticism and controversy.   Into a close examination of this discrepancy I will not now enter, but I would take this opportunity of remarking that, judging by the almost illegible manner in which is written the date '25 · 9bor,'[2] in the Hatfield MS., it is not certain whether, in any event, the confession belongs to the date assigned to it.[3]   His brother, and co-conspirator,

[1] These are preserved in the Record Office.
[2] In the copy made by Lord Salisbury's secretary, Munck, at the Record Office, the deed is dated November 23.
[3] Vide 'Thomas Winter's Confession,' by the Rev. John Gerard, S.J. (London, 1898).

JOHN WRIGHT,

One of the Conspirators in the Gunpowder Plot.

London. Published April 23.d 1794. by J. Herbert. No 6 Pall Mall.

wrote his name ' Wintour.'   But too much stress
must not be laid on this discrepancy in the
spelling, when we consider the various forms used
by some of Winter's most celebrated contemporaries.   Shakespeare, for instance, wrote his
name ' Shakspere ' and ' Shakespeare,'[1] and
Sir Philip Sidney has left behind him letters
wherein his name is signed by him in three
different ways.

[1] If not also ' Shakspeare.'

CHAPTER IV

GUY FAUKES AND THOMAS PERCY

THE name of the terrible hero of the popular feast, the anniversary of which is celebrated every fifth day of November, has been, and is written in several different forms. Sometimes it is written Fawkes,[1] with the Christian name as 'Guido.' Father Gerard calls him 'Mr. Guido Falks,' and by other writers he has been dubbed 'Guye Faux.' But, as he himself signed himself Faukes in his confession, I prefer to use that form of the surname, irrespective of the question as to his proper Christian name.[2]

Guy Faukes was born early in the year 1570, at York, where he was christened. He came of a race of ecclesiastical lawyers, which was also connected with one or two well-known county families. His parents were (from the accession of Elizabeth, at any rate) Protestants, and he was their only son. His father, Edward Faukes, Registrar of the Consistory Court, dying in 1578, his mother

[1] He is called Guy Fawkes in the official account of his trial.

[2] In an indenture, dated 1592, picked up for a few shillings in a second-hand book shop in London (1901), his name is signed in neat letters 'Guye Faukes.' After being tortured in the Tower, he wrote 'Guido,' but fainted before he could complete his surname.

38

GUY FAWKES.

Executed in the Year 1606.

for the GUNPOWDER PLOT.

Published April 1.1794 by t.Bœufield.

married a gentleman named Baynbridge, of Scotton, in the county. Guy seems to have been on good terms with his step-father, who is reported to have persuaded him to become a Roman Catholic; but soon after his coming of age he left Yorkshire for the Continent, and enlisted in the service of the Spaniards occupying Flanders.

His service in the Spanish army readily enough explains the change of his Christian name into 'Guido.' Whilst in Spain, Gerard reports that those who knew him 'affirm that as he did bear office in the camp under the English coronell[1] on the Catholic side, so he was a man every way deserving it whilst he stayed there, both for devotion more than is ordinarily found in soldiers, and especially for his skill in martial affairs and great valour, for which he was there much esteemed.' In 1595 he assisted in the capture of Calais. In 1604, at Catesby's request, he came over to England, Catesby and Winter having 'desired one out of Flanders to be their assistant.'[2] He had, before returning to England, been employed as a delegate of the Jesuits in the mission to obtain aid from Spain after the death of Queen-Elizabeth.[3]

[1] Sir William Stanley.

[2] As Faukes had left his native county for the Continent when quite a young man, he was consequently not known in London, and it was this reason that induced Catesby to allot to him the task of looking after the powder and of firing the mine, for his presence at Westminster would not attract attention.

[3] Guy Faukes was a tall and wiry man, with light brown hair, and auburn beard.

Thomas Percy was a person of great influence among the conspirators.   Indeed, next to Catesby, he was the most important amongst them.   He seems to have acted as Catesby's first lieutenant. It was he who hired within the precincts of Westminster Palace the little dwelling next to the Parliament House, and it was he who obtained possession of the cellar where the powder was eventually deposited.   As soon as the news of the abortive plot leaked out in London on November 5, it was described at first as Percy's conspiracy.   In common with so many of his confederates, Percy was of illustrious lineage, being a scion of the great feudal house of Northumberland.[1]   He was an agent of the head of the family, Henry, the ninth Earl, the political enemy of Robert Cecil, Earl of Salisbury. Authorities differ, however, as to how nearly he was related to the Earl.   The nearness of the connection has, I think, been exaggerated, and (so far as I can ascertain) he was no nearer in blood to the head of his house than a third or fourth cousin.   With this opinion Father Gerard agrees, when he declares that ' he was not very near in blood, although they called him cousin.'

' For the most part of his youth,' relates Father Gerard, 'he had been very wild more than ordinary, and much given to fighting ; so much that it was noted in him and in Mr. John Wright (whose

---

[1] From which the present Duke of Northumberland is only descended in the female line.

sister he afterwards married) that if they heard
of any man in the country to be esteemed more
valiant and resolute than others, one or the other
of them would surely have picked a quarrel
against him and fought with him. . . . He had
a great wit and a very good delivery of his mind,
and so was able to speak as well as most in the
things wherein he had experience.   He was tall,
and of a very comely face and fashion ; of age
near fifty,[1] as I take it, for his head and beard
was much changed white.'   Brought up a Protestant, it is difficult to ascertain when he became
a Catholic, according, vaguely, to Gerard ' about
the time of Essex his enterprise.'[2]   Of Lord
Essex he was a warm admirer and devoted
adherent.   On the accession of James I., whom
he had visited (shortly before Elizabeth's death)
with a view to getting from him a promise to help
the English Catholics—a promise which that
monarch deliberately broke—Percy became quite
a turbulent recusant, in spite of his position in
his patron's household.   By Lord Northumberland
he was enrolled one of the royal gentlemen
pensioners, but without swearing the usual oath.
On the discovery of the plot, the crafty and
unscrupulous Cecil seized upon this trivial circumstance as an excuse to imprison the innocent

[1] He could not have been so old as this at the date of his death,
for he was born at Beverley in 1559.

[2] I should, however, be inclined to assign an earlier date than
that, by some five years or so.

Northumberland in the Tower, and to impose upon him a colossal fine.

In private life, Thomas Percy was a very different person from the bigoted Guy Faukes. Percy was not even commonly honest in money matters, for he had robbed his patron over the collection of the Alnwick rents, and projected doing so again on a larger scale as a means of raising money for the plot. He was a restless, aggressive, inquisitive man, and led such a prominent public life that he was ill-fitted to play the part of a conspirator. To have refrained from receiving him as a member of the gang would, however, have been almost as dangerous as to admit him; for he would have racked his brains to find out what was going on, and his jealousy might have procured Catesby's arrest. Boisterous,[1] arrogant, and domineering, his movements were of the most rapid and untiring description; nothing stood in his way when he wanted anything done, or when he wanted to take a journey; one day he was in London dining with his patron, another he was *en route*, post haste, for Alnwick. That he stood high in his patron's favour is evident, otherwise his unpopularity, and indifferent character would have prevented him retaining his appointments under the northern Earl, whose retainers complained of Percy's harsh treatment of them; whilst on the eve of the Gunpowder

[1] Father Greenway, however, asserts that 'notwithstanding the boldness of his character, his manners were gentle and quiet.'

MAGNI BRITANNIÆ REGIS STIPENDIARIVS ANNO 1605 THOMAS PERSI NOBILIS ANGLVS

Hæc est vera & prima originalis editio Thoæ Perci

Os vultumꝗ vides Thomæ cognomine Percy
Inter Britannos nobiles notiſſimi
Queis rebus ꝓcœat ambitione superstitiofo
Animo nefandam machinatur dum necem
Regi Reginæ Ordinibus diſrenditur, ipsum
Deo volente ſcelus in auctorem vuiƚ

A Thomas ſcloⸯp̃ Captivorunt
B Tho. Ichrofe Regi adduxt
C Tho Perfi in Arce fugit
D Thomas Perfi fagittatus mortuus

Published July 20, 1801. by Wᵐ Richardson, York House, 31. Strand

Plot, he confessed that it was unsafe for him to visit Yorkshire, in which county he was accused of being ' the chief pillar of papistry.' By many of his co-religionists, too, he was distrusted, for they accused him of having deceived them in regard to his secret mission to the Scottish Court. But, to give Percy his due, it is certain that he was himself grossly deceived by James, who was, at that period, ready to promise anything to anybody, if by so doing he could strengthen his prospects of succession to the coveted throne of England.[1]

Such a man as Percy, therefore, it is not difficult to comprehend, was a fertile source of danger to his confederates. He was too busy and officious a person to play a part requiring the most consummate care and skill. He was, nevertheless, of great use to Catesby for three important reasons, namely, that by his position under Lord Northumberland he was enabled to hear what was doing at Court; by his ingenuity, possession of the vault was obtained underneath the Parliament House; and, by his position as Northumberland's agent, he was enabled to purloin large sums of money for feeding the conspiracy.

In the proclamation for his arrest, now

---

[1] The conduct of James in this matter is one of the most scandalous incidents in his scandalous life. His denial that he ever promised to help the Catholics was deliberate perjury. This treachery of James seems to have driven Percy to desperation, and to have strengthened his alliance with the Jesuit faction in consequence.

preserved at the Public Record Office, Thomas Percy is described as 'a tall man with a great broad beard, a good face, and hair, mingled with white hairs, but the head more white than his beard. He stoopeth somewhat in the shoulders, is well coloured in the face, long-footed, and small-legged.' To sum up his character briefly, he was a gentleman by birth and education, who had gradually become a rogue.

CHAPTER V

O F Christopher Wright,[1] the younger brother of John, little is known. He was actively engaged in the Essex revolt, and had been employed as one of the delegates of the Jesuits on the mission to the Court of Spain. Born in 1571, he seems to have followed faithfully the fortunes of his brother, but to have taken no leading part in the management of the plot. Robert Keyes, his friend, deserves greater attention, for he commenced life as a pronounced Protestant, his father being a Protestant clergyman, but his mother, a daughter of Sir Robert Tyrwhit, came of a Roman Catholic stock, though whether she influenced him in his resolve to become a Roman Catholic we are not told. He married Christiana, widow of Thomas Groome, and for some years previous to the plot lived with her at Turvey, Bedfordshire, the residence of Lord Mordaunt, a Catholic peer, to whose children his wife was governess.

---

[1] 'And soone after we tooke another unto us, Christopher Wright, having sworn him also, and taken the Sacrament for secrecie' (Guy Faukes's confession).

45

According to Father Gerard, he was ' a grave
and sober man, and of great wit and sufficiency,
as I have heard divers say that were well
acquainted with him. His virtue and valour
were the chiefest things wherein they could
expect assistance from him; for, otherwise, his
means were not great.' His close intimacy with
Lord Mordaunt brought that nobleman into grave
trouble with the Government, in the same way
as Percy's intimacy with his patron, Northumberland, proved injurious to that unsuspecting peer.
At Catesby's advice, the care of the conspirators'
house at Lambeth, used by them as their London
rendezvous, was entrusted to the stern and
undaunted Keyes.

Thomas Bates sprang from a very different
origin to that of his confederates. He was an
old and faithful servant of Catesby, to whom he
was devotedly attached, and by whom he was
admitted into the confederacy, as one upon whom
his powerful master could implicitly rely, and
who would prove useful as a humble messenger
carrying despatches between the conspirators.
According to Sir Edward Coke (Attorney-
General), who appeared for the Crown at
Bates's trial, the manner of his reception was
as follows—

'Concerning Thomas Bates, who was
Catesby's man, as he was wound into this treason
by his master, so was he resolved, when he
doubted of the lawfulness thereof, by the doctrine

THO.ˢ BATES

Executed in the Year 1606

for the GUNPOWDER PLOT.

of the Jesuits.[1]   For the manner, it was after this sort : Catesby, noting that his man observ'd him extraordinarily, as suspecting somewhat of that which he the said Catesby went about, called him to him at his lodging in Puddle-wharf; and in the presence of Thomas Winter, asked him what he thought the business was they went about, for that he of late had so suspiciously and strangely marked them.

'Bates answer'd, that he thought they went about some dangerous matter, whatsoever the particulars were : whereupon they asked him again what he thought the business might be; and he answered that he thought they intended some dangerous matter about the Parliament House, because he had been sent to get a lodging near unto that place.

'Then did they make the said Bates take an oath to be secret in the action ; which being taken by them, they then told him it was true, that they were to execute a great matter; namely, to lay powder the Parliament House to blow it up.'

John Grant was a Warwickshire gentleman, his residence, Norbrook, being situated between Warwick and Stratford.   He was well descended, and connected with several old families in the shires of Warwick and Worcester.   Although, according to Father Greenway, of a taciturn disposition, he was of a very fierce and mettlesome temper, in the opinion of Gerard.   He was implicated with

---

[1] Of this there is no proof beyond Coke's *ipse dixit.* He confessed, however, his intentions, and the design of the plotters, to Greenway.

his friends in the Essex rebellion.[1] Catesby's chief
reason for enrolling him as a member of the
confederacy, seems to have been the fact that
Grant's 'walled and moated' residence would
provide an excellent rendezvous for those of the
conspirators who were to foment an armed rising
in the Midlands. He was a devout Roman
Catholic, and on the eve of his death on the
scaffold expressed himself 'convinced that our
project was so far from being sinful,' as to afford
an 'expiation for all sins committed by me.'

Robert Winter was the elder brother of
Thomas, and was a son-in-law of John Talbot,[2]
of Grafton, an influential Roman Catholic, whom
the conspirators tried vainly to inveigle into
connection with their schemes. He possessed
the estate of Huddington, in Worcestershire.[3]
On first hearing of the plot, he expressed his
utmost detestation of the whole concern ; but
eventually permitted himself to be cajoled into
joining it, probably at the instance of his brother,
His heart, however, was never in the business,
and he took no part in stowing away the gunpowder. He deserted Catesby before the last
stand was made at Holbeach. He cannot be
considered in the light of either an active or a
willing conspirator, but merely of one who

[1] It is an extraordinary fact that so many of the plotters should
have been engaged in the Essex rebellion. This suggests that
Lord Essex was secretly supported by the Jesuits.

[2] Heir to the Earldom of Shrewsbury.

[3] Near Droitwich.

possessed an unhappy, though guilty, knowledge
of what was going on; for which, after months of
terrible anxiety and perplexity, he paid forfeit
with his life.

Ambrose Rookewood, born in 1577, was a
gentleman of an old family in Suffolk, which had
remained Roman Catholic, notwithstanding the
severe persecution of several of its members under
Elizabeth.[1]   Ambrose was the eldest son of his
parents, and on his father's death, some four
years before he joined the conspiracy, he became
a very wealthy man.   His wife, Elizabeth
Tyrwhit, was a lady of remarkable beauty, by
whom he had two sons.   The elder of these
quickly wiped out the stain on his name incurred
by his father's treason, and was actually knighted
by the very king whom his father had plotted to
destroy.   Rookewood was drawn into the plot by
Catesby, whom he 'loved and respected as his
own life,' and who overcame his scruples against
'taking away so much blood,' by assuring him,
so it seems, that the scheme had received the
approbation of his confessor.   In Rookewood's
stable at Coldham Hall there was an especially
fine stud of horses, and Catesby, who selected
each conspirator for some particular reason likely
to prove advantageous to his plans, had long
coveted Rookewood's steeds.

---

[1] Elizabeth's ingratitude to Edward Rookewood was base in the
extreme.   After being entertained by him at great expense, she
sent him to prison, and ruined him with fines.

D

That a man like Ambrose Rookewood should have been seduced into treason is to be deplored. Notwithstanding his persecution at the hands of the Government, he was so circumstanced as to have every expectation, after his father's death, of leading a happy and prosperous life. Married to a young and lovely wife, the bearer of an ancient name, the owner of a great estate, the father of two little boys, it was especially hard that, listening to the temptations of scoundrels, he should be hanged, like a common cutthroat or pickpocket, at the early age of twenty-eight.[1]

Unlike the majority of his confederates, Ambrose Rookewood, it should be noticed, had always been, without a break, a staunch and bigoted Roman Catholic, from his childhood upwards; and, in order to obtain a thorough religious education, in strict accordance with the tenets of his faith, he had been educated abroad. Ambrose Rookewood's mansion, Coldham Hall, still stands, and is remarkable for containing at least three secret chambers, which are reputed to have been used to conceal priests.   In the curious chapel, Mass was undoubtedly said in the presence of Ambrose and his family. On joining the conspiracy, Rookewood moved, in order to be within closer reach of the abodes of Catesby, Tresham, Digby, Grant, and the Winters, from

[1] Ambrose, nevertheless, was not the last conspirator of his ill-fated race, as his great-grandson, also named Ambrose, was hanged in 1696, for being concerned in a plot to kill or kidnap King William III.

Suffolk into Warwickshire, where he rented Clopton Hall. This house, besides 'priest's holes,' had a little chapel hidden in the roof, where Mass was often said.[1]

[1] For an account of the houses (containing secret chambers) used by the conspirators, the reader cannot do better than refer to Mr Allan Fea's superb book, *Secret Chambers and Hiding-Places*. (Mr. Fea is, however, in error when he states that Sir Everard Digby was captured at Holbeach.)

CHAPTER VI

O F the thirteen misguided men who are known for certain to have been engaged in hatching the Gunpowder Plot, and who duly paid forfeit for their treason with their lives, the fate of one only has excited an expression of regret from his posterity. This one is Sir Everard Digby, Kt., who is popularly considered to have been cajoled into joining the conspiracy, after much hesitation, against his better and prior inclinations to have nothing whatever to do with the deed; and who is also commonly supposed to have been far superior to his confederates in regard to his general character and abilities. Why Sir Everard should thus alone of the plotters have been singled out for so much commiseration, it is difficult for anybody who has tested the traditional story of the plot, as recorded in the original papers at the Record Office,[1] to comprehend. This popular sympathy seems, in fact, to have been accorded to Sir Everard on the absurdly mistaken grounds that

[1] The State Paper, or Public Record Office, Chancery Lane, London.

he was really the only gentleman in regard to birth, education, and behaviour amongst his fellow-conspirators. This theory is, of course, fallacious in the extreme. He was not, for instance, so well educated or so learned as Thomas Winter; he was no better born than at least six of his confederates—nor, indeed, so nobly descended as was Percy; in private life he was not more esteemed or better behaved than Ambrose Rookewood; whilst, as a soldier, his reputation was not equal to that of Guido Faukes, nor, as a swordsman, either to that of Catesby or John Wright. In a word, he is erroneously supposed by the man in the street to have been the only respectable person engaged in the Gunpowder Plot.

Sympathy, too, resting on no surer foundations, and wholly undeserved, has been extended towards him on account of his youth, and his being the husband of a young and comely wife,[1] by whom he was the father of two children.[2] Here again, however, his supporters are at fault. If, indeed, he was so fortunate as to be a happy husband and a proud father, so also was Rookewood, whose wife was, from all accounts, a lady of far greater personal attractions, and more highly accomplished than was Lady Digby. As to the question of his age, his admirers have been

[1] Lady Digby's chief attraction seems to have been her wealth.
[2] Both of whom were knighted, and one (Sir Kenelm) became particularly famous.

deceived by not knowing the date of his birth;[1] for he was not, as his principal biographer tells us, barely four and twenty[2] years of age at the period of the exposure of the plot, but over three years older.   Had he been barely twenty-four, he must have been married at the early age of fourteen.   But, in making these just comments, it must not be thought that the writer is influenced by any desire to make an attack on the character of Sir Everard, for such is not the case.   His sole aim in offering these criticisms is merely to show that Digby, whatever virtues he may or may not have possessed, is not entitled to receive any more sympathy from historians than, say, either Robert Winter, Thomas Winter, or Ambrose Rookewood.

Sir Everard Digby was born and brought up a Protestant, but reverted to the faith of his ancestors when still in his 'teens.   He became a favourite of Queen Elizabeth, and cut quite a gay figure at Court, his ample fortune, no doubt, being a considerable factor in his advancement.   His father, a gentleman owning estates in Rutlandshire, had died when Everard was quite a child, and had left him a ward of the Crown, or, as we should now term it, a ward of Chancery.   In 1596, he married Mary Mulshol, a notable heiress, of Goathurst, Bucks.   In 1603, he was knighted by James I.

---

[1] He was born in 1578.

[2] The usually correct Jardine, author of *A Narrative of the Gunpowder Plot*, states that he was born in 1581.

at Belvoir Castle.[1] His joining Catesby in such a scheme as the Gunpowder Treason was, therefore, an act of base ingratitude to a monarch who had been specially kind to him, notwithstanding his known recusancy. On arranging to join the conspirators, Sir Everard Digby contributed a sum, equivalent in our money to nearly ten thousand pounds, to its support.

Sir Everard Digby was, in personal appearance, tall and handsome, and of pleasing manners and address. He is described as having been ' extremely modest,' and as ' one of the finest gentlemen in England.' Father Gerard, his intimate friend, mentions that ' in gifts of mind he excelled much more than in his natural parts; although in those also it were hard to find so many in one man in such a measure. But of wisdom he had an extraordinary talent, such a judicial wit, and so well able to discern and discourse of any matter, as truly as I have heard many say they have not seen the like of a young man, and that his carriage and manner of discourse were more like to a grave Councillor of State than to a gallant of the Court.' This panegyric from a Jesuit[2] source must, however, be accepted *cum grano*, and I agree with Jardine that neither his conduct nor his letters justify this applause.' He appears, indeed, to have been a mere tool in

---

[1] As was his friend, Oliver Manners, the date of whose knighthood, as given in Burke's *Peerage*, being quite incorrect.

[2] By another Jesuit he is referred to as possessing ' a profound judgment, and a great and brilliant understanding.'

the hands of the Jesuits, as the references to
' Mr. Farmer' (Father Garnet), contained in his
correspondence, plainly prove. It was, however,
by the inspiring influence of Catesby that his
scruples were gradually overcome, and he consented to aid the conspirators.

Francis Tresham, who, according to the generally received tradition, was the Judas among the
conspirators, came from a race as wealthy and
illustrious as did Digby. Related to the Winters,
Catesby, and Lord Mounteagle, he was the eldest
son of Sir Thomas Tresham, of Rushton, Northamptonshire, a most ardent Roman Catholic, but
chiefly famous for his building operations, an
interesting account of which has been compiled
in an illustrated treatise by Mr. Alfred Gotch.[1]
One of the most remarkable results of his enterprise was the erection of a triangular lodge at
Rushton, built in honour of the Trinity, the idea
running through the whole building being Three ;[2]
e.g. the shape of the house being an equilateral
triangle, thirty-three feet in length, the floors
three in number, three windows on each floor,
triangular rooms, etc.

Sir Thomas Tresham was, altogether, a far
better man than his disreputable son Francis,
who was ever of a crafty and treacherous nature,
a fact well known to the arch-villain, Catesby,
who, however, was tempted, at the eleventh

[1] Published in Northampton, and in London, 1883.
[2] *Vide* Mr. Gotch's plans.

hour, to induce Tresham to join the plot for the sake of his wealth, his father having died some two months before the eventful 'fifth.' Tresham was born in 1568, educated at Gloucester Hall, Oxford, and was involved in the Essex rebellion; for which outbreak he, or rather his father, was very heavily fined, and he narrowly escaped execution. He had also been a party to Father Garnet's schemes for obtaining aid from Spain. How this miserable Tresham was the traitor who was mainly instrumental in betraying his fellow-plotters, I shall show later.

Finally, it will be seen from a perusal of the above memoirs of the different conspirators that Robert Catesby, unscrupulous and cunning as he was, selected each one to join the plot on account of his possession of some special quality that would particularly forward the interests of the great design. Thus, Thomas Winter was chosen on account of his skill in languages and his soldierly reputation; Ambrose Rookewood on account of his wealth and his horses; the dishonest Percy on account of his position at Court and in Lord Northumberland's household; Sir Everard Digby on account of his social position, his friendship with influential Roman Catholics, and his wealth; Grant on account of his fortified house; Robert Winter on account of his wealth and his relationship to the Talbots, and other great Roman Catholic families; Faukes on account of his military qualities, and his face being unknown to the government spies ; the turbulent Keyes, and the Wrights on account of their being stout-hearted and handy men ; the humble Bates on account of his being a useful and trustworthy messenger ; and Francis Tresham for the sake of his cash.

Drawn by *James Clay, 1808.* Engraved by J. Rock.

Interior of the Crypt called the POWDER PLOT CELLAR beneath the old Palace of Westminster,

looking toward Charing Cross — Taken down in June 1858.

"WILKINSON'S LONDINA ILLUSTRATA."

CHAPTER VII

THE vague idea of blowing up the Parliament House seems first to have occurred to Robert Catesby 'about Lent,' 1604. Roughly speaking, we may date the genesis of the actual conspiracy from about April in that year. The first formal meeting of the first three plotters (Catesby, Thomas Winter, and John Wright) was held at a house in Lambeth, probably at the end of March, 1604. Later on, after the admission of Percy into the conspiracy, an empty house, with a small garden, adjoining the Palace of Westminster, was hired.[1] This house rented in Thomas Percy's[2] name, was leased by one Ferris as tenant to Mr. Whyneard, keeper of the King's wardrobe. From a cellar in this house the conspirators began digging a mine through the wall into the contiguous vault beneath the Parliament House; but the work proved much harder than anticipated, as the wall was

---

[1] The decision to hire this abode was taken at a meeting of five of the conspirators held in a lonely house near Clement's Inn.

[2] 'Thomas Percy hired a house at Westminster' (Confession of Guy Faukes).

immensely thick—nearly nine feet—and all the rubbish displaced in the course of their toil had to be buried in the garden.   Whilst still at work (December, 1604), they suddenly learned that the meeting of Parliament had been prorogued from February 7 (1605), till October 3.   The conspirators, therefore, took a holiday until after Christmas before resuming their labours.

On returning to their terrible task, at the end of January, they found it no easier, till one day they were startled by hearing a peculiar rumbling noise over their heads.   Guy Faukes, who acted as a kind of outside porter and sentinel to the confederates engaged within, on inquiry found that the tenant of the cellar almost above them was removing, and his coals (in which he traded) were being taken away.   Percy immediately hired this cellar on the pretext that he wished to use it to keep fuel and coal.   He had not taken it more than a month before he and his confederates, having abandoned their now unnecessary task of digging through the lower wall, had succeeded in depositing within it barrels of gunpowder [1] brought by water from their house at Lambeth.   In May (1605) they separated, to meet once more in London at the end of September.

On their reunion, they received important

---

[1] Accounts differ as to the number of the barrels, and consequently as to the total weight.   The barrels were not, however, all of the same size.   We may, I think, put the total at not less than two tons' weight of powder.

news, the meeting of Parliament had again been postponed—until November 5.   This further prorogation considerably alarmed the con- spirators, many of whom were very superstitious, and looked upon this delay as ominous of ill-fortune. At first, they thought their project had been discovered ; but inquiries set on foot by Thomas Winter, Percy, and Faukes, failed to elicit that the Government had obtained any inkling of their scheme. This last prorogation, brief though it was, proved the death-warrant of all the con- spirators. Catesby, in need of more money for the furtherance of the rebellion in the Midlands, which was to take place after the explosion had occurred at Westminster, required more recruits. He, accordingly, selected two, Sir Everard Digby and Francis Tresham.   Both responded to his appeals for money, and to Digby, who was never prominently engaged in the Westminster part of the plot, was deputed the office of heading the rebellion in the Midlands.

In selecting Tresham as the last, but not the least, of his recruits, Catesby made his first—and fatal—mistake since he had started the conspiracy. He was well aware of Tresham's unreliable character, but the wealth that this new recruit could pour into the coffers of the conspiracy was too strong an inducement to be ignored. More- over, Tresham's friendship with several of the Roman Catholic Peers, two of whom had married his sisters, was a circumstance that Catesby thought would prove useful to the furtherance of the plotter's plans. As a matter of fact, these very reasons which led Catesby to act against his better judgment, in selecting Francis Tresham, were actually to prove the very reasons which induced Tresham to turn traitor. Tresham had too recently become a rich man to view with equanimity the prospect of spending much of his wealth on promoting so wild a scheme; whilst his relationship to Lords Mounteagle and Stourton only made him dangerously anxious to give them a hint of what was going on, in order to save their lives. Catesby soon discovered that he had committed a grievous error in choosing Francis Tresham, and is said to have bitterly repented of having let him into the secret of the plot. He caused a watch to be set upon Tresham's movements.

Meanwhile, by the middle of October, the plans of the conspirators were definitely decided upon. These plans comprised the following schemes :—

1. To blow up the King, Queen, Prince of Wales, Lords, and Commons, at Westminster, by means of the mine to be fired by Guy Faukes.

2. An attempt to capture the Duke of York (Prince Charles).[1]

3. An insurrection in the Midlands ; the meeting-place to be Dunsmoor Heath, whence

[1] Afterwards Charles I. The conspirators presumed that his elder brother Henry, Prince of Wales, would perish in the explosion.

Digby and his friends were to proceed to Lord
Harrington's house, Combe Abbey, near Coventry,
there

4. To seize the person of the little Princess
Elizabeth (afterwards Queen of Bohemia), who, in
the event of Prince Charles remaining untaken,
was to be proclaimed Queen.

5. To seize the person of the baby Princess
Mary.

Such had been the preparations made when
Catesby, Faukes, and Thomas Winter met on,
or about October 18, at a house called White
Webbs, on the confines of Enfield Chase; a
building, the secret chambers of which had more
than once afforded harbours of refuge to priests,
and especially Jesuits.[1]   Here they received a
visit from Tresham, who appeared to be very much
dejected.   He came to them, he said, in a state
of terrible anxiety.   His conscience pricked him.
He could obtain no peace of mind until they had
satisfied him on one important point, namely,
might he be allowed to warn his two noble relatives
of their danger?

Although greatly alarmed at Tresham's behaviour, Catesby proceeded to discuss the matter
calmly with him; but as to what was the exact
substance of the evasive reply he gave Tresham
we are still in the dark.   But that Tresham had
already approached Lord Mounteagle on the
subject of the conspiracy before going to White

---

[1] Garnet had been there very recently.

Webbs seems clear.   That Catesby suspected
this, but refrained from letting Tresham know
that he suspected this, seems equally plain.

Francis Tresham's object in going to White
Webbs was, without doubt, if possible to upset
the plot altogether.   He advised Catesby to
postpone the explosion to a later date, and to seek
safety by flying, *pro tem.*, with the majority of
the conspirators to Flanders, Faukes alone to
remain in London.   As to the balance of the
money which he had promised to provide, he
asserted that it could not be raised by the fifth of
the forthcoming month.

It is surprising, considering how thoroughly
alarmed were Catesby and his friends at White
Webbs at Tresham's fears and excuses, that they
should have let Tresham go back unharmed to
London.   They seem, at first, to have meditated
capturing him, and keeping him under lock and
key till after the fifth.   It would have been better
had they elected to do so; but they probably were
afraid that his visit to White Webbs was already
known to Mounteagle, or even to Cecil himself,
and that his non-return to London, in consequence might give the alarm.

On leaving White Webbs, the evil results of
Tresham's visit were quickly forthcoming; for on
Saturday, October 26, occurred an event which
will ever remain memorable in our history, since
it sealed the fate of all the conspirators engaged
in the Gunpowder Plot.   This event was the

receipt of the famous anonymous letter sent to Lord Mounteagle.

But, before dealing with the delivery of this mysterious letter, it should be stated that Mounteagle was by no means the only one of the Roman Catholic peers whom one or more of the conspirators had hoped to save, by giving them a hint to prevent their attending the opening of Parliament. The greater number of the conspirators were naturally unwilling to sacrifice members of their own communion, and were most desirous of giving them warning, without, at the same time, divulging the existence of the conspiracy. Among the names which have come down to us of the peers, Roman Catholic or Protestant, whom certain of the plotters implored Robert Catesby to save, we find mentioned the Earl of Northumberland, Lord Arundel, Lord Mordaunt, Viscount Montague, Lord Vaux, and Lord Stourton. At first, Catesby held out against giving any one of these a hint; declaring that the necessity of secrecy demanded that even the innocent should perish with the guilty, rather than the success of the plot should be endangered by disclosing its existence to outsiders. Of Lord Mordaunt he declared that he 'would not for a chamber full of diamonds acquaint him with their secret, for he knew he could not keep it.' At last, under pressure, he relented, and promised that those Roman Catholic peers who were likely to be present should be, by some means or

E

other, hindered from putting in an appearance.
'I do not,' records Sir Everard Digby,[1] 'think
there were three worth saving that should have
been lost; you may guess that I had some
friends that were in danger, which I prevented.'
But, by the time Catesby had consented to save
some of those for whom intercession had been
made by Keyes, Faukes, Digby, and Tresham,
the latter had rendered all their good intentions
void, by the delivery of the letter to Lord
Mounteagle, who passed it on to Cecil, by whom,
after examination before the Privy Council, it
was handed to King James.

[1] Writing, when in the Tower, to his wife. This callous
admission—that there were, perhaps, 'three' Catholics who would
have been killed—should be quoted in evidence against the fulsome
panegyrics which have been lavished by certain writers on the
character of Sir Everard Digby.

my lord out of the loue i beare ▮▮▮▮ to some of youere frendz
i haue a caer of your preseruacion therfor i would
aduyse yowe as yowe tender youer lyf to deuys some
exscuse to shift of youer attendance at this parleament
for god and man hathe concurred to punishe the wickednes
of this tyme and thinke not slightlye of this aduertisment
but retyere youre self into youre contri whaere yowe
maye expect the euent in safti for thowghe theare be no
apparance of anni stir yet i saye they shall receyue a terrible
blowe this parleament and yet they shall not seie who
hurts them this councel is not to be contemned becaus
it maye do yowe good and can do yowe no harme for the
dangere is passed as soon as yowe haue burnt the letter
and i hope god will giue yowe the grace to mak good
use of it to whose holy proteccion i commend yowe

Inscribed on the back.

To the right honorable
the lord mounteagle

FACSIMILE OF THE FAMOUS LETTER TO LORD MOUNTEAGLE.

CHAPTER VIII

THE LETTER TO LORD MOUNTEAGLE

OF all the mysterious incidents enveloped in the traditional story of the Gunpowder Plot, none has taken so strong a hold upon the popular imagination as has the famous warning letter, undated and unsigned, written to Lord Mounteagle. The receipt of this letter by Mounteagle is generally understood to have formed the sole means whereby the plot was discovered, and the lives of King, Lords, and Commons were saved ; but, as I hope to show later, the Government evidently had some knowledge of what was going on prior to the delivery of the letter to Mounteagle at Hoxton, on Saturday, October 26, 1605. ⌊At the same time, it is perhaps rather two wide a definition to refer to all the members of the Government as being possessors of this information. It would be more correct to name instead only Robert Cecil, Earl of Salisbury, who seems to have known of the existence of the plot quite six weeks before the receipt of the letter. It may even be argued that he was aware of it as much as three months earlier.

But its authorship is not the only puzzle that awaits solution in connection with this letter, for the personal character of Lord Mounteagle himself is almost as much a puzzle.

William Parker, Lord Mounteagle, inherited his title in right of his mother, Elizabeth Stanley, heiress of the third Lord Mounteagle, or Monteagle. He was the eldest son of Henry Parker, Lord Morley, who died in 1618. Mounteagle did not succeed to his father's title until thirteen years after the plot, and he is always known to historians by his earlier title. It would, however, be more correct to call him Lord Morley, for he was summoned to Parliament before he died as Baron Morley and Mounteagle, of which the first-named was by far the oldest dignity. He was, at the date of the receipt of the mysterious letter, about thirty-one or thirty-two years of age, and had married a sister of Francis Tresham, the conspirator, in company with whom he had joined in the Essex rebellion, and had been very heavily fined for his pains. A personal friend of both Father Henry Garnet and Robert Catesby,[1] it is clear that he sanctioned the Jesuit missions to the King of Spain, and until the accession of James I., remained a staunch Roman Catholic of the faction directed by Garnet and his colleagues.

[1] In a letter to Catesby, he says, 'In what languishment have we led our life, since we departed from the dear Robin (Catesby), whose conversation gave us such warmth as we needed no other heat to maintain our health.' After further expressions of flattery, he signs himself ' Ever fast tied to your friendship, W. Mounteagle.'

Why he should have suddenly changed his politics, and, ostensibly, at any rate, his religion on the accession of the King of Scots, it is difficult to tell; but he undoubtedly proffered the most fervent protestations of loyalty to the new monarch, to whom he pretended that he wished to become a Protestant. But that he ever was anything but a Roman Catholic at heart need not be disputed. He merely conformed outwardly to the dominant faith for political reasons, and for the protection of his purse. In this position he did not stand alone, for there were then in England hundreds of prominent Roman Catholics who pursued the same course. On his death-bed he received the last rites of the Roman Church.

Notwithstanding his altered life, Mounteagle did not cease to keep up his friendship with Catesby, Tresham, and the Winters. In fact, he frequently met Catesby from the time of the construction of the plot down till the autumn of 1605.[1] This is a circumstance that has been conveniently ignored by those writers who maintain that he was not in any way privy to what was going on among his old allies. That he may, all the time, have been acting, as has been suggested, as a spy on the part of Cecil is probable; but it would, indeed, be strange if a person connected as he was by ties of blood and

---

[1] In July, 1605, he had a meeting with Garnet, Catesby, and Tresham, in Essex, and had that same September met Catesby at Bath.

friendship with the chief conspirators, a friend of
the Jesuits, and a participator with the chief of
these conspirators in not one, but two or three
former plots, should have been utterly unaware
of this new design, invented and directed by a
man to whom he was in the habit of writing in
terms of the warmest admiration.

(Late on Friday, October 25, Mounteagle gave
orders that he would sup the following day at his
house at Hoxton.   This sudden notice seems to
have surprised his servants.   To Hoxton he and
his household repaired, and when 'ready to go to
supper at seven of the clock at night, one of his
footmen, whom he had sent of an errand over
the street, was met by an unknown man, of a
reasonable tall personage, who delivered him a
letter,' which letter was immediately brought to
Mounteagle, who handed it to a gentleman in his
household, named Warde, and told him to read it
aloud.   Its contents ran as follows [1] :—

'my lord out of the love i beare to some of
youere frends [2] i have a caer of youere preservacion
therfor i would advyse yowe as yowe tender
youer lyf to devyse some excuse to shift of
youer attendance at this parleament for god and
man hathe concurred to punishe the wickedness
of this tyme and thinke not slightlye of this
advertisment but retyere youre self into youre

----

[1] From the original at the Record Office.   There is also a copy
in Dom. S.P. James I., November, 1605, vol. xvi.

[2] The writer originally wrote 'you,' instead of 'some of your
friends,' but erased the word.

countri wheare yowe maye expect the event in safti for thowghe theare be no apparence of ani stir yet I say they shall receyve a terrible blowe this parleament and yet they shall not seie who hurrts them this councel is not to be contemned because it maye do yowe good and can do yowe no harme for the dangere is passed as soon as yowe have burnt the letter and i hope god will give yowe the grace to mak good use of it to whose holy proteccion i commend yowe.'

The ostentatious manner in which Mounteagle directed Warde—who was, it should be noted, an intimate friend of Thomas Winter—to read the letter, is in keeping with all his other actions in connection with this enigmatic epistle's arrival. By handing it to Warde to read aloud, he affected to pretend that such a letter was beneath his notice, and that he merely regarded the message as the production of a lunatic or a practical joker. Notwithstanding this apparent indifference, he hastily set out, after supper, for London, and gave the letter to Lord Salisbury, whom he found entertaining some of the principal Ministers of State, such as Suffolk, Northampton, Worcester, and Nottingham. The fact that all these statesmen were to be found late on a Saturday night with Cecil in London, clearly suggests that they had been brought together by Cecil for the special purpose of receiving this letter, the arrival of which was expected.

On October 27, Thomas Warde went secretly to his friend Winter, and informed him of the letter's delivery at Hoxton, and of its contents. Winter immediately communicated with Catesby. By letting Warde have the letter to read, Mounteagle evidently intended to allow the conspirators to know of their danger, for he naturally conjectured that Warde[1] would lose little time in putting himself into communication with his friend Winter. Thus, the eventual development of the situation came about precisely as Mounteagle had desired. By means of the letter, he was enabled to excuse himself from incurring deadly peril; he was enabled to enter into confidential relations with the all-powerful Salisbury; he was enabled, through the medium of Warde, to give warning to the conspirators at the very moment that he was bringing their treason to light, yet without in any way appearing to them in the guise of a traitor; and he was enabled to pose as the saviour of the nation.

So far, so good! Mounteagle, however, calculated that, after Warde had communicated with Winter, the conspirators would seek refuge in flight, and no blood, in consequence, would be shed of either Protestants or Roman Catholics. Such also were the calculations of Tresham. But both men, reasonable as were their anticipations of this result, were completely deceived. The conspirators, with almost incredible temerity,

---

[1] The exact state of the relations existing between Warde and some of the plotters is a mystery yet to be solved. Warde may have been entirely in his master's confidence, and may have expected the letter's arrival.

refused to budge, and awaited the completion of their plot.[1]

The authorship of the letter, strange to say, has never been discovered. Of the various claims made on behalf of certain persons, no convincing proof has ever been adduced in support of any one of them. That Percy was the author is not in the least likely. That the letter was not written by the person (or persons) who dictated, or inspired it, is almost certain. Neither Tresham, nor Mounteagle, would have been so foolish as to put pen to paper; yet either, or both, might have practically dictated it. According to one tradition, it was written by Anne Vaux, daughter of Lord Vaux, the faithful friend of Father Garnet; according to another, it was written by Mrs. Abington, another devout Roman Catholic lady friendly with the Jesuits, and sister to Lord Mounteagle.

That the letter was actually written by Father Oldcorne, S.J., is an unsupported theory, and it is not in his handwriting. I conclude that the letter was written very shortly after Tresham's futile visit to White Webbs;[2] for Tresham was not in London at the exact time of its delivery, and had evidently just gone into the country to establish an *alibi* should he, as indeed fell out,

---

[1] They had a ship, hired for their use, then lying in the Thames, intended probably for Faukes to use after the explosion.

[2] It is possible that this meeting took place earlier in the month than I have recorded. Tresham was in London, or its vicinity, within twenty-four hours of the letter's delivery.

be taxed, later on, by Catesby or Winter with being concerned in its delivery.

After consulting with Mounteagle, the latter probably went to Lord Salisbury, and all arrangements were made accordingly. It may be argued that if Salisbury knew of the existence of the plot, why should he have exacted the performance of such a farce as the production of this letter? But all the evidence tends to show that the letter was designed for Mounteagle's own protection, and that he could see no other way of clearing himself from being considered a traitor to his friends than by obtaining an anonymous warning of the kind actually received. Whoever drew up the letter, or was responsible for its contents, did his work with consummate skill. It was quite a model of what such a letter should have been.[1] It mentioned, no names, no dates, no facts. Whether Lord Salisbury knew that Warde was to be made a party to knowing its contents is doubtful; and if Mounteagle wished to save his friends, as he probably did, without Salisbury's knowledge, his object was only defeated by the insane folly of the chief conspirators.

It is quite possible that some third person, whose name has never been revealed, was accessory to its construction. This third party may have been a priest. Rigid Roman Catholic

[1] 'As a plan concocted by Mounteagle and Tresham to stop the plot, and at the same time secure the escape of their guilty friends, the little comedy at Hoxton was admirably concocted' (Gardiner).

as were all the persons involved in the conspiracy, such men, like all Jesuit-ridden individuals, would hardly have moved in any specially important undertaking without seeking the advice of their confessor. Tresham, therefore, probably consulted one of the Jesuits, either in or out of the confessional. Tresham's denial that he (Tresham) wrote the letter is, of course, valueless; for he naturally would never have confessed to an act which conduced to the capture of his friends. He was, moreover, an adept in the art of equivocation, in which he had been instructed by so proficient a tutor as Father Garnet himself. On his deathbed he astonished even Cecil by the recklessness of his perjury.

Meanwhile, to the ordinary reader of the traditional story, it must seem incredible that if on October 27 the leading conspirators realized that they had been betrayed, and if Cecil knew of the existence of their treason,—the conspirators should have proceeded with their scheme, with the Government making no attempt to arrest them. The reasons for both these extraordinary courses are easily forthcoming. Catesby, finding that no names had been mentioned in the letter, thought that Salisbury would never 'guess' the secret. He sent Faukes, apparently without telling him of the terrible risk he ran, to examine the premises beneath the Parliament House. Faukes reported he could tell, by means of certain secret marks invented by himself to discover whether the vault was visited in his absence, that nobody had approached the whereabouts of the gunpowder.

With this assurance Catesby was sufficiently satisfied as to abandon all idea of flight, little suspecting that Salisbury had completely out-witted him by postponing all action against the plotters until the eve of the very 'fifth' itself, in order to give his dupes time still further to incriminate themselves. The King, too, was out of town, and Lord Salisbury awaited his return from Royston [1] before taking the initiative. Salisbury, who was by this time, irrespective of the mysterious letter, cognisant of the whole scheme, still wished to conceal by what means he had become aware of the plot ; and determined to flatter the King's vanity by giving him some broad hints whereby he might display his sagacity to the Court, and suggest that the vaults under-neath the Parliament House should be searched.

That Lord Mounteagle must have been very deeply in Lord Salisbury's confidence before the receipt of the famous letter is not to be disputed. The rewards that were heaped upon him were extraordinary, and the money grants given to him would, according to our present value, work out to reach something like six thousand pounds per annum. But, if the Government had merely

[1] The king did not return till October 31. When Salisbury took him the letter two days after his return, no third party was present at their first meeting.

rewarded him for disclosing the letter, there would have existed little cause for comment. Yet the Government not merely rewarded him, but employed the most peculiar and coercive methods to prevent all knowledge of his former treasons being brought to light.[1]   All knowledge of these former treasons were carefully concealed from the ordinary public, and in a signed statement by Thomas Winter, and a similar statement by Francis Tresham, both made during their captivity about four weeks after the letter had been given to Salisbury, Mounteagle's name (mentioned unfavourably by both conspirators) was carefully erased from the original documents; whilst,[2] to strengthen his position, Tresham, who must have been well aware of the true nature of Mounteagle's intimacy with Salisbury, died very suddenly whilst a captive in the Tower.   His death was a lucky circumstance for Mounteagle, for that Tresham intended, unless his life were spared, to denounce his brother-in-law, is evident.[3] Even so submissive a tool in Salisbury's service as Sir William Waad, Lieutenant of the Tower, has left on record the fact that 'Tresham's friends were marvellous confident, if he had escaped this

---

[1] Especially at the trial of the conspirators, and at the trial of Garnet.

[2] In the originals at the Record Office, a slip of paper is pasted over Mounteagle's name.

[3] 'It is so lewdly given out that he (Mounteagle) was once of this plot of powder, and afterwards betrayed it all to me' (Salisbury's instructions to Coke).

sickness, and have given out words in this place that they feared not the course of justice.'

On November 1, Catesby (having sent for Tresham) interviewed him, in the presence of Thomas Winter, at Barnet. By both conspirators he was charged with having written the letter to Lord Mounteagle. He denied the accusation with many oaths, and they either were half persuaded to believe him, or from lack of evidence were unable to proceed further, and reluctantly let him go free. On November 3, however, another urgent message came from Warde ; and this time to the effect that, so far from the contents of the letter having been ridiculed at head-quarters, as the plotters had vainly imagined, it had actually been taken to the King. Now thoroughly frightened, Catesby and Winter sent again for Tresham, who had endeavoured to avoid them, and met him after dusk near Lincoln's Inn. Tresham, at this interview,[1] threw off the mask which he had worn so long, and, denouncing the plot, implored all his confederates to leave England at once. From the substance of Tresham's words, Catesby and Winter were at last convinced that he had lied to them on both the previous interviews at White Webbs, and that he had betrayed them.

Even now, however, they refused to escape to the Continent, and determined, whatever happened to prevent the success of the Westminster part

[1] Winter also saw Tresham again on the following day.

of the plot, to continue their preparations for heading a revolt in the Midlands.[1] The time was too short, moreover, to warn all their fellow-conspirators, some of whom were, of course, ignorant of the affair of the letter. It was finally settled that Faukes and Percy should remain in London, that Catesby should go into the country on the morrow, and that Winter should make ready to follow him, if necessary, a few hours after his departure. Keyes, Rookewood, and the Wrights were apparently to remain in London so long as they should think fit.

On November 4, early in the afternoon, Faukes whilst in his cellar was surprised by a sudden visit from Mounteagle[2] and the Lord Chamberlain,[3] who asked him to whom belonged this large store of fuel. Faukes, in the character of Percy's servant, replied that his master had need of so large a store. No attempt was made to look beneath the fuel, so that Faukes concluded that they had not suspected the presence of the powder, contained in thirty-six casks. Common sense, one would imagine, should have taught him that all, nevertheless, was discovered; but, faithful to the last, he stuck to his post, with the

---

[1] Some of the plotters, whose names are unknown, are said to have favoured flight, but were overruled by Percy and Catesby, both, as ever, confident of success.

[2] Both of these visitors, Mounteagle and the Lord Chamberlain, were intimate friends of Tresham.

[3] Thomas Howard, Earl of Suffolk; Knyvet, who captured Faukes, was his brother-in-law.

exception of a brief expedition undertaken to tell Percy of what had happened. Catesby and John Wright fled, thereupon, to join Digby, but the other conspirators remained.

At a little before midnight, Faukes was captured just outside the house, by a body of men under Sir Thomas Knyvet, and the gunpowder was discovered beneath the fuel. Thus were dissipated, before the Abbey clock boomed forth the hour which ushered in the morn of the eventful Fifth of November, 1605, all the vain and foolish hopes, which a handful of desperate fanatics had for so long cherished,[1] of destroying by one diabolical stroke, the power of Protestantism in Great Britain, for the purpose of restoring to its old and supreme position the fallen faith of Rome.

[1] 'When Faukes saw his Treason discovered, he instantly confessed his own guiltyness saying, if he had beene within the house when they first layed hands uppon him, hee would have blown up them, himselfe and all' (Stow).

CHAPTER IX

AFTER the capture of Guy Faukes, no time was lost in taking him before the Privy Council, and he was actually brought before the King in his bed-chamber before four o'clock, a.m. This feverish haste to question him is another point in favour of the supposition that the details of the plot were already well known to Cecil. But neither King nor Council could extract any information of value from the undaunted Guy. He confessed, however, that it was his object to have blown up the Parliament House, but refused to admit that he had any accomplices. One of his aims in firing the train was, he said, 'to blow the beggarly Scots back to their native mountains:' an answer which must have pleased some of those present, for the King's Scottish favourites, all notorious for their rapacity, had already made themselves very unpopular in London. As to his name and profession, Guy Faukes stated that he was one ' John Johnson, servant to Master Thomas Percy.' After leaving Whitehall, Guy Faukes was sent under a strong guard by water to the Tower, where the King

directed the Lieutenant that he was to be tortured.[1]

Those of the conspirators left in the metropolis
were not long in discovering that all was lost, for
soon after dawn the streets were filled with people
talking of the plot.   Horror and dismay were
depicted on every countenance, and it was
rumoured that a general rising of the Roman
Catholics was imminent.   The Spanish Ambassador's house was mobbed.   The train-bands were
called out, and the general alarm reminded the
Londoners of the preparations made in 1588,
against the coming of the Armada.   'Not only
that night,' writes the Venetian Ambassador, 'but
all next day, the citizens were kept under arms.'

The conspirators, quickly realizing that there
was no time to be wasted, made all haste to be
gone.   Percy[2] and Christopher Wright rode off
first, then Keyes ; then Rookewood, whose stud
now came in useful, followed, having relays of
horses waiting for him between London and
Dunchurch.[3]   Riding at a most extraordinary
rate of speed, he soon overtook and passed
Keyes on the road; and at Brickhill, Bucks,
came up with Catesby and John Wright, and

----

[1] James finished his written order with the canting sentence,
'And so God speede your good worke'!

[2] Percy was first reported in London to have made for
Gravesend (Dom. S.P., Nov. 5, 1605).

[3] Close to Rugby.   It was on the neighbouring Dunsmoor
Heath that Sir Everard Digby had summoned his 'hunting-party'
to meet on the fifth.

soon after with Christopher Wright and Percy, who had also been travelling very rapidly. All five then proceeded to Dunchurch, ~~via Ashby St. Legers, the house of Catesby's mother.~~ Rookewood having, by the time of his arrival at Ashby, completed something like eighty miles in less than eight hours! Such an adventure reminds us, curiously enough, of Ainsworth's account in his novel, *Rookwood*, of Dick Turpin's wholly mythical ride from London to York.[1] ~~Arrived at Ashby, the party found~~ Thomas Winter ~~there~~. With him they soon took to saddle again for Dunchurch, ~~where their dejected looks told Digby that all was up.~~ Of the Roman Catholic 'huntsmen,' the greater number disappeared when Catesby avowed his plan of raising the standard of rebellion, one of the first to depart being Digby's uncle, Sir Robert. ~~After much discussion,~~ Catesby resolved, ~~instead of seeking safety in flight, on marching towards~~ Wales, ~~traversing en route the counties of Warwick, Worcester, and Hereford or Stafford.~~ He ~~expected~~ that the local Roman Catholics would ~~rise and join him,~~ but in this ~~he was bitterly mistaken.~~

From the moment of his decision until the date of his death, the march was to prove hopelessly to be a forlorn hope, undertaken in the insanity of despair. The first check came

---

[1] Ainsworth, however, refers to Ambrose Rookewood's ride in his novel, *Guy Fawkes*.

from their own friends.   Mr. Talbot, of Grafton, near Bromsgrove—a member of the ancient house of Shrewsbury, and father-in-law of Robert Winter—not only refused them aid, or even lodging, but also threatened to detain the delegates sent to him.   The rebels proceeded first to visit Norbrook, Grant's fortified house, whence a message was despatched to Garnet, at Coughton,[1] telling him of what had occurred. From Norbrook they went to Huddington,[2] the Winters' home, where they were visited by Father Greenway, S.J.   On November 7 they attacked Hewell Grange, Lord Windsor's house, and seized all the armour they could find. Thence they marched to Holbeach, the home of their friend, Stephen Lyttleton.

So far but very few of the inhabitants had joined them, and those who had, belonged mainly to the lowest ranks of the unemployed.   The rainy weather, too, helped to impede their march and to damp their ardour; and the little band of well-horsed and well-armed gentlemen[3] that had set out so valiantly from Dunchurch, reached Holbeach in a most miserable plight.   At Holbeach they were deserted by Stephen

[1] Where Garnet had celebrated the Feast of All Saints. Digby's wife, and other relatives of some of the conspirators, were there.

[2] Here Mass was said by Father Hart, a Jesuit (*alias* Hammond), who heard the conspirators' confessions, and absolved them.

[3] About fifty in number.   About forty reached Holbeach.

Lyttleton, Robert Winter, and Thomas Bates. Here also Sir Everard Digby left them, and was speedily captured by the Sheriff of Worcestershire's men, hiding in a wood. Whether Sir Everard Digby actually deserted them, or was commissioned to obtain assistance from Roman Catholics living further afield, remains a disputed point.

Meanwhile, in London, great had been the stir when it was discovered that the birds had flown. The extraordinary rapidity of the mode of travelling adopted by Percy and Rookewood obtained for them a long start, but messengers were soon speeding into the Midlands, on their account, from Whitehall. Of the insurrection in the Midlands the Government was well aware; another proof that they had known for some time past of what was going on. For the conspirators did not really take the field until November 6, and yet on the 7th was printed in London a proclamation denouncing the revolt. In those days, it is hardly necessary to remark, there were no telegraphs, telephones, motor-cars, or trains, so that Lord Salisbury must have got his information in a very quick space of time, if he waited for advices from Warwickshire before printing the royal proclamation issued in London on the 7th.

This proclamation is interesting in the extreme. In it Thomas Percy is denounced as the leader, whilst there is no allusion to Sir

Everard Digby, Tresham, Keyes, or Bates. Special reference is made to the fact that the conspirators are acting on their own account, and without being in receipt of any assistance, advice, or approval from the Roman Catholic kingdoms on the Continent.

I append a verbatim copy of the proclamation, transcribed by me from the original at the Record Office :—

'BY THE KING.

'Whereas Thomas Percy Gentleman, and some other his confederates, persons knowen to be bitterly corrupted with the superstition of the Romish Religion, as seduced with the blindness thereof, and being otherwise of lewde life, insolent disposition, and for the most part of desperate estate, have beene discovered to have contrived the most horrible treason that ever entered into the hearts of men, against our Person, our Children, the whole Nobilitie, Clergie, and Commons in Parliament assembled, which howsoever cloaked with zeale of Superstitious Religion, aymed indeed at the Subversion of the State, and to induce an horrible confusion of all things.   In which they and all others of banke-rupt and necessitous estate, might have those of better abilitie for a pray to repaire their beggarly Fortunes, and have proceeded so farre some of them in their devilish Attempts as to assemble in Troupes in our Counties of Warwicke and Worcester, where they have broken up a Stable, and taken out horses of divers Noblemen and

Gentlemen, within our towne of Warwicke,[1] And no doubt but doe proceede further in their purposes, seeking to raise some Rebellion in our Realme, and will with many fained and false Allegations seek to seduce divers of our Subjects, especially with shew of Religion, Although wee are by good experience so well persuaded of the Loyaltie of divers of our subjects (though not professing true Religion) that they doe as much abhorre this detestable conspiracie as our Selfe, and will bee ready to doe their best endeavours (though with expence of their blood) to suppresse all Attemptors against our Safetie and the quiet of our State, and to discover whomsoever they shall suspect to be of Rebellious or Traiterous disposition : Yet have Wee thought good by this our open Declaration, to give warning and advertisement to all our Subjects whatsoever, of that horrible purpose of Percies and his complices, and to distinguish betweene all others, calling themselves Catholics, and these detestable Traitours : And therefore doe denounce and publish all the Persons hereunder named, Adherents to Percy, to bee Traitours knowen, and that all others are in the same case, who shall in any wise either receive, abbette, cherish, entertaine, or adhere unto them, or not doe their best endeavours to apprehend and take them.

'Wherefore Wee will and command all our Lieutenants, Deputy Lieutenants, Sheriffes, Justices of Peace, Mayors, Bayliffes, Constables, and all other our officers, Ministers, and loving Subjects, to take knowledge thereof, and to doe their best duties herein, as they will answer the

[1] They broke into Warwick Castle.

contrary at their uttermost peril : Not doubting, but that they all, without regard of their pretence of Religion, will with our hearts and will, employ themselves for the suppressing, apprehending, deterring, and discovering of all sorts of persons any wayes likely to be privie to a Treason so hatefull to God and man, and implying in it the utter subversion of this Realme, and dignitie thereof.

'And where Wee doe heare that many doe spread abroad, that this Conspiracie was intended onely for matter of Religion, and that Sovreine Princes our neighbours are interessed therein, which Rumors are divulged by busy Persons both to Scandalize the Amitie wherein We stand with all Christian Princes and States, and to give unto lewde Persons hope that they shall be backed in their enterprises by great Potentates. We doe declare that We cannot[1] admit so inhumane a thought, as to conceive that any Prince of what Religion soever, could give eare to so Savage and Barbarous an imagination.   And that by such examinations as hitherto have been taken, Wee finde them all, and their Ministers cleere from any suspicion of privity thereunto ; Whereof one infallible argument to us is, that all the Ministers of Sovraine Princes which are now here, made earnest sute to us to bee present in their place that day.   And wherefore We doe admonish and charge all our Subjects, that they shall not speake of any the Princes our neighbours, or their

[1] On December 24, I find the Venetian Ambassador to Spain writing to the Doge of Venice, ' I enclose the King of England's proclamation, exculpating foreign princes. They have printed and published it here (Madrid), and sold it publicly in the streets.'

Ambassadors, otherwise then reverently, upon paine of our displeasure, and to bee punished as persons seeking the disturbance of the Peace, wherein We live with our sayd Neighbours.

'Given at our Pallace of Westminster, the seventh day of November, in the third Yeere of our Reigne of Great Britaine, France, and Ireland.

GOD SAVE THE KING.

THOMAS PERCY Gentleman.
ROBERT CATESBY Esquire.
AMBROSE ROOKWOOD of Coldham hall in Suffolk Esquire.
THOMAS WINTER Gentleman, brother of ROBERT WINTER of Huddington in the Countie of Worcester.

EDWARD GRANT of Northbrooke in the County of Warwicke Gentleman.
JOHN WRIGHT.
CHRISTOPHER WRIGHT.
ROBERT ASHFIELD, servant to ROBERT CATESBY, Esquire.

Imprinted at London by Robert Barker.
Printer to the King's most Excellent Majestie,
Anno Dom. 1605.

On the day after this proclamation was issued an equally interesting pronouncement was dated and sent on its way from the scene of Catesby's operations up to London. This was a letter, signed by two Justices of the Peace (Sir Euseby Andrew and Sir Thomas Burnaby), to Cecil, describing the consternation created in the counties of Warwick and Northampton, by the whirlwind ride of the five conspirators from

London down to Ashby St. Legers.   This letter was accompanied by several depositions taken down from the lips of certain persons in the neighbourhood, who had witnessed the movements of Catesby and Percy on their arrival at Dunchurch.   Again, in this despatch, as in the royal proclamation, we cannot but remain astonished at the rapidity with which the news of Faukes's attempt to blow up the Parliament House had travelled; for here we have two country gentlemen, writing from Daventry (seventy miles from London), on the third day only after the 5th, talking plainly of the plot to destroy the Parliament.

I append a verbatim copy of this letter, transcribed by me from the original at the Record Office :—

'RIGHT HONORABLE,

'We having bine informed of a great concourse of horsemen on Tuesday the fifthe of November at Ledgers Ashby in the County of Northampton, betweene foure and tenne of the clocke in the afternoone, and likewise of the intended treason about the Parliament house, as also of five gentlemen, who came posting doune from London very suspiciously into our Countrie, and as farre as we can gather by Examinations wente presently to the saide Ledgers Ashby but there did not stay : Whereupon we having taken divers Examinations, we thought it our duty to sende the accompt thereof

unto your Lordship : And so referring our selves
wholly to your honored discretion, we humbly
take our leaves. Daventrie in Northam. this
VIIIth day of Novem : 1605.

      ' Your honours in all duty,
        ' EUSEBIE ANDREWE.
       'THO : BURNABYE.'

The prompt action of the country gentlemen,[1]
gave the conspirators but little breathing time,
and all the loyal fighting men in the shires of
Worcester, Warwick, and Northampton, including
even some Roman Catholics, took arms in
support of the Crown. Catesby's attempt to
turn Digby's 'hunting-party'[2] into a Roman
Catholic army, destined to pull down the
Government and the Established Church in
favour of a new sovereign and a new Creed, had
proved a prodigious failure. Holbeach provided
the last scene in the tragedy, and the fall of the
curtain was not long delayed. Sir Richard
Walshe, Sheriff of Worcestershire, hung on to
the skirts of the conspirators' force until it was
safe inside the walls of Holbeach House (four
miles from Stourbridge), in the proximity of
which he awaited with equanimity the arrival of
men marching to his aid, for he knew that the
little garrison inside was caught within a trap.

[1] Of whom Sir Richard Verney did the most effective service.

[2] 'To their dismay, every Catholic from whom they solicited
aid on the road shut his doors against them, and the sheriffs of
each county followed, though at a respectful distance, with an
armed force' (Lingard).

But before the attack on the house was made
by the sheriff, occurred an event, in the shape of
an accident, which had an extraordinary effect
upon the superstitious minds of the disheartened
traitors seeking a comfortless shelter within its
walls. This was no less than an explosion of
gunpowder. It was a case of the biter being bit,
with a vengeance! Catesby and company, who
had arranged to blow up to the skies their
enemies at Westminster, were now within an ace
of sharing the fate which they had projected for
their victims. Some powder, which the rebels
had brought with them, had got damp during
their dismal march, owing to the bad weather.
and whilst drying it, a live coal, jumping out,
touched the powder, and caused instant ignition,
Although nobody was killed, several had a most
narrow escape, and Catesby and Rookewood were
severely scorched.

This startling incident completely unmanned
the conspirators. Even Catesby at last lost heart,
and Robert Winter asserted that the whole catas-
trophe had been pictured to him in a terrible
dream which had visited him in his slumbers,
and in its realization, he declared he clearly
recognized the finger of Almighty God. That
morning he deserted his comrades, and slunk
away through the rain, cowed and trembling, as
did Thomas Bates.[1]   Rookewood and Catesby,

---

[1] Bates seems to have left the house without any attempt to
conceal his purpose, for in a letter he subsequently testified that,

deeming that the end was now very near, betook themselves to their prayers. Thomas Winter and Percy vowed to die, sword in hand, in one final, hopeless, helpless conflict with their foes. One and all were now convinced that Heaven had from the beginning been against their design,[1] and saw in many of the strange occurrences which had injured their cause during the past year the workings of Providence against them: the repeated prorogations of Parliament, the treachery of Tresham, the hostility of Mounteagle, the dreadful dream of Winter, the inclement weather of the last few days, the explosion of the powder, were now all attributed to the wrath of Heaven kindled against their plan.

A little after eleven a.m. on November 8, the Sheriff of Worcester, having encompassed Holbeach House, proceeded to storm the little garrison, which, by reason of its want of numbers and lack of ammunition, was unable to offer any prolonged resistance to the attack. With the utmost gallantry Percy,[2] Catesby, and the Wrights met their fate. Ambrose Rookewood and Thomas

when going away, 'Christopher Wright flung me out of an window an 100*l*.' The bulk of this sum was to be given to Wright's family. He was captured in Staffordshire, on November 12.

[1] 'The accident with the gunpowder at Holbeach turned the scale, and placed before them their acts as they really were' (Dr. Gardiner).

[2] Percy and Catesby were shot by John Streete, a trooper, who received a pension for life in reward (about fourteen shillings a day in our money).

Winter were badly wounded, but recovered. It was thought also that one or two amongst the slain might also have survived but for the action of the country people,[1] who began stripping their bodies and handling them roughly, for the sake of plunder, before they could receive the attentions of a surgeon. In support of the Jesuit story that Percy was shot down by orders from Salisbury, who had given directions that he was not to be taken alive, because he was in the position of a man who knew too much·about that minister's early knowledge of the plot, there exists not the very smallest original evidence. It surely was Lord Salisbury's object to capture rather than kill Percy,[2] who (as we have seen above) was the first person denounced in the royal proclamation, and whose capture might have helped to incriminate Salisbury's enemy, Lord Northumberland.

Rookewood, Thomas Winter, Grant, and Keyes were taken to London and lodged in the Tower. Keyes was not taken with the rest at Holbeach, but was captured in Warwickshire on November 9. He had parted with his friends at Dunchurch, but what he had been doing in the interval is unknown.

Of the thirteen conspirators originally engaged

---

[1] 'The rude people stripped the rest naked ; and their wounds being many and grievous, and no surgeon at hand, they became incurable, and so died' (letter from an eye-witness to Salisbury)

[2] Percy, as a matter of fact, was not killed outright, but died from his wounds three days later.

in the plot, no less than eleven were either captured
or killed within a period of five days from the fatal
Fifth of November. Of these eleven men, Catesby,[1]
Percy, and the Wrights were dead; Guy Faukes
was in the Tower; Digby, Thomas Winter,
Grant, Keyes, Bates, and Rookewood were on
their way thither under arrest. Of the remaining
pair, Francis Tresham was in London, but not
yet actually arrested; and Robert Winter was in
hiding. By November 12, Tresham also was
under lock and key, so that, if we omit the
fugitive Robert Winter (the least important of
the band), we find the Government's measures
for the repression of the conspiracy, both at
Westminster and in the Midlands, had been so
skilfully executed that it had only taken the
authorities seven days to kill or imprison all those
who had been actively engaged in the Gunpowder
Plot.

That the Government wished to take Percy
alive is further shown by reference to a letter
from the Venetian Ambassador to the Doge
of Venice, dated November 23,[2] in which he
writes :—

'Percy, head of the conspiracy, was wounded
by a musket, and along with five others was taken
alive. As soon as the King heard this, he sent
off two of his best surgeons, and a doctor,

---

[1] 'The heads of Percy and Catesby were cut off, and sett uppon
the ends of the Parliament house' (Stow).
[2] Cal. S.P., Venetian Series, vol. x., No. 447.

to attend the said Percy, and also a litter to convey him to London. His Majesty is extremely anxious to keep him alive, as he hopes to wring from him all the details of the Plot, for up to now he has been considered the leader.'

This extract, from a source above suspicion, proves the absurdity of the Jesuit fable that Percy was killed by orders of Lord Salisbury, and reveals that he was, as I have stated, considered, at first, by the Government to have been the leader among the conspirators.

ROBᵀ. WINTER.

Executed in the Year 1606.

for the GUNPOWDER PLOT.

Pubᵈ. April 1 1794 by T. Caulfield.

CHAPTER X

ALTHOUGH, as I have more than once hinted above, Robert Winter was probably the least important of the Gunpowder conspirators, the original account[1] of his escape from Holbeach, and his subsequent adventures before falling into the hands of his enemies, is so interesting, and savours so much of a romance, that a *précis* of the ' true historicall Declaration' of his ' Flight and Escape' is well worth notice here.

The two fugitives, Robert Winter and Stephen Lyttleton, left Holbeach immediately after the explosion of the gunpowder. That they must have exercised considerable ingenuity in getting away there can be little doubt; but, perhaps, during the confusion caused by the disaster, their retreat was rendered easier. Robert Catesby, luckily for them, was *hors de combat ;* had this not been the case, he would certainly have handled both delinquents very roughly, for he was not the man to tolerate so flagrant a case of desertion from his little force at the eleventh hour.

[1] *Vide* Harl. MSS. 360, pp. 103–108.

The deserters left the house separately, but met in a wood about half a mile or more away, and after being first at their wits' end to know where to go, decided to make for Hagley, the beautiful residence of Muriel Lyttleton. To do this, they had not only to make a considerable *détour*, in order to avoid the forces of the sheriffs, but had also to cross the river Stour, much swollen by the recent rain.   Proceeding towards Rowley Regis, in Staffordshire, they besought refuge from one Pelborough, a farmer, and tenant of the Lyttletons. Notwithstanding the risk, he willingly agreed to put them up, and provided them with food and clothing. Here they continued for over a week, hidden in a loft over one of the farmer's barns. From this farm they removed at night to that of another tenant of the Lyttletons, rented by a man named Perkes, whose house was close to Hagley Park. Here they lay hidden in a barn for about seven weeks. At the end of this time, suspecting that their retreat was, or would soon be, known, they went, at the invitation of Humphrey Lyttleton, to lodge in Hagley House itself.

Arriving at Hagley in the middle of the night, Humphrey Lyttleton elected—in order to obtain food the more easily for the fugitives—to acquaint John Fynwood, his cook, with the news of their presence. The cook promised faithfully not to betray his master's guests, and agreed to supply them secretly with food, whenever necessary,

unknown to the rest of his fellow-servants. On
the first available opportunity,[1] however, he sent
news to the nearest magistrate of their presence
in the house; for which act of treachery he was
officially rewarded with an annuity, or the promise of an annuity, of forty marks. The result of
his giving information was that Stephen Lyttleton and Robert Winter were quickly captured, and
sent to the Tower; whilst Perkes and Humphrey
Lyttleton were arrested, and taken to Worcester.

This act of the wily cook also conduced to
more important results than the seizure of the
fugitives, for it led directly to the capture of
the Jesuit Fathers, Garnet and Oldcorne, whom
the Government looked upon as a more important
prize than any one of the individuals directly
concerned in the plot.

Tried at Worcester, Humphrey Lyttleton was
found guilty, and sentenced to death. He offered,
however, if his life were spared, to give the
Government valuable information as to the whereabouts of some of the Jesuits, especially in regard
to 'Mr. Hall' (Father Oldcorne, S.J.). This
offer was accepted, provided that he made good
his promise. He, thereupon, not only gave an
account of some conversations he had had with
Oldcorne, but also stated that he had every reason
to believe that this Jesuit was lying concealed

---

[1] January 9, 1606. From a further account, which I shall
quote later on, it seems that another servant participated in the
betrayal.

at Hendlip Hall.   This news was sent to the,
searchers at Hendlip, near Worcester, and after
a long quest, not only was Oldcorne captured
there, but Father Garnet[1] also, who surrendered
himself into the hands of Sir Henry Bromley, a
local magistrate.

Thus, owing to the cupidity of a menial, was
effected, by a most extraordinary series of acci-
dents, the capture of Father Henry Garnet, the
Superior of the English Jesuits, who was put on
his trial for treason, and hanged in St. Paul's
Churchyard.

Humphrey Lyttleton's life was not spared,
after all, and he suffered the same fate[2] as the
priests he had betrayed.

Stephen Lyttleton was eventually executed at
Stafford.

The adventures of Robert Winter and Stephen
Lyttleton during the period (nearly two months)
which intervened between their escape from Holbeach and their capture at Hagley were of so
exciting and romantic a nature as to bear some
resemblance to those of Charles II. after the
Battle of Worcester.   Both Charles and the
plotters were saved more than once from capture

---

[1] Hallam makes a curious error when he says, in his *Constitu-
tional History*, that Garnet was 'taken at Henlip along with the
other conspirators.'

[2] In defence of the Government, it has been asserted that
Humphrey Lyttleton was merely offered a reprieve; but this seems
absurd, for no man would betray his best friends, unless he received
some very strong inducement to do so.

by farmers, and the first series of their adventures commenced in the same part of England. The anxiety which the fugitives from Holbeach were a prey to baffles description, for over and over again they fancied, when hiding beneath some hay in the barns, that they heard the footsteps of men coming to arrest them; and when, at last, they thought themselves safe, for a time, at Hagley Hall, they were betrayed by a servant in whom they had placed implicit trust.

CHAPTER XI

GUY FAUKES was the first of the plotters to be incarcerated in the Tower, which he actually reached not long after the time fixed for consummating his terrible scheme. As he had refused to incriminate his friends, he was speedily put to the torture, being by the King's direction subjected to the 'gentler' torments first, and then gradually to the more severe. His stubborn courage and strong frame were not proof against the series of torments under which he was placed, and he was compelled to confess.[1] But, in his confession, or confessions, he only told the Government what was practically known to them before; and in the delirium of pain he never fulfilled the desire of Salisbury's heart, namely, to denounce Father Henry Garnet. Even in admitting that he and his confederates had received the Sacrament at the hands of Father John Gerard, S.J., he denied that Gerard knew anything of the plot;

[1] He confessed 'when told he must come to it againe and againe, from daye to daye, till he should have delivered his whole knowledge' (Dom. S.P. James I. vol. xvi.).

but this most important statement was deliberately omitted by the counsel for the Crown at his trial, so that the spectators in Court went away under the impression that Gerard was an accessory to the crime. But, before dealing with the admissions wrung from the tortured Faukes, it will be best to notice the case of Francis Tresham, whose earthly career was now nearing its end.

It is a significant fact that Tresham's name was omitted from the proclamation quoted above. Probably, Lord Mounteagle did his best to screen his relative so long as he could, and it was not until more than a week after Guy Faukes's arrest that Tresham shared the same fate. In the Tower he soon became ill, and died on December 23.[1] The cause of his death has been, and is still, the subject of much debate. Both Lord Salisbury and Sir William Waad (the Lieutenant of the Tower) declared that Tresham died of an internal complaint, from which he had a long time been suffering, and that he was a dying man when he entered the Tower of London.

Rumour, however, attributed his end to poison. That his death was extremely opportune, so far as Mounteagle's position was concerned, need not be disputed. It is clear that Tresham not only 'knew too much' to suit both Salisbury and Mounteagle ; and of his possession of this knowledge he foolishly made no secret. Against the

---

[1] At about two o'clock a.m. The date of his death has been wrongly given as the 22nd.

theory of his being poisoned must, however, be stated the fact that his wife and servant were allowed free access to him, and used to nurse him. It is, at the same time, remarkable that, if Tresham was so ill before he entered the Tower, we should have heard nothing of this illness beforehand. Up to November 12, he led a most healthy life, without being in any way prevented from taking active exercise ; and yet, not six weeks later, we read of his being dead of a slow and wasting disease.

Francis Tresham was taken to the Tower on November 12, 1605, and on the same day, without being put to the torture, confessed that he had had many interviews of late with Robert Catesby, and with Fathers Gerard, Greenway, and Garnet, but declined to say what had occurred on these occasions. On the following day he was more communicative, and stated that Catesby revealed the plot to him, four weeks back ; but that he had done everything in his power to induce Catesby and his confederates to desist from their purpose. On November 29, he was again examined, but on this occasion chiefly with reference to the Jesuits' missions to Spain ; and stated that, in Elizabeth's reign, Thomas Winter had gone to Spain, to obtain military aid from the Spaniards, under the direct approval and advice of Catesby, Garnet, and Mounteagle—but the latter's name was obliterated from the paper on which the prisoner's deposition was reported. Soon after this he appears to have become too ill to be frequently examined ; but before dying he committed (in order to help Father Garnet) one of the most astounding acts of perjury on record, for he swore 'upon his salvation' that what he had previously said about Garnet and the Spanish treason was untrue, and that he had not seen Father Garnet for sixteen years.

This impudent perjury, instead of helping Garnet, only tended to hurt him, for Cecil had ample proofs that, so far from Tresham not having met Garnet for sixteen years,[1] he had actually met him often during the last sixteen months, and even weeks. In the form of an official rejoinder to this death-bed declaration was produced a copy of a 'Treatise of Equivocation,' found in Tresham's lodgings, in which notes of approval of the doctrine of 'mental reservation' were written in Garnet's own handwriting.[2] It was thus clear to all that Tresham was an able pupil of that past-master in the art of equivocation and dissimulation, Father Henry Garnet, S.J.

Let us now return to Guy Faukes, who had been all this time lodged in the Tower[3] in very much less comfortable quarters than Tresham ;

---

[1] Garnet, at his trial, acknowledged that Tresham probably 'meant to equivocate.'

[2] So late as December 9, Tresham actually denied all knowledge of the contents of this book, although it was found amongst his effects.

[3] He was placed in a subterranean cell under the White Tower, and afterwards in 'Little Ease.'

for instead of occupying a room large enough to admit of the presence of cheerful companions, he was locked up in a narrow and unlighted cell, beneath the surface of the ground, in immediate proximity to the place of torture. At first the Government were considerably baffled to discover the prisoner's real name; for, owing to his having spent his life (until burrowing like a mole in Percy's cellar) either in Yorkshire or abroad, his face was not known to Salisbury's spies. This circumstance reflects credit on the cleverness of Catesby, who had calculated on this from the first, and had specially selected Faukes in consequence for the task of remaining to the last moment at Westminster. On November 7, his name was discovered by means of a letter found upon his person, and he admitted that he was Guy Faukes, of York.

On November 6, he was examined, but refused to mention any names of his friends. ' The giving warning to one,' he pertinently remarked, in defence of this attitude, ' overthrew us all.'

On November 7, he was (after torture) more communicative. He confessed that the conspiracy had been contrived a year and half ago; that it was at first only manipulated by five persons; that the Princess Elizabeth was to be placed on the throne, and, as soon as possible, to be married to an English Roman Catholic nobleman.

On November 8, Sir William Waad writes to Cecil in a state of great disappointment. On the night previous he had found Faukes in a pliant mood, and expected that he would reveal everything on the morrow.   In the morning, however, he found that Faukes 'hath changed his mind, and is sullen and obstinate.'   On the same day, nevertheless (probably after torture) Faukes again changed his mind, and revealed much.   He repeated his previous story as to the seizure of the Princess Elizabeth, and stated that Thomas Winter was the man who had induced him to join the plot.   He also freely 'gave away' the names of Percy, Digby, Tresham, Keyes, Grant, Rookewood, and the Wrights.

On November 9, Faukes promised to make further revelations, provided that he might disclose them, unwritten, to Salisbury in private. Waad advised Salisbury to see the prisoner, but there is no record of his having done so.   On the same day Faukes disclosed full details of the meeting at the house near St. Clement's Inn, where Gerard gave them the Sacrament, and of the subsequent proceedings of the conspirators.[1] This last deposition was not formally attested and signed till November 17, and so weak was the shattered frame of the tortured man that he only scrawled the word 'Guido,' and then, after making two faint dashes, swooned away.

[1] A freshly worded, and more concise *précis* of this confession was made before this deed was signed on November 17 by Faukes. The conspirators at Holbeach had, of course, by then been taken, and if Faukes knew this, he may have felt little scruple in mentioning their names, now common property.

On November 16, Guy Faukes had declared
that Catesby had tried to warn Lord Montague
against being present on the fifth; that Lord
Mordaunt would, in any event, have not been
present; that Lord Stourton was to be detained
by an artifice; that Tresham wished to warn
Lord Mounteagle, as did all the conspirators the
Earl of Arundel.

On December 8, it was ascertained that
Faukes's mother was alive, and that he had been
at school with Greenway (the Jesuit) and the
Wrights. On January 9, 1606, Faukes gave
an account of how Catesby sent Sir Edward
Baynham to Rome to complain of the way the
English Catholics were persecuted.

On January 25, a conversation was reported,
in which Guy Faukes was overheard to have
discussed with Robert Winter their forthcoming
trial; and to have said that Lord Mounteagle
had asked the King to save some of their
confederates' lives.[1]

Let us now turn our attention to Thomas
Winter, who, since Catesby was dead, in point of
seniority, ranked as the chief of the conspirators.

On November 12, Winter was examined for
the first time. He admitted that Robert Catesby
was the chief spokesman at the first meeting of
the conspirators. He denied that they had the

---

[1] On January 26, Faukes was examined as to this conversation.
On the 27th, he was put on his trial. On the 20th, Faukes had
reaffirmed what he had said on November 16, about warning
certain noblemen.

assistance of any priest, and that he had ever sworn an oath of secrecy.

On November 23 (?), he made his famous confession, already referred to above, and which will later be dealt with in detail. On the 25th, he incriminated both Tresham and Mounteagle, but the latter's name was partly obliterated in the deposition.

On December 5, he confessed that he had tried to obtain Mr. Talbot of Grafton's assistance; but that the latter had refused to help him or his.

On January 9, 1606, he confessed that the conspirators had received the Sacrament from Father Gerard, who was ignorant of the plot. On January 17, he mentioned his visit to Rome (1599–1600), and said that Sir Edward Baynham was to have informed the Pope, had the explosion taken place.

Sir Everard Digby seems to have made no effort to conceal anything from his interrogators, and was treated by them less roughly than Faukes or Winter. On November 19, under examination, he stated that he had gone into Warwickshire, and lived at Coughton, at Catesby's advice. Catesby, in order to induce him to take the field after the failure of the Plot, had prevaricated, and told him the King and Cecil were dead. Confronted with Faukes, he admitted his knowledge of the plot.

On November 23, he wrote to Cecil, stating that he wished to reveal everything, but really knew little more than he had previously mentioned. On December 2, he stated that Catesby revealed the plot to him in October; that Garnet was frequently with him at Coughton; that Catesby had agreed to warn the Romanist Peers. On December 10, he repeated his story as to Catesby having announced the King's death. On January 9, he said that Catesby had administered the oath to him, but he did not receive the Sacrament after it.

In the examinations of Robert Winter,[1] Grant, Keyes, and Rookewood there is nothing very remarkable to be noticed, but those of Bates are worth comment. On December 4,[2] he revealed how Catesby, his master, had induced him to join the plot; how he had spoken of the plot in confession to Father Greenway, who had approved of it; how that, terrified by the explosion, he went away from Holbeach; that from Holbeach a message had been sent to Talbot of Grafton. On January 13, he gave an account of his being sent from Norbrook with a letter from Sir Everard Digby to 'Mr. Farmer' (Father Garnet) at Coughton. Garnet and Greenway both read the letter, and the latter returned with him to see Catesby at Huddington. Garnet, according to Bates, said to Greenway, on reading the letter, that 'they (the conspirators) would have blown up

---

[1] On January 17 (1606), R. Winter gave the account of how the conspirators had been absolved by Father Hart, *alias* Hammond, S.J., who knew of the plot having failed.

[2] In this confession his name is written 'Bate.'

the Parliament House, and were discovered, and were all utterly undone.'   After leaving Hudding-ton, Father Greenway left for Mr. Abington's house (Hendlip), to raise recruits for Catesby's force.

The importance of this last confession was great in the extreme, for it not only proved Greenway to be guilty of treason, but also tended to show that Greenway had seen the conspirators at Huddington with the approval and permission of his superior, Garnet.   That Bates was speak-ing the truth, however, has been denied by Jesuit writers, who urge that Greenway subsequently denied that Bates ever mentioned the subject of the plot to him in the confessional; and that Garnet, whilst questioning the accuracy of Bates's version of the Coughton story, complained that he was being condemned on the evidence of a dead man.   But notwithstanding the denials of these priests, it is probable that Bates's story, although extracted from him under terror of torture, was in the main part true; and both Greenway and Garnet were such notorious pre-varicators that no reliance can be placed on any of their statements, unless corroborated by indis-putable evidence forthcoming from other sources.

Finally, in concluding this chronological record of the conspirators' confessions, it will be well to reproduce from the version in King James's Book on the Plot the important deposition of Guy Faukes, as signed by him on November 17, and witnessed by Sir William Waad, Sir Edward

Coke, Sir John Popham, and the Lords Dunbar,
Mar, Salisbury, Nottingham, Suffolk, Worcester,
Devonshire, Northampton.

'I confess that a practice in general was first
broken unto me, against his Majesty, for relief
of the Catholick cause, and not invented or
propounded by myself. And this was first
propounded unto me by about Easter last was
twelvemonth beyond the seas, in the low-countries,
of the arch-duke's obeisance, by Thomas Wynter,
who came thereupon with me into England, and
there we imparted our purpose to three other
gentlemen more, namely, Robert Catesby, Thomas
Percy, and John Wright, who, all five, consulting
together, of the means how to execute the same;
and taking a vow, among ourselves, for secrecy,
Catesby propounded to have it performed by
gunpowder, and by making a mine under the
upper house of Parliament; which place we made
choice of, the rather, because, religion have been
unjustly suppressed there, it was fittest that justice
and punishment should be executed there.
'This being resolved amongst us, Thomas
Percy hired an house at Westminster for that
purpose, near adjoining to the Parliament House,
and there we began to make our mine about
December 11, 1604. The five that first entered
into the work were Thomas Percy, Robert
Catesby, Thomas Winter, John Wright, and
myself, and soon after we took another unto us,
Christopher Wright, having sworn him also, and
taken the Sacrament for secrecy. When we came
to the very foundation of the wall of the house,
which was about three yards thick, and found it

a matter of great difficulty, we took unto us another gentleman, Robert Winter, in like manner, with the Oath and Sacrament as aforesaid. It was about Christmas, when we brought our mine unto the wall, and about Candlemas, we had wrought the wall half through; and, whilst they were in working I stood as a sentinel, to descry any man that came near, whereof I gave warning, and so they ceased, until I gave notice again to proceed. All we seven lay in the house, and had shot and powder, being resolved to die in that place, before we should yield or be taken. As they were working upon the wall, they heard a rushing in a cellar, of removing of coals; whereupon we feared we had been discovered, and they sent me to go to the cellar, who finding that the coles were a selling, and that the cellar was to let, viewing the commodity thereof for our purpose, Percy went and hired the same for yearly rent. We had before this provided and brought into the house twenty barrels of powder, which we removed into the cellar, and covered the same with billets and faggots, which we provided for that purpose.

'About Easter, the Parliament being prorogued till October next, we dispersed ourselves, and I retired into the Low-Countries, by advice and direction of the rest, as well to acquaint Owen[1] with the particulars of the plot, as also lest by my longer stay I might have grown suspicious, and so have come in question. In the meantime, Percy, having the key of the cellar,

---

[1] Captain Hugh Owen, a Jesuit agent, whom the Government much wished to prove guilty of being accessory to the plot.

H

laid in more powder and wood into it. I returned about the beginning of September next, and, then, receiving the key again of Percy, we brought in more powder and billets to cover the same again, and so I went for a time into the country, till October 30.

'It was further resolved amongst us that the same day that this action should have been performed, some other of our confederates should have surprised the person of the Lady Elizabeth, the King's eldest daughter, who was kept in Warwickshire, at the Lord Harrington's house, and presently have proclaimed her for Queen, having a project of a proclamation ready for the purpose; wherein we made no mention of altering of religion, nor would have avowed the deed to be ours until we should have had power enough to make our party good, and then we would have avowed both.

'Concerning Duke Charles, the King's second son, we had sundry consultations how to seize on his person, but because we found no means how to compass it, the duke being kept near London, where we had not forces enough, we resolved to serve our turn with the Lady Elizabeth.

'The Names of other principal persons that were made privy afterwards to this horrible conspiracy.[1]

  — Everard Digby Knight,
  — Ambrose Rookewood,
  — Francis Tresham,
  — John Grant,
  — Robert Keyes.'

[1] The name of Bates is omitted.

WESTMINSTER HALL AND PALACE YARD.

(Fawkes, T. Winter, Rookwood, and Keyes were executed in this yard.)

CHAPTER XII

OUT of the original number of thirteen, only eight of the conspirators survived to be committed for trial. These eight, namely, Thomas Winter, Guy Faukes, John Grant, Robert Winter, Ambrose Rookewood, Thomas Bates, Robert Keyes, and Digby, were arraigned at Westminster Hall, on January 27, 1606, before a Commission consisting of the Lord Chief Justice (Sir John Popham), the Lord Chief Baron (Sir Thomas Fleming), Sir Peter Warburton (a Judge), and the Earls of Salisbury, Northampton,[1] Nottingham, Suffolk, Worcester, and Devonshire. Sir Everard Digby was separately arraigned, and tried and sentenced immediately after the conclusion of the case against his friends. The Counsel for the Crown were Sir Edward Philips and Sir Edward Coke.

The prisoners were not represented by counsel. All of them, however, with the sole exception of Sir Everard Digby, pleaded 'Not Guilty.' This bold policy of refusing to plead 'Guilty' was

---

[1] Northampton was a Roman Catholic, although by no means a strict or devout member of that religion.

apparently taken by them on account of the manner in which the indictment had been framed, the absent priests (Garnet, Greenway, and Gerard) all being mentioned by name as participators in the plot. When asked, therefore, 'why he pleaded Not Guilty,' [1] Faukes only voiced the opinion of his confederates, when he replied, 'That he had done so in respect of certain conferences mentioned in the indictment, which he said that he knew not of : which were answered to have been set down according to course of law, as necessarily pre-supposed before the resolution of such a design.'

The trial from beginning to end was a mere farce. The prisoners, after having to listen to a very long, by no means truthful, and very violent speech from Sir Edward Coke, and having heard 'their several Examinations, Confessions, and voluntary Declarations, as well of themselves, as of some of their dead Confederates,' read out, were merely asked, ' What they could say, where-fore Judgment of Death should not be pronounced against them ?' [1] and the trial was virtually over, so far as the hearing of their case was concerned.

Thomas Winter, on being asked what he had to answer for himself, ' only desired that he might be hanged both for his brother and himself.'

Robert Keyes said, 'That his estate and fortune were desperate, and as good now as at another time, and for this cause rather than for another.'

[1] *State Trials*, vol. ii., edited by Cobbett.

Thomas Bates and Robert Winter 'craved mercy.' John Grant ' was a good while mute; yet after, submissively said, he was guilty of a conspiracy intended, but never effected.'

Ambrose Rookewood ' first excused his denial of the Indictment, for that he had rather lose his life than give it. · Then did he acknowledge his offence to be so heinous, that he justly deserved the indignation of the King, and of the Lords, and the hatred of the whole commonwealth; yet could he not despair of mercy at the hands of a prince, so abounding in grace and mercy; and the rather, because his offence, though it were in-capable of any excuse, yet not altogether incapable of some extenuation, in that he had been neither author, nor actor, but only persuaded and drawn in by Catesby, whom he loved above any worldly man : and that he had concealed it not for any malice to the person of the King, or to the State, or for any ambitious respect of his own, but only drawn with the tender respect, and the faithful and dear affection he bare to Mr. Catesby, his friend, whom he esteemed dearer than anything else in the world. And this mercy he desired not for any fear of the image of death, but for grief that so shameful a death should leave so perpetual a blemish and blot unto all ages, upon his name and blood. But, howsoever that this was his first offence, yet he humbly submitted himself to the mercy of the King; and prayed that the King would herein imitate God, who sometimes doth punish *corporaliter, non mortaliter*, "corporally, yet not mortally."[1]

'. . . Here also was reported Robert Winter's dream, which he had before the blasting with powder in Lyttleton's house, and which he himself confessed and first notified, viz. That he thought he saw steeples stand awry, and within those churches strange and unknown faces. And after, when the aforesaid blast had the day following scorched divers of his confederates, and much disfigured the faces and countenances of Grant, Rookewood, and others ; then did Winter call to mind his dream, and to his remembrance thought, that the faces of his associates so scorched, resembled those which he had seen in the dream.'

Sir Everard Digby pleaded guilty, stating, *inter alia*, that his firm friend, Catesby, had introduced him to the conspirators, whom he had joined 'for the restoring of the Catholic religion in England.' He requested that all his property might be preserved for his wife and children, and that he might be beheaded, instead of hanged. The last request would,[1] in all probability, have been granted, had not Digby, most unfortunately for himself, made reference to the fact 'that promises were broken with the Catholics.' This was too open a criticism of the King's duplicity not to be understood by all in Court, and brought Cecil to his feet, who denied that James had ever committed himself so far as to promise toleration to the Roman Catholics.

[1] Aubrey (who calls Sir Everard 'the handsomest gentleman in England') states that ' King James restored his estate to his son and heir.'

The winter's afternoon was by now so far advanced that darkness had set in, and in that dimly lighted, sombre Court the jury quickly found all the accused men guilty, and the Lord Chief Justice passed sentence of death.[1]

'Upon the rising of the Court, Sir Everard Digby, bowing himself towards the Lords, said, "If I may but hear any of your Lordships say you forgive me, I shall go more cheerfully to the gallows." Whereunto the Lords said, "God forgive you, and we do."'[2]

The conspirators met their fate with courage, considering the terrible nature of their punishment. Tied to separate hurdles, they were dragged, lying bound on their backs, through the muddy streets to the place of execution, there to be first hanged, cut down alive, drawn, and then quartered.

Guy Faukes, weak and ill though he was, seems to have suffered the least, for he was dead by the time his body was taken down. Ambrose Rookewood lived until he reached the quartering-block. Keyes, breaking the rope, was probably killed by the knife; whilst Sir Everard Digby was in full possession of all his senses on being cut down, and even felt the pain of a bruise on the head when his body fell to the ground.

[1] Hanging, drawing, and quartering.

[2] Anything more absolutely in accord with the traditional story of the Plot than the above confessions of Rookewood, Thomas Winter, and Digby it is difficult to conceive; yet, with almost incredible audacity, some Jesuit writers have had the hardihood to question whether there was a Plot at all.

CHAPTER XIII

OF intense interest and importance is the correspondence, that has been preserved to us, of Sir Everard Digby when a prisoner in the Tower of London. He found means, probably by bribing his gaolers, to smuggle letters out of the Tower of London without detection. These letters were scribbled on scraps of paper, and were generally left unaddressed and unsigned, whilst they were often written with lemon juice in lieu of ordinary ink. They were not discovered until seventy years after his death, when they were found amongst the papers of his famous son, Sir Kenelm, and were published by a contemporary writer,[1] from whose original edition I reprint them below.

These letters have been ignored, as much as possible, by Jesuit writers, for the good reason that they reveal, on the whole, their favourite, Digby, in a not very pleasant light.

[1] They were printed in the Appendix to Thomas Barlow's (Bishop of Lincoln) account of the *Gunpowder Treason*, published at the Bishop's Head, St. Paul's Churchyard, February, 1679. In a later edition, published in 1850, no less than five of the letters are omitted.

As will be seen by their perusal, Digby, notwithstanding the clever way in which he fenced with the Lords of the Council, had frequently been, during the nine months preceding the plot, in the company of Fathers Garnet and Greenway, as well as of Gerard. Moreover, he does not seem to consider that his share in the plot was a crime, and expresses his intense surprise that the majority of his co-religionists regarded the proceedings of himself and his friends with horror. Beyond all doubt, too, he seems to have thought that the English Jesuits not only knew of the plot, but secretly approved of it, for he writes of his ' certain belief that those which were best able to judge of the lawfulness of it, had been acquainted with it, and given way unto it. More reasons I had to persuade me to this belief than I dare utter!' When, therefore, the Jesuit apologists pretend that Father Garnet did not receive a fair trial, and was unjustly condemned, they should remember that had this paper of Digby's, from which the above extract is taken, been produced at Garnet's trial, it would have afforded damning evidence against him, in regard to his being absolutely possessed of certain information as to Catesby's conspiracy.

THE LETTERS

' The Several Papers and Letters of Sir Everard Digby which are (as we have been credibly informed) the Original Papers and

Letters written by him, concerning the Gunpowder Treason, were found by us, Sir Rice Rudd, Baronet, and William Wogan, of Grays-Inn, Esquire; in the presence of Mrs. Ursula Giles, and Mr. Thomas Hughes, about the month of September, 1675, at the House of Charles Cornwallis, Esq.; who was Executor of Sir Kenelm Digby (Son and Heir to the said Sir Everard) tied up in two Silk Bags, amongst the Deeds, Evidences, and Writings of the said Sir Kenelm Digby.'

PAPER I

Jesus

'I have not named any either living or dead, that should have hurt my Lord Salisbury: and only intended these general informations to procure me access of some friend, that I might inform my knowledge, for I never intended to hurt any creature, though it would have gained me all the world. As yet they have not got of me the affirming that I know any Priest particularly, nor shall ever do to the hurt of any but myself.

'At my first examination, the Earl of Salisbury told me that some things should be affirmed against me by Gerrat[1] the Priest, who (saith he) I am sure you know well. My answer was, that if I might see him, I would tell him whether I

---

[1] Gerard.

knew him or no, but by that name I did not know him, nor at Mrs. Vauxe's, as he said I did, for I never saw a Priest there. Yesterday I was before Mr. Attorney and my Lord Chief Justice, who asked me if I had taken the Sacrament to keep secret the plot as others did. I said that I had not, because I would avoid the question of at whose hands it were. They told me that 5 had taken it of Gerrard, and that he knew of the Plot, which I said was more than I knew.

'Now for my intention let me tell you, that if I had thought there had been the least sin in the Plot, I would not have been in it for all the world: and no other cause drew me to hazard my Fortune, and Life, but Zeal to God's religion. For my keeping it secret, it was caused by certain belief, that those which were best able to judge of the lawfulness of it, had been acquainted with it, and given way unto it. More reasons I had to persuade me to this belief than I dare utter, which I will never, to the suspicion of any, though I should be to the rack for it, and as I did not know it directly that it was approved by such, so did I hold it in my conscience the best not to know any more if I might.

'I have, before all the Lords, cleared all the Priests in it for anything that I know, but now let me tell you, what a grief it hath been to me, to hear that so much condemned which I did believe would have been otherwise thought on by Catholics; there is no other cause but this, which hath made me desire Life, for when I came into prison death would have been a welcome friend unto me, and was most desired; but when I heard how Catholics and Priests thought of the matter, and that it should be a great sin that should be the cause of my end, it called my conscience in doubt of my very best actions and intentions in question : for I knew that my self might easily be deceived in such a business, therefore I protest unto you that the doubts I had of my own good state, which only proceeded from the censure of others, caused more bitterness of grief in me than all the miseries that ever I suffered, and only this caused me with life till I might meet with a ghostly friend. For some good space I could do nothing, but with tears ask pardon at God's hands for all my errors, both in actions and intentions in this business, and in my whole life, which the censure of this contrary to my expectance caused me to doubt : I did humbly beseech that my death might satisfy for my offence, which I should and shall offer most gladly to the Giver of life.

'I assure you as I hope in God that the love of all my Estate and worldly happiness did never trouble me, nor the love of it since my imprisonment did ever move me to with life. But if that I may live to make satisfaction to God, and the world where I have given any scandal, I shall not grieve if I should never look living creature in the face again, and besides that deprivation endure all worldly misery. I shall not need to clear any living body either private or public, for I never named any body, but reported that those that are dead did promise that all forces in those parts about Mr. Talbot[1] would assist us, but this can hurt nothing, for they openly spoke it. You must be careful how you send, for Mr. Lieutenant hath stayed the . . . book,[2] but take no notice of it. Let my Brother see this, or know the contents, tell him I love his sweet comforts as my greatest jewel in this Place, if I can, I will convey in the tables a copy of a letter which I sent yesterday ; it is as near as I can understand the meaning of the instruction. I perceive it works with the Lords, for I shall be sent to them. Oh how full of joy should I die if I could do anything for the cause which I love more than my life ! Farewell my '

PAPER II

' Besides the trunk of armour which was sent to Mr. Catesbye's I did carry but one other trunk with me, which had in it cloathes of mine, as a white satin doublet cut with purple, a jerkin and hose of de-roy colour satin laid very thick with gold-lace ; there were other garments in it of mine, with a new black winter gown of my wife's, there was also in the trunk £300 in money, and

[1] John Talbot, of Grafton.
[2] The original MS. was here imperfect.

this trunk did I see safe at Mr. Lyttleton's house after the blowing up of the powder.

'Since that Mr. Addis cannot spare time from his business to sell such goods as shall be necessary to defray the expense of my Wife, children, and family, and my own charges, my desire, therefore, is that one Andrew Knight of Newport, dwelling near the house where these goods are, should have power given him to make sale of such things as shall be thought necessary for these purposes.'

 'by me EVERARD DIGBY,

  'W. WAAD, *locum ten. turris.*'[1]

PAPER III

'Since the writing of the other which I sent you, I have been with the Lords, whose chiefest questions were what I meant by the message, which I should send you to Coughton, about laying up that which I delivered, which, said the Lords, were either a Priest or money, but I denied the sending of any such message ; they asked me of Father Wallies[2] being there, which I denied ; also they asked me what letter Mr. Catesby did send to him, but could tell them of none : it seemeth that Bate[3] hath confessed thus much, whether he hath been tortured or no I do not know ; they asked me what company I kept the

---

[1] This letter was evidently despatched with the sanction of the Lieutenant of the Tower.

[2] Garnet.

[3] Bates.

Sunday sevenight before the day: to which I
could not answer, for I did not remember; but
they told me I was in the company of Father
Walley,[1] Father Greenway, and Father Gerrard
at Mrs. Vauxe's; I told them I had been in their
companies, but not there, or anywhere else with
others but myself; they said Mr. Greenway came
to Huddington[2] when we there, and had speech
with Mr. ——,[3] but I told them it was more than
I took note of, and that I did not know him very
well, that he would be very careful of himself;
my lord of Salisbury told me he had received
my letter,[4] but if the King should propose such
a course he had no need of me. I was not much
pressed in these matters, and so they dismissed
me for this time. Farewell my dearest.'

Paper IV

'Since my late writing, I have been examined
about the knowledge of Foster and Hamon. I
give my Brother many thanks for his sweet
comforts, and assure him that now I desire
death; for the more I think on God's mercy the
more I hope in my own case: though others
have censured our intention otherwise than I
understood them to be, and though the act be

[1] Garnet.

[2] On his own admission, Greenway actually said Mass for the
conspirators at Huddington.

[3] Evidently Catesby, who introduced Greenway to the conspirators as 'A gentleman who would live and die with them!'

[4] The text of this letter will be reproduced later in this chapter.

thought so wickid by those of judgment, yet I hope that my understanding it otherwise, with my sorrow for my error, will find acceptance at God's hands. I have not as yet acknowledged the knowledge of any Priest in particular, nor will do to the hurt of any but myself, whatsoever betide me. I could give unanswerable reasons both for the good that this would have done for the Catholic cause, and for my being from home, but I think it now needless, and for some respect unfit. I do perceive the Lords will come hither no more, which caused me to write, which copy I send you. I have some guess that it worketh, but the Lieutenant maketh all show to me of the contrary; for, saith he, the Catholics are so few in number as they are not to be feared on any terms, for on his knowledge there were not above 4000[1] in all England. Besides, he said, they were easily pacified. I would not at all argue the matter with him, but if the number should be objected by the Lords unto me, why may I not answer it thus, that it is certain that there are at least 400 priests in England, therefore by all consequence there must be more Catholics: if there be inconvenience in it let me know and I have done. If I be called to question for the Priest, in my letter I purpose to name him Winscombe, unless I be advised otherwise.

[1] This estimate of the number of the English Roman Catholics is, of course, far too low.

' I do desire my brothers advice for Sir Oliver,[1] for his rents I never received any, and only owe £200, which I kept in my hands for the good of the best cause, out of which I had paid £30. There is £100 yet to be paid to my cousin John to him, and the bonds for that and three more he hath paid, are in my gilt-box, at least there I left them : I durst not make a perfect note for his estate, because I know not his course, and whether it would be hurtful for me to put it from myself to him, as.'

PAPER V

' I do not well conceive my brother, for I did never say that any other told me but Mr. Catesby about the Lords' particulars ; and for affirming that a priest in general said something of Intentions of redress, I did understand Tar : notice to give approbation, I have not been asked his name, which if I had, should have been such a one as I knew not of. Howsoever my brother is informed, I am sure they fear him for knowledge of the Plot, for at every examination I am told that he[2] did give the Sacrament to five[3] at one time, who they say have confessed it —I do not know who they may be ; sure I am

---

[1] Sir Oliver Manners, son of the fourth, and brother of the fifth and sixth Earls of Rutland. He was received into the Church of Rome, and became a priest.

[2] Father Gerard, S.J.

[3] Of the conspirators.

that I never yet did confess to know him nor any of the three.   I do it not in regard of myself, as it shall appear at the bar, for whatsoever I could do for him or any of his, I would do it though it cost me never so much sufferance; but I have been sparing in that, because I may do more in public, which will, I think, be best, as you wish I will do, and what else may clear me from scandal, not with any hopes or desire of favour; my little friends' courtesy is very comfortable, entreat them to pray for the pardoning of my not sufficient striving against temptations since this business was undertook.   Farewell, God send you can read.'

Paper VI

'You forgot to tell me whether Winscombe be a fit name: I like it, for I know none of it.   You need not fear this lord, for he never looks in the tables, nor dare shew them to any.   Tell my brother I do honour him as befits me, but I did not think I could have increased in so much, loving him more as his charitable lessons would make me.   Your information doth much comfort me, but I pray you after my death, let me not want good prayers, for my need is great, though my trust in God is not small, as occasions fall out you will know.   Farewell.'

Paper VII

'I have found your pennywares, but never that in the waistcoat till this night. The substance of my last writing was strictly examined about Mr. Darcy,[1] who they said, the first time, was Blackwell,[2] but after they told me it was Walley or Garnet. I told them it was more than I knew, for I did not take him to be a priest. They also urged me with Brooke, Fisher, and Browne, and said they were priests, and that Brooke was Gerrard, but I answered I did not know so much; they told me that I had been at Mrs. Vauxe's with this company, and that I knew Gerrard there, but I denied it. They did in a fashion offer me the torture, which I will rather endure than hurt anybody, as yet I have not tried it . . . the next time I will write more, I could scarce.'

Paper VIII

'You shall find in this paper with . . . the reasons of my not acquainting an inward friend with the business, was not for any particular

[1] Garnet.

[2] Mr. George Blackwell, Archpriest of the Romanists in England. He was a mere tool of the Jesuits, and his appointment as Archpriest, together with his relations with the Jesuits, produced great dissensions amongst the English Romanists, especially among the Secular priests. He was deprived of his office by Pope Paul V. in 1608. The Secular clergy sent reprentatives to Rome to appeal against the tyranny of Blackwell and his Jesuits.

wilfulness, or ill end ; but I thought it not best for the Cause, nor did not think it ill, which was to be done, since necessity compelled, as I thought somewhat to be done.   I saw the principal point of the case, judged in a latin book of M.D.,[1] my brother's father-in-law, I neither can nor will draw in suspect for a world, but if he were deceived in that point by a prefixed day, let him think I had more cause than he.'

PAPER IX

'My Dearest the . . . I take at the uncharitable taking of these matters, will make me say more than ever I thought to have done.   For if this design had taken place, there could have been no doubt of other success : for that night, before any other could have brought the news, we should have known it by Mr. Catesby, who should have proclaimed the Heir Apparent at Charing Cross, as he came out of Town ; to which purpose there was a Proclamation drawn ; if the Duke [2] had not been in the House, then there was a certain way laid for possessing him ; but in regard of the assurance, they should have been there, therefore the greatest of our business stood in the possessing the Lady Elizabeth, who lying within eight miles of Dunchurch, we would have easily surprised before the knowledge of any

[1] Father Martin del Rio, S.J.
[2] Charles I. (then Duke of York).

doubt : this was the cause of my being there. If she had been in Rutland, then Stoaks [1] was near, and in either place we had taken sufficient order to have been possessed of her ; there was also courses taken for the satisfying the people if the first had taken effect, as the speedy notice of liberty and freedom from all manner of slavery, as the ceasing of Wardship and all Monopolies, which with change would have been more plausible to the people, if the first had been than it is now. There was also a course taken to have given present notice to all Princes,[2] and to associate them with an oath answerable to the League in France. I have not uttered any of these things, nor ever thought to do ; for my going from Dunchurch I had this reason. First, I knew that Faukes could reveal me, for I must make choice of two besides Mr. Catesby, which I did of him and Mr. Winter.[3] I knew he had been employed in great matters, and till torture sure he carried it very well. Secondly, we all thought if we could procure Mr. Talbot to rise that . . . party at least to a composition . . . that was not little, because we had in our company his son-in-law,[4] who gave us some hope of, and did not much doubt it. I do answer your speech with Mr. Browne thus. Before that I knew anything of

[1] Stoke.
[2] The Catholic Powers on the Continent.
[3] Thomas Winter.
[4] Robert Winter had married Talbot's daughter.

this plot, I did ask Mr. Farmer[1] what the meaning of the Pope's Brief was; he[1] told me that they were not (meaning Priests) to undertake or procure stirs: but yet they would not hinder any, neither was it the Pope's mind they should that should be undertaken for Catholic good. I did never utter thus much, nor would not but to you; and this answer with Mr. Catesby's proceedings with him and me, give me absolute belief that the matter in general was approved, though every particular was not known. I dare not take that course that I could, to make it appear less odious; for divers were to have been brought out of the danger, which now would rather hurt them than otherwise. I do not think that there would have been three worth saving that should have been lost; you may guess that I had some friends that were in danger, which I had prevented, but they shall never know it. I will do as much as my partner wisheth, and it will then appear, that I have not hurt or accused one man, and howsoever I might in general possess them with fear, in hope to do the Cause good, yet my care was ever to lose my own life, rather than hurt the unworthiest member of the Catholic Church. Tell her I have ever loved her and her house, and though I could never shew it, I will not live to manifest the contrary. Her Go: I hope will

---

[1] Father Garnet, S.J. In spite of this decisive evidence against him, Jesuit writers have pretended that Garnet never used the alias of 'Farmer'!

remember me, who I am in temporal respects indebted to : your sister salute from me, whose noble mind to me in this misery I will never . . . my lord of Arundell may do much with the Lord and the Queen. One that you write of which dearly loveth him, and is dearly loved of him again, can tell him that I love him, and did manifest it in his fight, and he might have found it; last time as I saw him, was in his company, as I think. I am sure when this was, he was there. If your mother were in town you should . . . Farewell, and where you can understand, send to me by your next, and I will explain.'

In addition to the above there were also found among the papers of Sir Kenelm Digby a letter by Sir Everard to his children, dated ' from my prison this 23. of Jan. 1605,' and two poems, evidently by the same pen. As these three contain, however, no matter of any importance touching upon the plot, there is no need to insert them here.

In Digby's third letter (Paper III.), he mentions 'my lord of Salisbury . . . received my letter.' Of this letter I reproduce the greater part below, as its contents decidedly merit reproduction. Before doing so, however, it is only fair to state that so great an authority as Dr. S. R. Gardiner ('What Gunpowder Plot Was'), considers that this letter was not sent by Digby whilst in the Tower, but was written by him at some unknown date, between May 4 and

September, 1605. This view is also held by
Father John Gerard, S.J., in his 'What Was the
Gunpowder Plot?' I, however, humbly beg to
agree with Mrs. Everett Green (Editor, Dom. S.
P. James I.), that this letter must have been
despatched from the Tower early in December,
1605, and penned, therefore, whilst Digby was a
prisoner. The whole tone of the text seems to
bear upon the recent plot and the terrible position
of the writer, who, in evident reference to his
impending fate, says, ' I shall be as willing to die
as I am ready,' etc., and signs himself, 'Your
Lordship's poor Bedesman, Ev. Digby.' Father
Gerard's statement that it cannot have been
written by a prisoner, because ' it was sealed with
a crest or coat-of-arms,' is absurd in the extreme.
Digby was lodged like a gentleman in the Tower,
finding means to write to his friends, to buy good
food, and to wear fine clothes ; why, therefore, in
the name of common sense, should he have been
deprived of the use of so simple and usual an
article in those days as a signet ring, or ordinary
seal ? Moreover, only as recently as November
23, he had been allowed to write direct to Salisbury, asking, *inter alia*, that the royal clemency
might be extended to his family.

'. . . I do assure myself that His Holiness
may be drawn to manifest so contrary a disposition
of excommunicating the King that he will proceed
with the same course against all such as shall go
about to disturb the King's quiet and happy

reign; and the willingness of Catholics, especially of Priests and Jesuits, is such as I dare undertake to procure any Priest in England (though it were the Superior[1] of the Jesuits) to go himself to Rome to negotiate this business, and that both he and all other religious men (till the Pope's pleasure be known) shall take any spiritual course to stop the effect that may proceed from any discontented or despairing Catholics. And I doubt not but his return would bring both assurance that such course should not be taken with the King, and that it should be performed against any that should seek to disturb him for religion. If this were done, there could then be no cause to fear any Catholic, and this may be done only with those proceedings (which as I understand your lordship) should be used. If your lordship apprehend it to be worth the doing, I shall be glad to be the instrument, for no hope to put off from myself any punishment, but only that I wish safety to the King and ease to the Catholics. If your lordship and the State think fit to deal severely with the Catholics, within brief time there will be massacres, rebellions, and desperate attempts against the King and State. For it is a general received reason amongst Catholics that there is not that expecting and suffering course now to be run that was in the Queen's time,[2] who was the last of the line, and last in expectance to run violent courses against Catholics; for then it was hoped that the King that now is

[1] Father Garnet was then the Superior of the Jesuits in England, but he was subservient to Father Parsons, who resided abroad, and was the real head of the English Jesuits.

[2] i.e. the later period of Elizabeth's reign.

would have been at least free from persecuting, as
his promise was before his coming into his Realm,
and as divers his promises have been since his
coming, saying that he would take no soul money
nor blood.   Also, as it appeared, was the whole
body of the Council's pleasure when they sent for
divers of the better sort of Catholics, as Sir Tho.
Tressam [1] and others, and told them it was the
King's pleasure to forgive the payment of
Catholics, so long as they should carry themselves
dutifully and well.   All these promises every
man sees broken, and to trust them further in
despair most Catholics take note of a vehement
look, written by Mr. Attorney,[2] whose drift, as I
have heard, is to prove that the only being a
Catholic is to be a traitor, which look coming
forth after the breach of so many promises, and
before the ending of such a violent Parliament,
can work no less effect in mens' minds that every
Catholic will be brought within that compass
before the King and State have done with them.
And I know, as the Prince himself told me, that
if he had not hindered there had somewhat been
attempted " before our offence," [3] to give ease to
Catholics.   But being so prevented, and so
necessary to avoid, I doubt not but your lordship
and the rest of the Lords will think of a more
mild and undoubted safe course, in which I
will   undertake   the   performance   of   what   I

---

[1] Father of the conspirator.

[2] Sir Edward Coke.

[3] The words 'before our offence' must naturally refer to the
Plot. It is curious that Dr. Gardiner should have overlooked this
sentence, which proves my contention that the letter must have
been written from the Tower, and not before November 5.

have promised and as much as can be expected, and when I have done, I shall be as willing to die as I am ready to offer my service, and expect not nor desire favour for it, either before the doing it, nor in the doing it, nor after it is done, but refer myself to the resolved course for me. . . .'

Further proof in favour of my contention that this letter was written from the Tower is supplied by Digby's own words (Paper III.), to the effect that Lord Salisbury had received his letter, 'but if the King should propose such a course, he had no need of me.' The answer to Digby's offer of 'service' was, therefore, in the negative, which is not surprising, when we read his bold, but only too true and just comments on the broken promises of James to the persecuted Romanists in England, made prior to his succession to the southern throne.

That the importance of the matter contained in Digby's letters from the Tower has hitherto been underestimated by writers dealing with the Gunpowder Plot need not be questioned.[1] Had the letters been stopped by the Lieutenant and produced at Garnet's trial they would have established the impossibility of the accused having only heard of the Plot through the medium of the confessional. Digby's statements that he had the very strongest reasons for believing that

[1] In the *Dictionary of National Biography*, the writer of the Memoir of Sir Everard Digby never even once mentions the existence of these letters, and terms Sir Kenelm Digby 'the younger son' of Sir Everard, instead of, as he was, the elder

'those who were best able to judge,' *i.e.* the Jesuit Fathers, tacitly approved of it, clearly explain and sum up the whole situation.   In the event of the Plot proving a success, the Jesuits would have taken all the credit for themselves at Rome, and would have claimed that it was worked under their direction.   In the event of the Plot proving a failure, the Jesuits were prepared to denounce it, and to deny all knowledge of its construction. As for Digby himself, he seems to have been a mere silly puppet in the hands of Fathers John Gerard and Henry Garnet.   'My brother,' so constantly referred to by Digby in his correspon- dence, is, of course, Father Gerard, who (in his autobiography) often refers, in his turn, to 'my brother Digby.'   'He was,' says Gerard, 'a most devoted friend to me, just as if he had been my twin-brother.   And this name of brother we always used in writing to each other.'

CHAPTER XIV

THE position of Father Garnet after the capture of the rebels at Holbeach, and the flight of his colleague, Oswald Green-way, became one of great peril, for he knew full well that the Government would strain every nerve to seize him, and, if possible, convict him as an accessory, either before or after the fact, to the Plot. For some time he remained concealed at Coughton, but on December 6,[1] removed by night to Hendlip, nearly four miles north-east of Worcester, where his friend, Father Oldcorne, *alias* Hall, lay concealed. He removed thither in company with his faithful and devoted penitent, Anne Vaux, whose intimacy with him caused considerable scandal at the time of his trial, although there can be little doubt but that this connection was an innocent one, and such as often exists between fanatical, superstitious women and their presuming 'directors.' Before leaving Coughton, he sent a letter to Cecil, protesting his

---

[1] Most writers (Jardine included) state that he did not reach Hendlip till a fortnight later; but my authority is Garnet's own statement, made when examined in the Tower.

innocence of Catesby's proceedings both in regard to the plot at Westminster and the operations in the Midlands. He would have done far better had he left the neighbourhood altogether, with the idea of eventually following Greenway's example, and escaping to the Continent. Probably, however, a sense of duty induced him to remain, for the benefit of those few who were wont to receive the Sacraments from him.

Hendlip Hall,[1] the property of Thomas Abington, was a most remarkable house, though comparatively new, the whole of it having been erected since 1570. It was filled with priests'- holes, most of which had been cunningly contrived by the Jesuit lay-brother, the famous Nicholas Owen, who, acting as servant to Garnet, now came to reside with him, once more, at Hendlip. Of Owen, Father Gerard, in his 'Narrative,' furnishes a very interesting account.

'. . . One Nicholas Owen, commonly called, and most known by the name of Little John. By which name he was so famous and so much esteemed by all Catholics, especially those of the better sort, that few in England, either priests or others, were of more credit . . . his chief em- ployment was in making of secret places to hide priests and church-stuff in from the fury of searches; in which kind he was so skilful both to devise and frame the places in the best manner, and his help therein desired in so many places

---

[1] Now pulled down, and a modern mansion erected on the old site.

that verily I think no man can be said to have
done more good of all those that laboured in the
English Vineyard. For, first, he was the immediate occasion of saving the lives[1] of many hundreds
of persons, both ecclesiastical and secular, and of
the estates also of these seculars, which had been
lost and forfeited many times over if the priests
had been taken in their houses ; of which some
have escaped, not once but many times, in several
searches that have come to the same house, and
sometimes five or six priests together at the same
time. Myself have been one of the seven that
have escaped the danger at one time in a secret
place of his making. . . . One reason that made
him so much desired by Catholics of account, who
might have had other workmen enough to make
conveyances in their houses, was a known and
tried care he had of secrecy, not only from such
as would of malice be inquisitive, but from all
others to whom it belonged not to know; in which
he was so careful that you should never hear him
speak of any houses or places where he had made
such hides. . . .'

Owen is also said to have planned Father
Gerard's extraordinary escape from the Tower of
London in 1597.

Thomas Abington, the owner of Hendlip, was,
like his guest Owen, a very remarkable person.
He had been for over five years imprisoned in

---

[1] He may perhaps have saved the life of King Charles II., who
(after the flight from Worcester) found safety from his pursuers in
a priests' hole, attributed to Owen's skill for its construction, for
both at Boscobel and at Trent House, where Charles hid, were
'holes' contrived by Owen.

the Tower after the failure of Babington's conspiracy in favour of the Queen of Scots.   On his
release, he retired to Hendlip, where he devoted
himself to archæology, taking great interest in
antiquarian lore connected with Worcestershire
and Staffordshire.   But, notwithstanding his love
of learning, his zeal for religion still moved him
to commit imprudent but generous acts, and many
a hunted priest found a safe refuge in one of the
numerous ' holes' at Hendlip.   Moreover, he
maintained, at the time of the Plot, so dangerous
a person in his service as the Jesuit Oldcorne,
who acted as his chaplain, and who invited Garnet
to come, with Owen and another lay-brother,[1]
to Hendlip, after Coughton had become too
dangerous a retreat for Garnet to stay at much
longer.   The invitation was probably due to the
intercession of Abington's wife, a devout Romanist,
and sister to Lord Mounteagle,[2] whose relationship
to Abington was the means of saving the latter's
life, and that on probably more than one occasion.

For about six weeks, Father Garnet remained
hidden in peace at his new headquarters, before
being perturbed by the pressing attentions of his
enemies.   On Sunday, January 19, 1606, however,
Sir Henry Bromley, a magistrate, appeared before
Hendlip, early in the morning, ' accompanied with

[1] George Chambers.
[2] By many writers she is considered to have been the author of
the famous warning letter.   But this theory cannot be entertained,
for she was brought to bed of a boy shortly after the receipt of
the letter by the King.   This son became a famous poet.

above a hundred men, armed with guns and all kinds of weapons, more fit for an army than an orderly search.'　He came, acting under the direct instructions of Salisbury, but it is a disputed point whether he expected to find Garnet concealed in the house.　That he fully expected to find Oldcorne is an established fact, but I rather incline to the idea that the other, and more important quarry, for whom he had come in search, was Greenway, and not Garnet.　Hendlip, standing on high ground, afforded good opportunities for those on the watch, to observe the approach of an enemy, so that by the time Bromley battered at the door, all four Jesuits had been hidden away : Fathers Garnet and Oldcorne together in one 'hole,' Brothers Chambers and Owen together in another.　Mr. Abington was not at home when Bromley arrived, but his wife gave over to Bromley all the keys of her mysterious house, Mr. Abington not returning till the following night.[1]

Under Bromley's supervision, the most rigorous and drastic inspection was made of the house. ' He began,' writes Gerard, ' after the accustomed manner to go through all the rooms of the house, which were many and very large ; he had with him Argus' eyes, many watchful and subtle companions, that would spy out the least advantage or cause of suspicion ; and yet they searched and

---

[1] *Vide* letter from Bromley to Salisbury : 'Mr. Abington . . . was gone to Mr. Talbot's, and came home on Monday night.'

sounded every corner in that great house till they were all weary, and found no likelihood of discovering that they came for, though they continued the daily search, and that with double diligence all the week following. But upon Saturday, two laymen that did usual attend upon the two priests, and were hid in a place by themselves, being almost starved to death, came out of their own accord.' But Gerard is not, as is often the case, strictly accurate here, for the 'two laymen,' Brothers Owen and Chambers, came out of their hole on Thursday morning, January 23. Had they succeeded in fighting their cold, hunger, and confinement a little longer by remaining huddled up in their 'hole,' it is possible that the lives of all four might have been saved, for Bromley was getting very tired of his search,[1] which he was quite willing to abandon, at any rate for a time, if not altogether.

Father Gerard goes on to make the absurdly unwise statement that Owen and Chambers only gave themselves up because they thought the searchers might take them for priests, and, being satisfied with their capture, then leave the house, and thus enable Garnet and Oldcorne to escape. The very opposite of this was, of course, the case. The appearance of the lay-brothers only induced Bromley to continue the search ; for if, he argued,

---

[1] As a matter of fact, Bromley had gone home when the lay-brothers appeared, his (Bromley's) brother being left in charge of the searchers, *pro tem.*

two men could be forced by hunger to appear
from places where he thought it was impossible
for a human being to lie hid, why should not
there be other men concealed in some equally
strange hiding-place, and likewise be starved into
revealing themselves? Moreover, Gerard con-
fesses that Owen and Chambers had 'but one
apple between them.' His attempt, therefore, to
make them act the part of martyrs, sacrificing
their lives to save those of their masters', is
merely a fable of his own invention.

Writing to Lord Salisbury, on Thursday
evening, Bromley says—

'two are come forth for hunger and cold that
give themselves other names; but surely one of
them, I trust, will prove Greenway, and I think
the other be Hall.[1] I have yet presumption that
there is yet one or two more in the house;
wherefore I have resolved to continue the guard
yet a day or two.'

But hardly had this letter reached Salisbury,
than fresh and unexpected information reached
Bromley, who had by this time discovered that
he had not captured the two priests, as he sur-
mised. This information was sent to him from
Worcester, and was to the effect that Humphrey
Lyttleton had stated, in prison, 'that he believed
Oldcorne to be at Hendlip.' On receiving this
information, therefore, Bromley and his brother
set to work again with renewed hope and energy.

[1] Oldcorne.

According to Gerard, after 'five or six days . . . it pleased God to deliver them (the Priests) into their hands by permitting the searchers at last to light upon the very place itself.' This statement of Gerard is, nevertheless, untrue.[1] Bromley never hit upon the hiding-place,[2] for the two priests surrendered themselves voluntarily, as had their servants. The two fathers had, it appeared, suffered so much from cramp and want of air that they could hold out no longer, and were obliged to give in. Garnet, writing, when a prisoner in the Tower, on March 2, to Anne Vaux,[3] thus tells the story in his own words, and his account flatly contradicts Gerard's version as reported above, viz.—

'I purpose, by God's grace, to set down here briefly, what hath passed since my apprehension, lest evil reports, or untrue, may do myself or others injury.

'After we had been in the hole 7 days and 7 nights, and some odd hours, every man may well think we were wearied; and indeed so it was, for we continually sat, save that some times we could half stretch ourselves, the place being not high enough; and we had our legs so

[1] Gerard's error has been blindly copied by nearly all the writers who have told the story of Garnet's apprehension

[2] The fact that neither of the two holes was discovered by Bromley shows with what marvellous skill they had been devised and located by Owen..

[3] The original MS. is dated 'Shrovetuesday,' and addressed by Garnet 'For Mrs. Vaux or one of our's. Keep all discreetly secret.'

straightened, that we could not sitting find place for them,' so that we both were in continual pain of our legs, and both our legs, especially mine, were much swollen, and mine continued so till I came to the Tower.

'If we had had but one half day's liberty to come forth, we had so eased the place from the books and furniture that, having with us a close-stool, we could have abidden a quarter of a year. . . . We were very merry and content within, and heard the searchers every day most curious over us, which made me, indeed, think the place would be found. And if I had known in time of the proclamation against me, I would have come forth and offered myself to Mr. Abington, whether he would or no to have been his prisoner.

'When we came forth we appeared like 2 ghosts; yet I the stronger, though my weakness lasted longest. The fellow that found us ran away for fear, thinking we would have shot a pistol at him; but there came needless company to assist him, and we bad them be quiet, and we would come forth. So they helped us out very charitably; and we could not go; but desired to be led to a house of office. So I was, and found a board taken up, where there was a great down-fall, that one should have broken his neck if he had come thither in the dark, which seemed intended of purpose. We had escaped, if the two first hidden soldiers had not come out so soon,

¹ 'Marmalade and other sweetmeats were found lying by them; but their better maintenance had been by a quill or reed, through a little hole in a chimney that backed another chimney into a gentlewoman's chimney, and by that passage cawdle, broths, and warm drinks had been conveyed to them.'

for when they had found them they were curious to find their place.   The search at Hendlip was not for me but for Mr. Hall,[1] as an abettor of Robert Wintour.   Then came a second charge to search for Mr. Gerard.   Of me never no expectation.'

From this account, it is plain that Garnet and Oldcorne (Hall) gave themselves up, without any discovery being made of their 'hole,' which, if it had not been so much filled up with 'books and furniture,'[2] might have afforded them a safe refuge till Bromley had departed.   Garnet is evidently in error as to the 'second charge to search' being 'for Mr. Gerard,' for we know that this further charge was the result of Lyttleton's implicating Oldcorne.   Garnet's theory that 'we had escaped' but for the 'hidden soldiers,' is curious, but hardly tenable when we consider how weak he and his comrade must have been.   It is, however, a fact that Owen and Chambers were actually within an ace of escaping, when they quietly emerged from their hiding-place.   According to Gerard (who here completely contradicts his own story of their voluntary surrender), 'They,[3] perceiving, that some of the searchers did continually by turns watch and walk up and down the room where they were hidden, which was a long gallery foursquare going round the house, watched their time when the searchers were

---

[1] Oldcorne.

[2] Probably, Prayer-books and articles used when saying Mass, or even vestments.

[3] Owen and Chambers.

furthest off, and came out so secretly and quietly and shut the place again so finely, that they were not heard or perceived when or where they came out, and so they walked in the gallery towards the door, which they thought belike to have found open.   But the searchers being turned back in their walk, and perceiving two strange men to be there, whom they had not seen before, presently ran unto them and asked what they were ?   They answered that they were men that were in the house, and would be content to depart if it pleased them. . . . Then being asked where they had been all the while, they answered they had hid themselves, being Catholics, to avoid taking.'

Father Garnet, after having been identified [1] by Bromley—but not without much difficulty, various persons being summoned to look at him —was taken up to London, in company with his fellow prisoners.[2]   The story of this journey is best told in Garnet's own words (Dom. S.P. James I., vol. xix.)—

'We were carred to Worcester in his [3] coach, where he had promised to place us in some bailey's, or other citizen's house; but when we came there he said he could not do as he wished, but must send us to the gaol.

'I said, "In God's name, but I hope you will provide we have not irons, for we are lame

[1] Oldcorne was identified at once.

[2] Abington, Oldcorne, Owen, Chambers, and two servants. Mrs. Abington and Anne Vaux started for London about three weeks later.

[3] Bromley's.

already and shall not be able to ride after to London."

' "Well," said he, "I will think of it," and set me to rest in a private chamber, with one to look to me, because he would avoid the people's gazing. When he had despatched his business, he sent for me, and told me we should go with him to his house. So we did in the coach, and were exceedingly well used, and dined and supped with him and his every day.

'On Candlemas day, he made a great dinner to end Christmas; and in the midst of dinner he sent for wine to drink health to the King, and we were all bare. . . . All the way to London, I was passing well used at the King's charge, and that by express orders from Lord Salisbury.[1] I had always the best horse in the company. . . . I had some bickering with Ministers by the way. Two very good scholars and courteous, Mr. Abbott and Mr. Barlow, met us at an inn; but two other rude fellows met us on the way, whose discourtesy I rewarded with plain words, and so adieu! They were discharged by authority.'

Garnet's arrival in London created a great sensation, for a Jesuit Superior was a captive out of the ordinary, and the common herd flocked to see him as if expecting to find some new species of wild beast. After examination at Whitehall, Garnet was sent to the Tower. He says in his own words—

[1] This attestation of Garnet, concerning the kind treatment he received by direction of the Government is, of course, never admitted by Jesuit writers. In a letter to Salisbury, dated February 5, Bromley mentions that 'Mr. Garnet is but a weak and wearisome traveller.'

'On St. Valentine's day I came to the Tower, where I have a very fine chamber; but was very sick the two first nights with ill lodging. I am allowed every meal a good draught of excellent claret wine, and I am liberal with myself and neighbours for good respects, to allow also of my own purse some sack.'[1]

Finally, before closing this account of Garnet's capture and progress to London, it is worth quoting the following interesting, but not quite correct, reference to his capture made by the Venetian Ambassador in a letter, dated February 24, to the Doge of Venice—

'They have, at last, captured the two Jesuits, who had already been proclaimed as guilty of conspiracy; they had taken shelter in a cave in the country, and were besieged there, and finally driven out by the hunger and suffering which they had endured. One of them is the Provincial of the Jesuits in England, and it is thought that in putting him to death with cruel torments they will wreak all their hatred of his religion and of himself. But he will not be executed in public, for he is a man of moving eloquence and vast learning, and they are afraid that his constancy, and the power of his speech, may produce just the reverse of what they desire.'

[1] During the whole time he was in the Tower, Garnet indulged freely in wine, and is reported to have been overcome by the effects of his potations on more than one occasion. The Jesuit story that this is mere Protestant calumny is controverted by the fact that an agent was sent from Rome to England by Father Parsons to inquire into Garnet's conduct, owing to the reports which had reached head-quarters of his drunkenness and immorality.

CHAPTER XV

I

ALTHOUGH Father Garnet reached the metropolis early in February (on, apparently, the 8th, or even the 7th of that month), he was not brought to trial until March 28. During this interval, he was frequently examined before the Privy Council, the results of which examinations, or rather the most important of them, may be set down briefly as below.

On February 13, he admitted that he had for a period of nearly twenty years been the Superior of the Jesuits in England. He denied, however, all knowledge of the Powder Plot, and that he had tried to help the conspirators when they were marching to Holbeach. He confessed that he had corrected the book on equivocation, found in Tresham's desk, but had refused to have it printed. As to its doctrines, he could see no harm in them, although they had never been formally approved by the Holy See, in spite of their having been countenanced by certain divines.

154

Si quid patimini propter iustitiam, beati: petri:.
Henricus Garnetus anglus e societate IESV gassus
3 May 1606

Publish'd Oct.ʳ 1ˢᵗ 1802. by Wᵐ Richardson, York House, 31 Strand.

FATHER GARNET.

On March 5, he denied that he had held any secret conversations with his fellow-captive, Father Oldcorne, in the Tower. This denial was, as his interrogators well knew, a falsehood, for the conversations had been overheard.

On March 6, he stated that he went to Hendlip on December 4. As to White Webbs, he said that the expenses of keeping up an establishment there had been borne conjointly by himself, Anne Vaux,[1] and Mrs. Brooksby. He confessed that he had met Guy Faukes in London, at Eastertide, 1605, and that he had met Catesby twice in the same year.

On March 12, he mentioned that the Plot had been revealed to him in July, 1605, by Father Greenway, who had heard it from Catesby or Thomas Winter[2] in confession, but that the penitent had wished Greenway to report the information to Garnet. As to the correspondence which passed between him and Father Robert Parsons, he said that he kept no copies of the letters he wrote to Parsons, whose letters, in return, he burned after reading them. Although Greenway had repeated his penitent's confession, it was understood that Garnet was only to know it under the seal of confession, and was not to be allowed to pass on the information to anybody else.

---

[1] Anne Vaux, examined on March 11, maintained that she alone had borne the expenses of the establishment.

[2] Probably from both.

On March 13 and 14, he confessed that before the late Queen died, he had received two breves from Rome, one addressed to the Romanist laity, the other to the Romanist clergy.   These breves commanded all English Catholics not to acknowledge any Protestant as Elizabeth's successor. These breves he showed to Tresham, Catesby, Thomas Winter, and Percy.[1]   As to the information regarding the Plot given him by Greenway, the latter had only revealed the bare outlines of the scheme, and had not gone into details.

On March 24, he subscribed as correct a statement by Anne Vaux to the effect that Francis Tresham had often visited Garnet and herself at White Webbs.[2]   Garnet, said Anne Vaux, had always on these occasions advised Tresham not to do more than lead a quiet life, without taking part in politics.

On March 26, Garnet stated that the Pope was to be informed at once, so soon as 'that miserable woman[3] died.'

On April 1, Garnet (now under sentence of death) denounced the penal laws against Catholics, which he said could not be obeyed.   As to equivocation, he maintained that it was both useful and lawful under certain conditions.

---

[1] He might have added the name of Digby to the list.   He mentioned, also, ' I do not remember that ever Lord Mounteagle saw the breves.'

[2] And yet Tresham swore on his death-bed that he had not seen Garnet for sixteen years !

[3] Queen Elizabeth.

On April 25, he was bold enough to swear 'on his priesthood' that he had not seen, or communicated with Greenway since November 6.[1]

On April 28, he was told that his last statement was known to be false, and was asked how he could reconcile it with his conscience to tell such a lie ?   He answered that such perjury was permissible when 'just necessity so required,' and actually blamed the Council for blaming him.

Garnet's colleague, Oldcorne, was also submitted to frequent examinations, and to torture. He was eventually sent down to Worcester, and there executed on April 7.   The treatment received by him in the Tower was, I think, most unjust ; for it is difficult to see why he should have been so harshly dealt with, when his fellow-prisoner, Garnet, was lodged in comparative comfort, and was not put to the torture.   Moreover, Oldcorne did not stoop to such reckless perjury as his friend ; and he, at least, deserves credit for having had the courage to offer Garnet an asylum at Hendlip.   He probably lost his life entirely owing to this self-sacrificing and generous attempt to shelter his friend.[2]

---

[1] According to Bates, he and Greenway had talked about the Plot on November 7, when residing in the same house.   Oldcorne also admitted this in examination.

[2] The principal charge in the indictment was based on Oldcorne's invitation to Garnet to come to Hendlip.   He was not accused of complicity in the Plot, but of having expressed his approval of its purpose.   He has not received justice at the hands of our historians.

Had the Government depended solely on what they could elicit in cross-examination from Garnet as evidence to be used against him at his trial, they would hardly have been able to secure a conviction.   They, however, invented a far more subtle plan for incriminating him than this method of continued personal examination.   Garnet and Oldcorne were incarcerated in adjoining chambers, and were told by a janitor that by pulling open a kind of secret panel in a wall they could converse (provided they did so quietly) together, and without fear of detection.   It seems extraordinary that astute men like these hunted Jesuits, who had for many years had to defend themselves against innumerable tricks and strategems laid for them by their enemies, should have fallen into so simple a trap.   But they did, and relying on their janitor's word and fidelity, opened up a series of conversations by removing the stone in the wall, utterly unsuspecting that this same hollow wall concealed the persons of two agents of the Privy Council, who wrote down every word they heard of these conversations.[1]   What was over-heard of the conversations by the Government's agents proved fatal to Garnet, although some allowance must be made for the probability that the listeners did not always hear quite so plainly as they pretended.   So unsuspicious were the two Jesuits of the open trap into which they had

[1] The same trick—though with less success—is said to have been previously played on Faukes and Robert Winter.

walked, that they both subsequently swore that these conversations had never taken place. After having denied them, Garnet was shown the copies of the reports written by the men concealed in the wall. Oldcorne, under torture, eventually confessed to them, but Garnet persisted in his denial until he found the game was up. In (an intercepted) letter,[1] written on Palm Sunday, he says with reference to his perjury, 'When the Lords inquired of me concerning my conference with Hall, I denied it. They drove me to many protestations, which I made with equivocation. They then said that Hall had confessed the conference. . . . As soon as I found they had sufficient proofs, I held my peace : the Lords were scandalized at this.'

For the reader's convenience, I subjoin the most important items reported to the Privy Council as overheard by their agents hidden in wall, Lockerson and Forset.

Garnet. 'I had forgot to tell you I had a note from Rookewood,[2] and he telleth me that Greenway is gone over;[3] I am very glad of that. And I had another from Mr. Gerard, that he meaneth to go over to Father Parsons, and therefore I hope he is escaped; but it seemeth he hath been put to great plunges.

---

[1] Garnet's letters, generally written with orange-juice, were often intercepted, and several are now in the Record Office.

[2] A priest, and relative of the conspirator of that name.

[3] *i.e.* escaped to the Continent.

'I think Mrs. Anne[1] is in the town. . . .
I gave him (the keeper) an angel yesterday;
. . . and now and then at meals, I make very
much of him, and give him a cup of sack, and
send his wife another. . . . You should do well
now and then to give him a shilling, and sometimes send his wife somewhat. He did see me
write to Mr. Rookewood. . . .

'I must needs confess White Webbs, that we
met there; but I will answer it thus, that I was
there, but knew nothing of the matter. . . .

'Perhaps, they will press me with certain
prayers that I made, against the time of the
Parliament, for the good success of that business,
which is indeed true.[2] But I may answer that
well, for I will say, it is true that I doubt that at
this next Parliament there would be more severe
laws made against the Catholics; and, therefore,
I made those prayers; and that will answer it
well enough. . . .

'For my sending into Spain before the
Queen's death, I need not deny it; but I care
not for those things; he knoweth I have my
pardon for that time, and therefore he will not
urge them to do me hurt.

'If I can satisfy the King well in this matter,
it will be well; but I think it not convenient to
deny we were at White Webbs, they do so much

---

[1] Anne Vaux.

[2] On All Saints' Day (November 1, 1605) Garnet's congregation
sang—

> 'Gentem auferte perfidam
> Credentium de finibus.
> Ut Christo laudes debitas
> Persolvimus alacriter.'

insist upon that place. Since I came out of Essex, I was there two times; and so I may say I was there. . . .'

The above conversation is reported to have been overheard on February 23, 1606; the following, on February 25.

Garnet. 'They pressed me with a question, what Noblemen I knew that have written any letters to Rome, and by whom? Well, I see they will justify my Lord Mounteagle of all this matter.[1] I said nothing of him, neither will I ever confess him. . . .

'There is one special thing of which I doubted they would have taken an exact account of me; to wit, of the causes of my coming to Coughton, which indeed would have bred a great suspicion of the matter. . . .

'They mentioned the letters sent into Spain; but I answered that those letters were of no other matter but to have pensions.'

On February 27, the priests were again overheard talking.

'It seemed to us,' wrote the agents, 'that Hall told Garnet how he answered the matters of White Webbs, which Garnet said it was well; but, said he, of the other matter, of our meeting on the way, it were better to leave it in a contradiction, as it was, lest perhaps the poor fellow shall be tortured for the clearing of that point. . . .

[1] This tends to confirm my opinion, stated above, of Mounteagle's treachery. Garnet, throughout, seems to have thought it hopeless to get Cecil to let the truth be known about Mounteagle.

L

'Garnet said he was asked again about the prayer which he was charged to have made,[1] and then did name the prayer by a special name to Hall, thereby putting Hall in remembrance thereof; but, said he, I shall avoid that well enough. . . .'

On March 2, another report follows:—

'"Hark you, is all well?" said Garnet. "Let us go to confession first if you will."

'Then began Hall to make his confession, who we could not hear well; but Garnet did often interrupt him, and said, " Well, well."

'And then Garnet confessed himself to Hall, which was uttered very much softer than he used to whisper in their interlocutions, and but short; and confessed that because he had drunk extraordinarily he was fain to go, two nights, to bed betimes.'

The Government agents seem to have heard little that was said by Oldcorne, as (according to their reports) Father Garnet had done most of the talking.   In any event, they overheard nothing very damaging against Oldcorne, whose treatment after his capture was both brutal and unjust, and his execution little short of murder.

II

The trial of Father Henry Garnet took place on March 28, 1606, at the Guildhall.[2]   The

[1] On All Saints' Day (1605).

[2] Not at Westminster Hall, as has often been erroneously stated.

Commissioners who sat as his judges were the
Lord Mayor of London, Sir Leonard Holyday,
the Lord Chief Justice, Sir John Popham, the
Lord Chief Baron of the Exchequer, Sir Thomas
Fleming, Sir Christopher Yelverton, a Judge of
the Court of King's Bench, and the Earls of
Nottingham, Salisbury, Suffolk, Worcester, and
Northampton.[1]

The proceedings commenced soon after eight
o'clock in the morning, and were not concluded
till close on seven in the evening.   Among those
present in court, as spectators, were the King,[2]
some of the Ambassadors, Lady Arabella Stuart,
and a large number of the nobility.

The indictment charged 'this Garnet, otherwise Wally, otherwise Darcy, otherwise Roberts,
otherwise Farmer, otherwise Philips,' with traitorously conspiring and compassing, with the
assistance of Catesby and Greenway :—

'1. To depose the King and to deprive him
of his Government;

'2. To destroy and kill the King, and the

---

[1] Of these Commissioners, all, except the Lord Mayor and Sir
Christopher Yelverton, had presided at the trial of the gunpowder
conspirators.

[2] The Venetian Ambassador, writing to the Doge, says : 'His
Majesty was present *incognito*. The interrogation did not afford
that satisfaction which Catholics expected, nay, he (Garnet) has
scandalized the very heretics, and greatly disgusted his Majesty.
For besides being, on his own confession—not wrung from him by
torture, as he affirms, but compelled by irrefutable evidence—
cognizant of the plot, he further endeavoured to excuse his previous
perjury,' etc.

noble Prince, Henry, his eldest son : such a King,
and such a Prince, such a son of such a father,
whose virtues are rather with amazed silence to
be wondered at, than able by any speech to be
expressed ;

'3. To stir sedition and slaughter throughout
the kingdom ;

'4. To subvert the true religion of God, and
whole Government of the kingdom ;

'5. To overthrow the whole state of the
Commonwealth.

'The manner how to perform these horrible
treasons, the serjeant said "Horreo dicere," his
lips did tremble to speak it, but his heart praised
God for His mighty deliverance.   The practice so
inhuman, so barbarous, so damnable, so detestable,
as the like was never read nor heard of, or ever
entered into the heart of the most wicked man to
imagine.   And here he said, he could not but
mention that religious observation so religiously
observed by his religious Majesty, wishing it
were engraven in letters of gold, in the hearts of
all his people ; the more hellish the imagination,
the more divine the preservation.

'This Garnet, together with Catesby and
Tesmond, had speech and conference together of
these treasons, and concluded most traitorously
and devilishly : That Catesby, Winter, Faukes,
with many other traitors lately arraigned of high
treason, would blow up with gunpowder in the
Parliament-House, the King, the Prince, the lords
spiritual and temporal, the judges of the realm,
the knights, citizens, and burgesses, and many
other subjects and servants of the King assembled
in parliament, at one blow, traitorously and

devilishly to destroy them all, and piecemeal to tear them in asunder, without respect of majesty, dignity, and degree, age, or place.   And for that purpose, a great quantity of gunpowder was traitorously and secretly placed and hid by these Conspirators under the Parliament-House.'

To this indictment, 'Garnet did plead Not Guilty,' and the trial proceeded.

That Garnet was not likely to receive a fair trial was evident even from the absurd terms of the indictment, in which he was actually treated as an open conspirator, whose active complicity in the plot was as pronounced as that of Guy Faukes.   Notwithstanding the nature of the odds against him, the prisoner defended himself with skill, so far as his connection with the plot was concerned; but the chief difficulty he experienced in clearing himself resulted from the effects of the perjury committed by him in the Tower.   He had, indeed, lied through thick and thin to such an extent that at last he found himself caught in the meshes of his own nets.   It was impossible to place the least reliance on anything he said, or had said.   Romanists were disgusted as much as Protestants with his perjury.   That he had known of the plot outside the Confessional admitted of no doubt, and that, although he disapproved tacitly of the whole business, he had done nothing to prevent its being brought to maturity also admitted of no doubt.   The man who was so horrified at Father Watson's proceedings that he betrayed him and them to the Government, never made any attempt to avert the greater treason concocted by his own friends. To cut a long story short, that he was guilty of high treason need not be doubted. Nevertheless, he received anything but a fair trial, and it would have been a gracious, merciful, and good act to have commuted the death sentence, which was not carried out until five weeks had elapsed after the trial.

Although Garnet was only charged in the indictment with complicity in the Gunpowder Plot, Sir Edward Coke opened the trial with copious references to the prisoner's former treasons in connection with his communications with Spain. That Garnet was guilty of having invited the Spaniards to invade England, and that on more than one occasion, was indisputable. Coke also accused him of being mainly responsible for sending Sir Edward Baynham, 'the Prince of the Damned Crew,'[1] to Rome, and there can be no doubt that Coke was correct in stating that Baynham carried letters of introduction written in Garnet's own hand to the Pope's Nuncio in Flanders.

After being sentenced to death, Garnet was

---

[1] Most writers seem to have laboured under the impression that the 'Crew' refers to the Gunpowder conspirators. But this is not so. Baynham was a leading member of a gang of men (similar to the 'Mohocks') called 'The Damned Crew,' and Coke more than once at the trial named Baynham as the leader of this band.

again examined many times by the Privy Council, especially in regard to his notorious opinions on equivocation, with the view probably towards discrediting him in the eyes of his co-religionists. The continued postponements of the execution, together with the intercession in his favour by the Spanish Ambassador, induced Garnet to think that his life would be spared, and he seemed to have cherished this hope until within a few minutes of his death ; but the only grace granted to him was that he should be allowed to hang until dead, *i.e.* that his body should not be taken down and submitted to the executioner's knife until life was extinct.   By this concession he escaped the butchery undergone by his friends, Winter, Digby, Keyes, and Grant.

III.

'On the 3rd of May,' says the official account, ' Garnet, according to his judgment, was executed upon a scaffold, set up for that purpose at the West-end of St. Paul's Church.[1]   At his arise up the scaffold, he stood much amazed, fear and guiltiness appearing in his face.   The Deans of St. Paul's and Winchester being present, very gravely and christianly exhorted him to a true and lively faith to God-ward, a free and plain acknowledgment to the world of his offence ; and if any further treason lay in his knowledge, to unburden his conscience, and show a sorrow and detestation of

---

[1] Old St. Paul's Cathedral.

it : but Garnet, impatient of persuasions, and ill-pleased to be exhorted by them, desired them not to trouble him, he came prepared and was resolved.

'Then, the Recorder of London, who was by his Majesty appointed to be there, asked Garnet if he had any thing to say unto the people before he died : it was no time to dissemblè, and now his treasons were too manifest to be dissembled; therefore, if he would, the world should witness what at last he censured of himself, and of his fact; it should be free to him to speak what he listed. But, Garnet, unwilling to take the offer, said, His voice was low, his strength gone, the people could not hear him, though he spake to them; but to those about him on the scaffold he said, The intention was wicked, and the fact would have been cruel, and from his soul he should have abhorred it had it been effected; but he said he had only a general knowledge of it by Mr. Catesby, which in that he disclosed not, nor used means to prevent it, herein he had offended; what he knew in particulars was in Confession, as he said.

'But the Recorder wished him to be remembered, that the King's Majesty had under his hand-writing these four points amongst others:

'1. That Greenway told him of this, not as a fault, but as a thing which he had intelligence of, and told it him by way of consultation.

'2. That Catesby and Greenway came together to be resolved.

'3. That Mr. Tesmond and he had conference of the particulars of the Powder-Treason in Essex long after.

'4. Greenway had asked him who should be the Protector?[1]

' But Garnet said, That was to be referred till the blow was past. These prove your privity besides Confession, and these are extant under your hand. Garnet answered, Whatsoever was under was true. And for that he disclosed not to his Majesty the things he knew, he confessed himself justly condemned; and for this did ask forgiveness of his Majesty. Hereupon the Recorder led him to the scaffold to make his confession publick.

' Then Garnet said, "Good countrymen, I am come hither this blessed day of the Invention of the Holy Cross, to end all my crosses in this life: the cause of my suffering is not unknown to you; I confess I have offended the King, and am sorry for it, so far as I was guilty, which was in concealing it; and for that I ask pardon of his Majesty. The treason intended against the King and State was bloody, myself should have detested it, had it taken effect. And I am heartily sorry that any Catholicks ever had so cruel a design."

' Then turning himself from the people to them about him, he made an apology for Mistress Anne Vaux, saying, "There is an honourable gentlewoman who hath been much wronged in report: for it is suspected and said, that I should be married to her, or worse. But I protest the contrary: she is a virtuous gentlewoman, and for me a perfect pure virgin."

' For the Pope's breves, Sir Edward Baynham's

---

[1] After the explosion had taken place at Westminster.

going over seas, and the matter of the Powder-treason, he referred himself to his Arraignment and his Confessions : "for whatsoever is under my hand in any of my confessions," said he, "is true."

'Then addressing himself to execution, he kneeled at the ladder-foot, and asked if he might have time to pray, and how long. It was answered, He should limit himself, none should interrupt him. It appeared he could not constantly or devoutly pray ; fear of death, or hope of pardon, even then so distracted him : for oft in those prayers he would break off, turn and look about him, and answered to what he overheard, while he seemed to be praying. When he stood up, the Recorder finding in his behaviour as it were an expectation of a Pardon, wished him not to deceive himself, nor beguile his own soul ; he was come to die, and must die ; requiring him not to equivocate with his last breath ; if he knew anything that might be danger to the King or State, he should now utter it.

'Garnet said, "It is no time now to equivocate; how it was lawful, and when, he had shewed his mind elsewhere ; " but, saith he, "I do not now equivocate, and more than I have confessed I do not know." At his ascending up the ladder, he desired to have warning before he was turned off. But it was told him, he must look for no other turn than death. Being upon the gibbet, he used these words : "I commend me to all good Catholicks, and I pray God preserve his Majesty, the Queen, and all their posterity, and my lords of the Privy Council, to whom I remember my humble duty, and I am sorry that I did dissemble with them. But I did not think they had such proof against me,[1] till it was shewed me ; but when that was proved, I held it more honour for me at the time to confess, than before to have accused. And for my brother Greenway, I would the truth were known ; for the false reports that are, making him more faulty than he is. I should not have charged him, but that I thought he had been safe. I pray God the Catholics may not fare the worse for my sake ; and I exhort them all to take heed they enter not into any treasons, rebellions, or insurrections against the King." And with this ended speaking, and fell to praying ; and crossing himself, said, " In nomine Patris et Filii, et Spiritus Sancti ;' and prayed " Maria Mater Gratiæ, Maria Mater Misericordiæ, Tu me a malo protege, et hora mortis suscipe." Then "In manus tuas, Domine, commendo spiritum meum ; " then, " Per crucis hoc signum (crossing himself) fugiat procul omne malignum. Infige crucem tuam in corde meo, Domine : Let me always remember the Cross : " and so he turned again to " Maria Mater Gratiæ," and then was turned off, and hung till he was dead.'[2]

In closing this account of how Father Garnet met his fate, it is worth recording the official description of Garnet's personal appearance, as inserted in a Government proclamation, dated some five weeks only before he died :—

[1] Referring to the overheard conversations with Oldcorne in the Tower.

[2] My statement above that he was allowed by the Government to die before being cut down is contradicted by a Roman Catholic account, which says that 'the people would not allow the executioner' to cut him down.

'Henry Garnet, *alias* Walley, *alias* Darcey, *alias* Farmer:

'Of a middling stature, full-faced, fat of body, of complexion fair: his forehead high on each side, with a little thin hair coming down upon the midst of the fore part of his head : the hair of his head and beard grizzled; of age between fifty and three score: his beard on his cheeks cut close, on his chin but thin and somewhat short: his gait upright and comely for a fat man.'

CHAPTER XVI

WAS FATHER GARNET GUILTY?

HENRY GARNET, Superior of the Jesuits in England, was aged about fifty, or fifty-one, at the time of his death. He was the son of a schoolmaster at Nottingham; was brought up a Protestant, and educated at Winchester, where (according to Dr. Robert Abbott) he won a good name for himself as regards his scholarship, but a very bad one indeed as regards his moral conduct. His gross immorality was, it is asserted, so notorious that the authorities at Winchester intervened to prevent him going up to Oxford (New College). He proceeded, therefore, on leaving school, to London, where he became a corrector of the Press. After serving a printer for two years, he went abroad,[1] became a Romanist, and in 1575 entered the Society of Jesus. Studying at Rome, Garnet soon became famous for his learning, and it was great regret on the part of those who knew him best in the Eternal City[2] that he was eventually withdrawn

[1] First to Spain, and thence to Italy.
[2] At Rome he won the esteem of such men as Bellarmine, Suarez, and Clavius.

from this studious life and sent as a missionary (in 1586) to England, travelling thither in company with his colleague, Father Southwell, the poet. In 1587, he was appointed Superior of the Jesuits in England. From the date of his appointment until the year 1605, he lived chiefly in the neighbourhood of London, but acted entirely under the directions of Father Parsons from abroad. Such is, roughly speaking, briefly the history of the life of the man whose share in the Gunpowder Plot has proved one of the vexed questions of historical controversy.

His position as Superior of the Jesuits proved no easy one. The Jesuits were not only detested by the Protestants, but were also greatly disliked by most of the Roman Catholics themselves. Father Parsons, the greatest Englishman who has ever entered the Society, had to leave England because he knew that his presence had exasperated his co-religionists to such an extent that they threatened to betray him to the Government if he did not return at once to Rome.[1] Father Weston, Garnet's immediate predecessor, was a man of very peculiar character, superstitious, silly, and obstinate, and even hated by the Secular clergy, whom he endeavoured to place under the yoke of the Jesuits, with the result that open war was declared between the

---

[1] Father Heywood, his successor, was so unpopular with the English Romanists that he was recalled. He was imprisoned for seventeen months before returning to Rome.

Jesuits and the rest of the English priests. One
of Weston's peculiarities was that he believed
strongly in 'casting out devils,' and used to perform the most extraordinary exorcisms upon
credulous persons. He even claimed to know
the names [1] of the evil spirits whom he expelled
from the bodies of the sufferers.

Garnet, therefore, as may be imagined, had
no easy task in filling a post which had been
previously vacated by persons of such marked
unpopularity as the unscrupulous Parsons, the
extravagant Heywood, and the half - witted
Weston. On the whole, his reign was more
successful than, under the circumstances, might
have been expected, and it lasted for as long a
period as eighteen years. Amongst that small,
but strong faction of the English Roman Catholics
which favoured the Jesuits, Garnet was popular,
whilst his erudition and pleasant manners made
him many friends even in exterior circles hostile
to his Society. But the fact that he was practically
nothing more than a tool in the hands of Father
Parsons served to render his chances of gaining
the goodwill of the majority of his co-religionists
in England practically hopeless, whilst strange
stories about his intemperate habits were widely
circulated. His connection, too, with Anne Vaux,
however innocent, was not calculated to win

---

[1] Some of these went by the following curious appellations :—
'Flibertigibet,' 'Hobbydicat,' 'Lusty Dick,' 'Killicorum,' 'Wilkin,'
'Smolkin,' 'Captain Philpot,' and 'Captain Pippin.'

either for him or for his Society the esteem of the strictest members of his religion. For it was well known that he had placed this weak and foolish woman under a vow of obedience to him, whereby she was compelled to become little better than a servant to him and his colleagues, who had the disposal of her fortune.

In answer to the oft-repeated question, 'Was Father Garnet guilty?' we may, at this late date, with all the evidence before us, safely assert that he was undoubtedly guilty of having committed high treason, and that the sentence of death passed on him at his trial was the inevitable result of his having known all about the plot from Greenway,[1] and that, too, outside the Confessional. He made no attempt to inform the Government of what was going on. Moreover, he actually was a party to sending Sir Edward Baynham to Rome.[2] In being hanged for treason, he only encountered the same fate which had been served out to William Watson, whom he himself had helped to betray to the Government, merely because he and his fellow Jesuits were jealous of Watson and the anti-Jesuit party behind him. Garnet's fate, therefore,—in the light of his betrayal of Watson, and his constant correspondence with Spain, and Spain's most

---

[1] If not also directly from Catesby, which is most probable.

[2] The Venetian Ambassador calls Baynham the 'special messenger sent to beg his Holiness to incite the Catholics to assist and support the good effects' of the proposed explosion at Westminster.

faithful agent, the notorious Parsons, to say nothing of his not having given the Government due warning as to Catesby's intentions,—cannot be commiserated.

That he died a martyr for the seal of the confessional, as has been asserted by Roman Catholic writers, is absurd, as may be seen by a perusal of the official account of his trial, when all the evidence gathered against him was conclusively shown to have no connection with what passed between him and Greenway *sub sigillo*, whilst his conversation with Catesby, in a house in Thames Street, London, on June 9, 1605, was also quite sufficient to incriminate him.

It is lucky for Garnet's admirers that the letters of Sir Everard Digby, written in the Tower, were not intercepted. Had they been seized, and produced at Garnet's trial, the question of the prisoner's moral guilt would have, there and then, been settled once and for ever.

Sufficient prominence has not been given to these letters in the works of writers on the Plot, and they have, of course, been ignored by Garnet's apologists altogether. The whole tone of Digby's disclosures suggests clearly that the writer laboured under the impression that the Jesuit[1] leaders knew of the plot and tacitly approved of its purpose—

'For my keeping it secret,' says Digby, 'it was caused by certain belief, that those which

[1] It must be remembered that every one of the plotters had a Jesuit for his confessor.

M

were best able to judge of the lawfulness of it had been acquainted with it, and given away unto it.   More reasons I had to persuade me to this belief than I dare utter.'   Later on, he writes, ' Before that I knew anything of the plot, I did ask Mr. Farmer (Garnet) what the meaning of the Pope's brief was ; he told me that they were not (meaning Priests) to undertake or procure stirs, but yet they would not hinder any, neither was it the Pope's mind that they should.'

This confession by Digby is also supported by a statement in Garnet's own hand-writing, which completely contradicts the story of his having died a martyr in defence of the seal of confession.   Writing on April 4, 1606, to the Privy Council, he declares—

' And whereas, partly upon hope of prevention, partly for that I would not betray my friend, I did not reveal the general knowledge of Mr. Catesby's intention which I had by him, I do acknowledge myself highly guilty.'

All the sympathy that Garnet might have received from his co-religionists (exclusive of those submitting to the Jesuit yoke), after he had been sentenced to death, was destroyed by the general feeling of detestation against him excited by his continued equivocation.   He literally lied himself to death.   For him there was no escape. Lie after lie was detected, and the utter folly of putting faith in his protestations exposed.   How great a factor his indulgence in equivocation was in causing his death, and how strongly he disgusted

Roman Catholics as well as Protestants by his perjury, is touched upon by nearly all the leading historians who have dealt with his trial.   I quote the following criticisms from their works :—

Dr. Lingard[1] :—' Three days later, he was interrogated a second time respecting the doctrine of equivocation, and boldly declared that the practice of requiring men to accuse themselves was barbarous and unjust ; that in all such cases it was lawful to employ equivocation, and to confirm, if it were necessary, that equivocation with an oath ; and that if Tresham, as had been pretended, had equivocated on his death-bed, he might have had reasons which would justify him in the sight of God.   To these and similar avowals I ascribe his execution.   By seeking shelter under equivocation, he had deprived himself of the protection which the truth might have afforded him ; nor could he in such circumstances reasonably complain if the King refused credit to his asseverations of innocence,[2] and permitted the law to take its course.'

Dr. Gardiner :—' Garnet was again examined several times after his conviction, and there may possibly have been some inclination on the part of the King to save his life.   But the Jesuitical doctrine on the subject of truth and falsehood, which he openly professed, was enough to ruin any man.'

J. R. Green :—' Garnet, the Provincial of the

[1] Lingard, it is hardly necessary to state, was a Roman Catholic priest.

[2] Garnet, said the Venetian Ambassador, ' scandalized the very heretics ' at his trial, by ' excusing his previous perjury.'

English Jesuits, was brought to trial and executed. Though he had shrunk from all part in the plot, its existence had been made known to him by another Jesuit, Greenway; and, horror-stricken as he represented himself to have been, he had kept the secret and left the Parliament to its doom.'

Dr. Franck Bright :—' The trial of Garnet was more difficult, but his knowledge of the plot was at last proved by a conversation between himself and one of his fellow-prisoners, treacherously devised and overheard.   It is probable that he might even then have escaped his fate, had it not been for his open avowal of the lawfulness of equivocation and mental reservation on any point which might criminate himself.   This destroyed all credit in his assertions, and took from him all chance of popular sympathy.'

Father E. L. Taunton [1] :—' There seems to have been some kind of desire on the part of the King not to proceed to extremities; but Garnet's avowals on the subject of equivocation practically settled his fate; for it was found obviously impossible to believe a word he said.'

Hallam :—' Whether the offence of Garnet went beyond misprision of treason has been much controverted.   The Catholic writers maintain that he had no knowledge of the conspiracy, except by having heard it in confession.   But this rests altogether on his word; and the prevarication of which he had proved to be guilty (not to mention the damning circumstance that he was taken at Henlip in concealment along [2]

---

[1] *History of the Jesuits in England.*
[2] This is, of course, an error on Hallam's part.

with the other conspirators), makes it difficult for
a candid man to acquit him of a thorough
participation in their guilt.'

Winwood [1] (letter from Mr. John Chamber-
laine to Winwood, April 5, 1606) :—' Garnet, the
Jesuit, was arraigned at Guildhall, the 28th of
the last. . . . The King was present, but unseen,
as likewise divers Ladies. . . . The sum of all
was, that Garnet coming into England in 1586,
hath had his finger in every Treason since that
time, and not long before the late Queen's death,
had two Breves sent him by the Pope, the one to
the nobility and gentry, the other to the Arch-
priest and clergy of England, that *quandocumque
contigerit miseram illam feminam ex hac vita
migrare* they should take care, *neglectâ propinqui-
tate sanguinis*, or any other respect, to make
choice of such a Prince, as either should be Catholic,
or else promise and swear not only to tolerate,
but to further that religion to his utmost. But
for these matters he was not now to be touched,
having taken the benefit of the King's pardon
the first year of his reign. But for the late
hellish conspiracy he was proved to be privy to
it, both from Catesby, and Tesmond or Greenway a Jesuit. To which he answered, that from
Catesby he had it but in general terms, and
from Tesmond *sub sigillo confessionis*. To which
answer, though it were insufficient, yet it was
replied, that Catesby having imparted to him
the particulars of the very same plot to be performed in the Queen's time, [2] it was not likely he

---

[1] *Memorials of State collected by Sir R. Winwood in the Reigns
of Q. Elizabeth and K. James I.*

[2] There undoubtedly had been a wild scheme, formed during the

would conceal them from him now ; and the continual intercourse 'twixt him and the chief actors,
with his directions and letters by Winter and
Wright to the King of Spain, by Fawkes to the
Archduke, and by Sir Edward Baynham (Captain
of the Damned Crew) to the Pope, shew that he
could not but be acquainted, and one of the
principal directors in it. . . .

'Garnet, being brought into a "fool's paradise,"
had divers conversations with Hall, his fellow-
priest in the Tower, which were overheard by
spies set on purpose.　With which being charged,
he stifly denied it ; but being still urged, and
some light given him that they had notice of it,
he persisted still, with protestation upon his soul
and salvation, that there had passed no such
interlocution : till at last, being confronted with
Hall, he was driven to confess.'

Garnet's manifold perjuries cannot, of course,
possibly be excused or defended, and there is
some satisfaction in knowing, as the above
authorities demonstrate, that his lying did him
and his a great deal of harm.　At the same time,
the stratagems to which the Government had
recourse, in the efforts to entrap him, can hardly
be commended, and Dr. Gardiner only speaks
the plain truth when he exclaims : ' If all liars
had been subject to punishment, it would have
gone hard with those members of the Government, whoever they were, who, in order to
involve the Jesuits in the charge of complicity

last years of Elizabeth's reign, with the object of blowing her
alone up with powder.

with the plot, deliberately suppressed the words in which both Winter and Faukes declared that Gerard, when he administered the Sacrament to the original conspirators, was ignorant of the oath which they had previously taken.'

Finally, in dismissing the case of Father Garnet, for the convenience of the reader it is worth while to name the principal charges brought against the Jesuit Superior, of all of which he was shown to have been guilty,[1] and therefore to have committed high treason ; viz. :—

' 1. He had been a party to sending Sir Edward Baynham to Rome.   Baynham, a man of bad character, was (as Faukes explained) to inform the Pope of the result of the Plot, had it succeeded.

' 2. He had heard of the Plot (outside the confessional) from Father Greenway.

' 3. He knew, from two conversations with Catesby, that the plot was in active progress.

' 4. He sent Father Greenway to visit the conspirators at Huddington.

' 5. On All Saints Day, 1605 (Nov. 1st), he asked his congregation at Coughton, " to pray for some good success for the Catholic cause at the beginning of Parliament" (Nov. 5th).

' 6. He made no (known) attempt to save the Parliament from its doom.'

In conclusion, although we may regret that King James and his Government did not temper justice with mercy and commute the death-sentence passed on Garnet to banishment, it must

---

[1] Irrespective entirely of all the treasonable acts he had committed, as regards his correspondence with Spain, prior to 1605.

not be forgotten that, in those harsh times, there would have been no precedent for such a course. Moreover, Garnet, as the head of a branch of a Society determined on subjugating England, was as much a national enemy as any Spaniard. The Jesuits were fighting hard to destroy the liberties of England, and it was necessary, therefore, to deal with them severely. In the interests of their Society, they would stop at no offence, however shocking, when occasion served. In removing Garnet, then, the Government of James I. only put to death a man whose existence at large in London constituted a ceaseless danger to the commonwealth. Moreover, it must not be forgotten, so far as our means at this late date of arriving at a correct idea of Garnet's position are concerned, that several of the most damning pieces of evidence against him have been removed by the loss of certain documents, taken by the Jesuits from the Collection of State Papers during the reigns of Charles II. and James II. As to this, Mr. David Jardine, in a letter[1] to Mr. R. Lemon, dated November 17, 1857, says—

'That thievery of some kind abstracted such documents as the *Treatise on Equivocation*, with Garnet's hand-writing on it, the most important of the Interlocutions between Garnet and Hall in the Tower, and all the examinations of Garnet respecting the Pope's Breves, is most clear !'

[1] This letter, preserved in the *Gunpowder Plot Book* (1) at the Record Office, relates to the operations of 'those fellows the Jesuits.'

CHAPTER XVII

ROBERT CECIL, Earl of Salisbury, Secretary of State, has left behind him an account of the Plot, which may certainly claim to be the earliest historical record of the great event, for the manuscript is dated only four days later than the fatal fifth of November. This account is contained in a letter sent by him to Sir Charles Cornwallis, the British Ambassador in Spain.[1] I reproduce below the whole of the despatch, which is of great interest and historical importance—

'It hath pleased Almighty God out of his singular goodness to bring to light the most cruel and detestable Conspiracy against the person of his Majesty and the whole state of this Realm that ever was conceived by the heart of man, at any time or in any place whatsoever. By the practice there was intended not only the extirpation of the King's Majesty and his royal issue, but the whole subversion and downfall of

---

[1] Cornwallis was our Ambassador from 1605 till 1609. In 1614 he was imprisoned in the Tower. He died in December, 1629. A man of straightforward character, he was badly treated by King James.

this Estate; the plot being to take away at one instant the King, Queen, Prince, Council, Nobility, Clergy, Judges, and the principal gentlemen of the Realm, as they should have been altogether assembled in the Parliament-House in Westminster, the 5th of November, being Tuesday. The means how to have compassed so great an act, was not to be performed by strength of men, or outward violence, but by a secret conveyance of a great quantity of gunpowder in a vault under the Upper House of Parliament, and so to have blown up all out of a clap, if God out of his mercy and just revenge against so great an abomination had not destined it to be discovered, though very miraculously, even some 12 hours before the matter should have been put into execution.   The person that was the principal undertaker of it is one Johnson, a Yorkshire man, and servant to one Thomas Percy, a Gentleman-Pensioner to his Majesty, and a near [1] kinsman to the Earl of Northumberland.

'This Percy had about a year and a half ago hired a part of Vyniard House in the Old Palace, from whence he had access into this vault to lay his wood and coal; and, as it seemeth now, had taken this place on purpose to work some mischief in a fit time.   He is a Papist by profession, and so is his man Johnson,[2] a desperate fellow, who of late years he took into his service.   Into this vault Johnson had at sundry times very privately conveyed a great quantity of powder, and therewith

---

[1] This he was not, and the false statement illustrates Salisbury's unscrupulous methods of incriminating the innocent Northumberland.

[2] Guy Faukes.

FAUKES' LANTERN.

filled two hogsheads, and some 32 small barrels;
all which he had cunningly covered with great
store of billets and faggots; and on Monday, at
night, as he was busy to prepare his things for
execution, was apprehended in the place itself,[1]
with a false lantern,[2] booted and spurred. There
was likewise found some small quantity of fine
powder for to make a train, and a piece of match,
with a tinder-box to have fired the train when
he should have seen time, and so to have saved
himself from the blow, by some half an hour's
respite that the match should have burned.

'Being taken and examined, he resolutely
confessed the attempt, and his intention to put
it into execution (as is said before) that very day
and hour when his Majesty should make his
oration in the Upper House. For any complices
in this horrible act, he denieth to accuse any;
alleging, that he had received the Sacrament a
little before of a Priest, and taken an oath never
to reveal any; but confesseth that he hath been
lately beyond the seas, both in the Low Countries
and France, and there had conference with divers
English priests; but denieth to have made them
acquainted with this purpose.

'It remaineth that I add something, for
your better understanding, how this matter came
to be discovered. About 8 days before the
Parliament should have begun, the Lord Mounteagle received a letter about six o'clock at night
(which was delivered to his footman in the dark

[1] This does not tally with other accounts, which say that he
was captured outside the building.

[2] This lantern is now preserved in the Ashmolean collection at
Oxford.

to give him) without name or date, and in a
hand disguised; whereof I send you a copy, the
rather to make you perceive to what a strait I
was driven.   As soon as he imparted the same
unto me, how to govern myself, considering the
contents and phrase of that letter I knew not;
for when I observed the generality of the
advertisment and the style, I could not well
distinguish whether it were frenzy or sport;
for from any serious ground I could hardly
be induced to believe that that proceeded, for
many Reasons; 1st., because no wise man could
think my Lord[1] to be so weak as to take any
alarm to absent himself from Parliament upon
such a loose advertisement: secondly, I considered, that if any such thing were really
intended, that it was very improbable that
only one nobleman should be warned and no
more.   Nevertheless, being loath to trust my
own judgment alone, and being always inclined
to do too much in such a case as that is, I
imparted the letter to the Earl of Suffolk, Lord
Chamberlain, to the end I might receive his
opinion;[2] whereupon perusing the words of the
letter, and observing the writing (that the blow
should come without knowledge who hurt them),
we both conceived that it could not be more

---

[1] Lord Mounteagle.

[2] Cecil's story that the receipt of the letter took him entirely by
surprise, and that its contents proved an enigma to him, is very
cleverly told, but is a concoction not to be believed. He omits
the fact that, although the letter was received late at night, he lost
not a minute in placing it before his colleagues, who were all
(suspiciously) close at hand when Mounteagle arrived post haste
from Hoxton.

proper than the time of Parliament, nor by any other way like to be attempted than with powder, whilst the King was sitting in that Assembly; of which the Lord Chamberlain conceived more probability, because there was a great vault under the said chamber, which was never used for any thing but for some wood and coal, belonging to the Keeper of the Old Palace. In which consideration, after we had imparted the same to the Lord Admiral, the Earl of Worcester, the Earl of Northampton, and some others, we all thought fit to impart it to the King, until some 3 or 4 days before the Sessions. At which time we shewed his Majesty the letter, rather as a thing we could not conceal because it was of such a nature, than anything persuading him to give further credit unto it until the place had been visited.

'Whereupon his Majesty, who hath a natural habit to contemn all false fears,[1] and a judgment so strong as never to doubt anything which is not well warranted by Reason, concurred thus far with us, that seeing such a matter was possible, that should be done which might prevent all danger or nothing at all. Hereupon it was moved, that till the night before his coming, nothing should be to interrupt any purpose of theirs that had any such devilish practice, but rather to suffer them to go on till the end of the day.[2] And so, Monday, in the afternoon, the Lord Chamberlain, whose office is to see all places of assembly put

---

[1] This the King most certainly had not. He was ever suspicious, and prone to take unnecessary alarm.

[2] This stratagem resulted in the capture of the plotters, for it deceived them into thinking that their particular plan had not been discovered, and encouraged them to persevere to the end.

in readiness when the King's person should come, taking with him the Lord Mounteagle, went to see all the places in the Parliament House, and took also a slight occasion to peruse the vault; where, finding only piles of billets and faggots heaped up, his Lordship still inquiring only who owned the same wood, observing the proportion to be somewhat more than the housekeeper was likely to lay in for his own use : And when answer was made that it belonged to one Mr. Percy, his Lordship straight conceived some suspicion in regard of his person; and the Lord Mounteagle taking some notice, that there was great profession between Percy and him, from which some inference might be made that it was the warning of a friend, my Lord Chamberlain resolved absolutely to proceed in a search, though no other materials were visible. And being returned to the Court, about 5 a clock took me up to the King and told him, that though he was hard of belief that any such thing was thought, yet in such a case as this, whatsoever was not done to put all out of doubt was as good as nothing. Whereupon it was resolved by his Majesty, that this matter should be so carried as no man should be scandalized by it, nor any alarm taken for any such purpose. For the better effecting whereof, the Lord Treasurer, the Lord Admiral, the Earl of Worcester, and we two agreed, that Sir Thomas Knyvet, should under a pretext for stolen and embezzled goods both in that place and other houses thereabouts, remove all that wood, and so to see the plain ground under it.

'Sir Thomas Knyvet going thither about midnight unlooked for into the vault, found that fellow Johnson newly come out of the vault, and without asking him more questions stayed him; and having no sooner removed the wood he perceived the barrels, and so bound the catiff fast; who made no difficulty to acknowledge the act, nor to confess clearly, that the morrow following it should have been effected. And thus have you a true narration from the beginning of this, which hath been spent in examinations of Johnson, who carrieth himself without any fear or perturbation, protesting his constant resolution to have performed it that day whatsoever had come of it; principally for the institution of the Roman religion, next out of hope to have dissolved this Government, and afterwards to have framed such a State as might have served the appetite of him and his complices. And in all this action he is no more dismayed, nay scarce any more troubled, than if he were taken for a poor robbery upon the highway. For notwithstanding he confesseth all things of himself, and denieth not to have some partners in this particular practice, (as well appeareth by the flying of divers Gentlemen upon his apprehension known to be notorious Recusants), yet could no threatening of torture draw from him any other language than this, that he is ready to die, and rather wisheth ten thousand deaths, than willingly to accuse his master or any other; until by often reiterating examinations, we pretending to him that his master was apprehended, he hath come to plain confession, that his master kept the key of that cellar whilst he was abroad; had been in it since the powder was laid there, and inclusive confessed him a principal actor in the same.

'In the meantime, we have also found out, (though he denied it long) that on Saturday night the third of November, he[1] came post out of the north; that this man[2] rid to meet him by the way; that he dined at Sion[3] with the Earl of Northumberland on Monday; that as soon as the Lord Chamberlain had been in the vault that evening, this fellow went to his master about six of the clock at night, and had no sooner spoken with him but he fled immediately, apprehending straight that to be discovered, which at that time was held rather unworthy belief, though not unworthy the after trial. In which I must need do my Lord Chamberlain his right, that he could take no satisfaction until he might search that matter to the bottom; wherein I must confess I was much less forward; not but that I had sufficient advertisement, that most of those that now are fled (being all notorious Recusants) with many other of that kind, had a practice in hand for some stir this Parliament; but I never dreamed it should have been in such nature, because I never read nor heard the like in any State to be attempted ingross by any conspiration, without some distinction of persons.

'I do now send you some proclamations, and withal think good to advertize you, that those persons named in them, being most of them gentlemen spent in their fortunes, all inward with Percy and fit for all alterations, have gathered themselves to a head of some four score or 100 horse, with purpose (as we conceive) to pass over

[1] Thomas Percy.   [2] Faukes.
[3] Sion House, Isleworth.

Robert Cecil, Earl of Salisbury.

From the original of Zucchero in the Collection of

The Most Noble The Marquis of Salisbury.

Drawn by Wᵐ Hilton. R. A & Engraved (with Permission) by C. Picart

London, Published March 1 1806 by Lackington, Hughes, Harding, Mavor & Jones, and Longman Hurst, Rees, Orme & Brown.

Seas; whereupon it hath been though meet in policy of State (all circumstances considered) to commit the Earl of Northumberland to the Archbishop of Canterbury, there to be honourably used, until things be more quiet: Whereof if you shall any judgment made, as if his Majesty or his Council could harbour a thought of such a savage practice to be lodged in such a Nobleman's breast, you shall do well to suppress it as a malicious discourse and invention, this being only done to satisfy the world, that nothing be undone which belongs to policy of State, when the whole Monarchy was proscribed in dissolution; and being no more than himself discreetly approved as necessary, when he received the sentence of the Council for his restraint.

'It is also fit that some martial men should presently repair down to those countries where the "Robin Hoods" are assembled, to encourage the good and to terrify the bad. In which service the Earl of Devonshire is used, and commission going forth for him as General; although I am easily persuaded, that this faggot will be burned to ashes before he shall be 20 miles on his way. Of all which particulars I thought fit to acquaint you, that you may be able to give satisfaction to the State [1] wherein you are; and so I commit you to God.

'Your assured loving friend,
'(Signed) SALISBURY.

'From the Court at Whitehall.

[1] Spain.

N

' POSTSCRIPT.

'Although all ports and passages are stopped for some time as well as for Ambassadors as others, yet I have thought good to advertize you hereof with the speediest, the rather because his Majesty would have you take occasion to advertize the King his brother [1] of this miraculous escape.

' POSTSCRIPT.

'Since the writing of this letter, we have assured news that those traitors are overthrown by the Sheriff of Worcestershire, after they had betaken themselves for their safety in a retreat to the house of Stephen Lyttleton in Staffordshire. The house was fired by the Sheriff; at the issuing forth Catesby was slain; Percy sore hurt, Grant and Winter burned in their faces with gunpowder; the rest are either taken or slain; Rookewood or Digby are taken.'

It is much to be deplored that this letter to Cornwallis has not met with closer attention at the hands of historians, for to those able to read, as it were, between the lines, the contents reveal some important facts about the discovery of the Plot.

For example, this letter completely contradicts the old story that the Government knew nothing of a Plot till the arrival of Mounteagle's letter, for Lord Salisbury distinctly says, ' I had sufficient advertisement that most of those that

[1] The King of Spain.

now are fled (being all notorious Recusants) with many other of that kind, had a practice in hand for some stir this Parliament.' As to the writer's excuse that he was less forward in causing a strict inquiry to be made than the Lord Chamberlain, it is easy to see that Lord Salisbury's object was not to show his hand too much, but to let others obtain some credit for discovering what was already known to him. That Lord Salisbury was well posted up in the facts, and felt quite secure as to the result of his preparations, is 'evident from the account he renders as to how he determined not to inform the King until the last moment. His astuteness in making no open move thus deceived Catesby, and culminated in the ruin of the unsuspecting conspirators.

Salisbury's language in regard to Percy ends, if further contradiction were necessary, the absurd theory propounded by a Jesuit author that the Government did not wish Percy to be taken alive because he ' knew too much.' Lord Salisbury's anxiety, on the contrary, to capture Percy alive is obvious. He evidently hoped that under examination, and probably after torture, Percy would be compelled to incriminate his patron, Lord Northumberland. How little the Government knew of Faukes, well posted up though they were as to the antecedents of the other plotters, can be gathered from the circumstance that Salisbury terms him ' Johnson' throughout the letter.

CHAPTER XVIII

LASTING EFFECTS OF THE GUNPOWDER TREASON

OF the vast importance of the Gunpowder Treason, considered as an historical event, there can be no doubt. The consequences of its conception and failure are felt by English Roman Catholics even to this day. It determined for ever the question whether they could possibly recover the ground they had lost since the death of Queen Mary. The complete exposure of the conspirators' schemes was the one thing needed by the Protestant Government[1] to serve as an excuse to crush, not a section only, but the whole of the Romanist party in England. Loyal Romanists, and disloyal, one and all had to suffer for the sins of a desperate gang of fanatics belonging to the Jesuit section; and the terror excited by the revelation of Catesby's plans lived on so forcibly in the public mind that when Titus Oates appeared, in the reign of James' grandson, with his improbable story, the fear that what had been attempted in the autumn of 1605 was being attempted again in London in the autumn of

[1] 'It fixed the timid and wavering mind of the King in his adherence to the Protestant party' (Jardine).

1678, under the direction of the Jesuits, drove half the population of London off their heads. As a result a number of completely innocent people were butchered on the scaffold for no other reason than they were members of the same religion as had been Thomas Percy, Robert Catesby, Guy Faukes, Oswald Greenway, and Henry Garnet.

The hardships undergone by the English Romanists during the seventeenth century, from the date of the meeting of the adjourned Parliament (which Faukes strove to destroy), are manifest when we read of the fresh laws passed against all the avowed members, rich or poor, of the old religion. The following were some only of the schemes that came into operation for placing the ' Recusants' under the iron rule of the Government :—

1. They (Roman Catholics) were forbidden to appear at Court ;

2. They were forbidden to dwell within ten miles of London ;[1]

3. They were not allowed to remove five miles from their homes, without permission of the neighbouring magistrates ;

4. They were not allowed to become doctors, clerks, lawyers, or members of corporations ;

5. They were inhibited from presenting to Livings ;

[1] Unless employed in one of the very few professions open to them.

6. They were forbidden to act as executors or trustees ;

7. Married Roman Catholics, unless they had been united by a Protestant clergyman, held no legal right to property accruing to either party by marriage;

8. Every Roman Catholic, educated on the Continent, became *ipso facto* an outlaw ;

9. The houses of Roman Catholics might be broken open and searched,[1] on the order of a single magistrate, at any time, and under any pretext, however shallow ;

10. Every Protestant, entertaining a Roman Catholic visitor, or employing a Roman Catholic servant, was liable to a heavy fine;

11. Any Roman Catholic refusing to deny his or her belief in the Deposing Power of the Holy See became liable to perpetual imprisonment.

Soon after the death of Garnet, James offered some considerable relief to those Roman Catholics who refused to acknowledge the Deposing Power of the Roman Pontiffs, and many agreed to accept the proposal made to them.   But the authorities at Rome, backed up by the Society of Jesus—the everlasting curse of English Roman Catholicism —were determined to prevent the King's offer of relief being accepted by Romanists willing to take

[1] 'Every corner of the house was diligently searched. Even the bedrooms of the females were not spared. . . . The terror occasioned by these nocturnal visitations is not to be described' (Jardine).

the oath of allegiance to James as King. Black-well, the Arch-priest, was actually removed from his position[1] because he recommended his co-religionists to take this oath of allegiance, and a new Arch-priest, George Birkhead, was appointed in his stead, with instructions to endeavour to intimidate all Roman Catholics into denying the regal prerogative of James I. This senseless action on the part of the Pope (Paul V.) was the forerunner of fresh disasters for the wretched Roman Catholics in England, for it produced a schism amongst them, divided as they now were into two parties—the one ready to acknowledge James and abjure the Deposing Power of the Pope; the other refusing to acknowledge James, and ready to exalt the doctrine of the Deposing Power into the position of an obligatory Article of Faith. For the loyal English Roman Catholic gentry, therefore, there was no hope of peace. They were attacked on both sides—from Canterbury and from Rome. If they did not profess an outward belief in Protestantism by attending at their parish church, they were ruined with fines; if they acknowledged James as their King, they were condemned by the Head of that very Faith for which they had sacrificed so much.

Meanwhile, that eventful date, the fifth of November, was not allowed to be forgotten by the public. A special service of thanks to Heaven

---

[1] On his death-bed he again advised his friends to take the oath.

for the failure of Faukes' plan was added to the Book of Common Prayer, and every successive anniversary of the fifth [1] was celebrated as a feast-day, or rather, if we can coin such a word, feast-night, in every town and village throughout England.

Finally, in order that readers may be able to judge for themselves as to the nature of the terms of the relief offered to the 'Recusants' by the Government of James concerning the vexed question of the Deposing Power, I reproduce below the text of the oath which each responsible Roman Catholic was asked to swear :—

'I . . . do truly and sincerely acknowledge, profess, testify, and declare in my conscience before God and the world, that Our Sovereign Lord King James is lawful and rightful King of this Realm and all other His Majesty's Dominions and Countries ; and that the Pope, neither of himself, nor by any authority of the Church or See of Rome, or by any other means with any other, hath any power or authority to depose the King or to dispose of any of His Majesty's Kingdoms or Dominions, or to authorize any foreign Princes to invade or annoy him or his Countries ; or to discharge any of his subjects of their allegiance and obedience to His Majesty ;' or to give licence or leave to any of them to bear arms, raise tumults, or to offer any violence or

[1] The fifth of November was to become doubly a great date in Protestant annals when, eighty-three years later, William of Orange arrived in Torbay.

hurt to His Majesty's Person, State, or Government, or to any of His Majesty's subjects within His Majesty's Dominions.

'Also, I swear from my heart that, notwithstanding any declaration or sentence of excommunication or deprivation made or granted, or to be made or granted by the Pope or his successors, or by any authority derived, or pretended to be derived from him or his See against the said King, his Heirs or Successors, or any absolution of the said subjects from their obedience, I will bear faith and true allegiance to His Majesty, his Heirs and Successors, and Him and Them I will defend to the uttermost of my power against all conspiracies and attempts whatsoever which shall be made against Him or their Persons, their Crown and Dignity, by reason or colour of any such sentence or declaration or otherwise, and will do my best endeavour to disclose and make known unto His Majesty, his Heirs and Successors, all treasons and traitorous conspiracies, which I shall know or hear of to be against Him or any of them.

'And I do further swear that I do from my heart abhor, detest, and abjure as impious and heretical this damnable doctrine and position—That Princes, which may be excommunicated or deprived by the Pope, may be deposed or murdered by their subjects, or any other, whatsoever.

'And I do believe, and in my conscience am resolved that neither the Pope nor any person whatsoever hath power to absolve me of this oath or any part thereof, which I acknowledge by good and lawful authority to be lawfully ministered unto me ; and do renounce all pardon and dispensations to the contrary.

'And these things I do plainly and sincerely acknowledge and swear, according to these express words by me spoken, and according to the plain and common sense and understanding of the same words; without any equivocation, or mental evasion, or secret reservation [1] whatsoever.   And I do make this recognition and acknowledgment heartily, willingly, and truly, upon the true faith of a Christian.   So help me God.'

That the Holy See (and its Jesuit agents) acted with supreme folly in striving to prevent the English Romanists from taking such an oath as this is indisputable.   There was nothing in the text of the oath which attacked any Article of Faith contained in the Catholic creed.   The sole but slight objection that could be made to it was the rather strong, but very true, terms in which the Deposing Power claimed by the Popes was mentioned.[2]   It was, indeed, characteristic of the Society of Jesus that its members should have exerted themselves to prevent their co-religionists in England from becoming peaceful and patriotic citizens.   George Blackwell, the Arch-priest, plainly recognized this, for after being inclined at first to withstand the operation of the oath, he had the sense eventually to see how just was the

[1] The propounders of this oath had not forgotten Father Garnet's methods of equivocation.

[2] 'This damnable doctrine and position,' etc.

position opened up to Romanists by the Government, and defying (his former allies) the Jesuits and the tyrannical Pontiff, he died soon after, imploring his co-religionists to subscribe to the terms laid before them.[1]   In this appeal he was supported, it should be mentioned, by the King of France, who (Roman Catholic though he was) solemnly warned the Pope against driving the British Government to desperation.   But, unfortunately, this good advice produced no effect in changing the fatuous policy of the Vatican.

[1] The casual reader must be warned against the references to the text of the oath supplied by the Jesuit writer, Foley.   He dared not quote the actual text.

CHAPTER XIX

MORE LIGHT ON THE MYSTERIOUS LETTER

THE vexed question of the authorship of the famous anonymous letter deserves, without doubt, the closest attention from all students examining into the history of the Gunpowder Treason, for several important reasons, one of which is (even if we cannot ascertain the name of the letter's writer) that it sheds some light upon the part played in both the preparation and the discovery of the plot by Lord Mounteagle. But, before concerning ourselves again with the doubtful position of Mounteagle, it will be as well to deal first with those persons who have been named by various historians as having been concerned in the compilation of this letter. The list of those accused of the authorship may, I think, be said to comprise the following persons :—Thomas Percy, Christopher Wright, Father Oldcorne, Mrs. Abington, Thomas Tresham, Anne Vaux, and Lord Mounteagle himself.

Why the flimsy claims of Thomas Percy to be the author should ever have been seriously advanced it is difficult to imagine, for his conduct subsequent to its delivery shows that he was the very last person likely to have sent warning to Lord Mounteagle, and thence to the Government. He knew that no quarter would be given to him once the secret was out, and so soon as all was up, after the visit of the two lords to the underground chamber, he fled away to the Midlands,[1] without making any attempt to obtain mercy from the Government. Had he been the writer of the letter, he certainly would have pleaded that fact to save his life, instead of which he broke into open rebellion, and refused to surrender under any terms. In common with Christopher Wright, there is not a scrap of original evidence to support the theory that he may have written or dictated the letter.

That Father Oldcorne, S.J., was the author is another theory equally unsupported by evidence, and contrary to all probability. Had he written it, he would not have been severely tortured and then hanged. The letter, moreover, is not in his handwriting.

Mrs. Mary Abington's name has been freely mentioned by several writers as the authoress. Her relationship to Tresham and Mounteagle, and her friendship with Oldcorne, are facts quoted by some authorities as evidence that she must have been 'in the know.'

Anne Vaux has been thought by some to

[1] The Government offered £1000 reward to anybody who would take him alive.

have been the author, and her handwriting, to my mind, is by no means unlike that of the actual document, but when examined in the Tower she seems to have been treated, to a certain extent, as one who did not clearly know what had been secretly going on at Westminster, still she had been living for the last two years on terms of close friendship with nearly all the conspirators.

The claims of Francis Tresham to the authorship are very much stronger. 'That the writer of the letter,' says Dr. Gardiner, 'was Tresham there can be no reasonable doubt. The character of Tresham, the suspicions of his confederates, his own account of his proceedings, all point to him as the betrayer of the secret. If any doubt still remained, there is the additional evidence in the confidence which was after his death expressed by his friends, that if he survived the disease of which he died, he would have been safe from all fear of the confidences of the crime with which he was charged. This confidence they could only have derived from himself, and it could only have been founded on one ground.'

Dr. Gardiner's opinion is also shared by Lingard, who states, 'I will relate what seems, from Greenway's manuscript, to have been the opinion of the conspirators themselves. They attributed it to Tresham,[1] and suspected a

---

[1] 'He it was that wrote the letter to my Lord Mounteagle' (Goodman's *Court of James I.*).

secret understanding between him and Lord
Mounteagle ; and that such understanding existed
between the writer and Lord Mounteagle can be
doubted by no one who attends to the particulars.
They were convinced that Tresham had no
sooner given his consent than he repented of it,
and sought to break up the plot without betraying
his associates. His first expedient was to persuade
them to retire to Flanders in the ship which he
had hired in the river. He next wrote the letter,
and took care to inform them on the following
evening that it had been carried to the Secretary,
in hope that the danger of discovery would
induce them to make use of the opportunity of
escape. In this he would undoubtedly have
succeeded, had not his cunning been defeated by
the superior cunning of Cecil, who allowed no
search to be made in the cellar.'

My own opinion is that if Tresham did not
actually pen the letter himself, he dictated its
contents, but did so with the full approval and
cognisance of Lord Mounteagle, who arranged
with Tresham the farcical comedy of its reception
at Hoxton and transmission to Cecil.

Now, as to Lord Mounteagle ; that he knew
about the preparation of the plot I have not the
faintest doubt, and I base my opinion on the
following grounds, which seem to me to furnish
conclusive proof that he possessed a guilty
knowledge of the Gunpowder Treason, and saved
himself by betraying his confederates.

1. That he gave Sir Edward Baynham some letters to carry to Rome. (He was a party, therefore, to sending Baynham to the Pope.)

2. The extraordinary rewards received by him for taking the warning letter to Cecil.

3. Garnet's reluctance to mention Mounteagle's name, when examined by the council.

4. Garnet's remark (overheard in the Tower), ' I see they will justify my Lord Mounteagle of all this matter. I said nothing of him, neither will I ever confess him.' [1]

5. His relationship to the Winters, Tresham, Percy, Catesby, and others.

6. He had been concerned in former treasons with the Winters, Grant, Tresham, Garnet, Old-corne, Greenway, and Christopher Wright.

7. His secret meeting at Fremland (Essex), in July, 1605, with Catesby, Garnet, and others.

8. The Government made every attempt to suppress his name during the various examinations and the trial of the conspirators.

9. He seems to have been with Catesby, at Bath, shortly before Michaelmas, 1605, *i.e.* some six weeks before the 5th of November.

10. Popular contemporary opinion favoured the notion that Lord Mounteagle was concerned in the plot, for Cecil in his secret instructions to Coke, concerning the trial of the conspirators,

[1] On March 27, 1606, Garnet, however, confessed that 'Mr. Catesby did shew them (the Pope's Breves) to my Lo. Monteagle at the same time when Mr. Tressam was with him at White Webbs.'

confessed : ' It is so lewdly given out that he (Mounteagle) was once of this plot of powder, and afterwards betrayed it all to me.'

11. Thomas Warde, the 'confidential gentle-man' employed in Mounteagle's household, was a friend of several of the plotters, and gave them warning as to their danger.

12. Mounteagle's evident apprehension lest Tresham[1] (when in the Tower) should explain the secret relations existing between the pair during October (1605).

13. Mounteagle was an ally of the Jesuit faction among the English Romanists.

In face of these fatal thirteen reasons, therefore, strong as they are, it seems idle to pretend that Lord Mounteagle had no connection with the plot. His receipt of the warning letter was no sudden surprise, but the last act in a ' little comedy,' which he, Cecil, Tresham and (evidently) Warde, had been busily rehearsing for days past. Such a subtle method of clearing himself and currying favour with the Government was entirely in keeping with the character of this man. All his life he seemed to be sailing under false colours. He was untruthful and unfaithful in all matters of both public and private import. At heart a Roman Catholic, he, nevertheless, implored James to believe that he was a good Protestant.

[1] Tresham is thought by some writers to have been poisoned by Mounteagle.

It is possible that the handwriting of the mysterious letter may never be identified, but there need be no doubt that it was drawn up under the personal supervision of Lord Mounteagle or Tresham. As I have hinted above, a third party, probably a priest, may have assisted in its concoction. Who this priest was it is a little hard to establish. That Tresham may have mentioned intentions to Garnet in confession is very possible, and the Jesuit Superior may have thought the plan proposed a good way out of the terribly difficult situation wherein he was placed. It certainly would never have occurred to any priest (as it never occurred to Tresham himself) that the plotters would be such fools as to stay on in London after the delivery of the letter to the King. Their crass folly in refusing to leave London till all was lost was an act of incomparable madness which was never contemplated by Warde,[1] Tresham, and Mounteagle. 'Those whom the gods wish to destroy they first turn mad!' is a proverb certainly applicable to those of the gunpowder conspirators who refused to listen to the urgent warnings given to them by Thomas Warde.

Lord Mounteagle must, in any event, be deemed a very fortunate person to have been treated with such marked favour and liberality by

---

[1] 'One Thomas Warde, a principal man about him (Mounteagle), is suspected to be accessory of the treason' (Letter from Sir E. Hobart to Sir T. Edmonds, November 19, 1605).

the Government after the failure of the Gunpowder Plot. It must have been some extremely important service secretly rendered to the Government that enabled him to wipe out the stain of his past treasons, and bask in the sunshine of the royal favour. He had, perhaps, been for months past (prior to November, 1605) employed by Cecil as a spy upon the plotters. There is every reason to believe that about Michaelmas (1605) he was staying with Catesby and Percy at Bath. It was probably an additional stroke of fortune for him that Catesby was killed at Holbeach, for that arch-conspirator, 'the deare Robine' of Mounteagle's affection, must have become at the last pretty well acquainted with his friend's intrigues. Percy, slain at Holbeach, might have revealed something, for he also was with Mounteagle at Bath. It is noteworthy, too, that after being at Bath Catesby admitted into the conspiracy, Rookewood, Sir Everard Digby, and Tresham. In fact, it was resolved at Bath by Catesby and Percy, in consultation, to appeal to the trio just mentioned with a view to getting them to join the plot. Why, then, should not Percy and Catesby have taken Mounteagle, with whom they were staying, into their confidence regarding their idea of approaching Rookewood, Digby, and Tresham, all three of whom were known to their host, and one of whom was his relative? Moreover, Baynham seems to have been sent to Rome as the result of the deliberations of Garnet, Catesby, and Mounteagle, when meeting together at Fremland (Essex), in July, 1605.

Thomas Winter, in his confession, refers explicitly to this meeting at Bath in September, when he says, 'abought this time did Mr. Catsby and Mr. Percy meet at the bath wher they agreed t' the company being as yett butt few Mr. Catesby should have the others authority to call in any two whom he thought fit, by which authority he called in after Sir Everatt Digby, though at what time I know not, and last of all Mr. Francis Tressham.'

To sum up : the whole of the case against Lord Mounteagle seems strong in the extreme. That a man with such bad antecedents, and connected by such close ties with the principal plotters, could have been ignorant of what was going on, it would seem futile to conjecture. That he was a party to writing the famous letter addressed to himself can no longer be disputed ; and the evidence—circumstantial though it be— in favour of his having been an accessory both to the compilation of this letter and to the betrayal of the plot to Cecil, appears to me beyond all doubt.

That Lord Mounteagle's connection with the plot was not openly revealed by the conspirators, when imprisoned in the Tower, was due to two considerations : (1) all attempts to incriminate him were checked by the Government, and (2) a lingering hope was entertained by some of the conspirators that Mounteagle (if not accused by them) would intercede for their lives. As to the first of these considerations, proof is fully forthcoming when we notice that, in some cases, the agents of the Council refused[1] to write down Mounteagle's[2] name in the depositions, and in other cases they calmly erased or papered over his name if entered in the prisoner's confessions. As to the second of these considerations, ample proof is to be found by reading the report of the conversation (overheard in the Tower) on January 25, 1606, between Guy Faukes and Robert Winter.

[1] On more than one occasion Garnet was given a very broad hint not to mention Mounteagle's name on any account whatever.

[2] In one very important instance Mounteagle's name is altered to 'Montague.' There was a Romanist peer called Viscount Montague, but this special confession certainly refers only to Mounteagle. Lord Montague was fined £4000 after the failure of the plot.

CHAPTER XX

THE formal confession of Thomas Winter is a most important document. Some controversy has arisen about it owing to the fact that, although the handwriting of the original text is undoubtedly Winter's, his surname is not written in the usual manner, the signature affixed to the confession being spelled 'Winter,' instead of 'Wintour.' This circumstance, however, is of no great moment when we consider how various were the forms of spelling used by Winter's contemporaries. People of far greater genius than this conspirator, living under Elizabeth and James I., did not—if we may jocularly express it thus—know how to spell their own names. Ralegh, Shakspeare, and Sidney, have left behind them their signatures spelled in various forms,[1] so that the fact of Winter signing himself as his name is now known to us is of no consequence to those acquainted with the social history of his age.

In nearly all respects the document can

---

[1] As has Sir William Waad, Winter's gaoler.

undoubtedly be pronounced genuine, although
here and there the wretched man may have been
forced either to insert or to omit a sentence
which he would have much liked not to do, but
the confession may, nevertheless, be pronounced
a frank and veracious story of the plot. The
insinuation that Winter could not have penned
this confession because his arm had not recovered
from the wound received at Holbeach is absurd ;
since we have still with us to-day the original
manuscript accounts bearing witness that he was
then not only quite well enough to write, but
that he had even written at some length two or
three days before he began compiling this formal
confession.

Sir Edward Waad, Lieutenant of the Tower,
writing to Cecil on November 21, 1605, mentions
that 'Thomas Winter doth find his hand so
strong, as after dinner he will settle himself to
write that he hath verbally declared to your
Lordship, adding what he shall remember.'
Winter, therefore, was well enough to write by
November 21, that is to say, four days before
the date attached to his longest confession,[1]
which runs as follows :—

'The Voluntary Declaration of Thomas
Winter, of Hoodington, in the County of
Worcester, gent., the 25th of Nov., 1605, at

[1] The 23rd seems to have been the date on which he wrote, but
the '23rd' on the Hatfield original copy has been altered into the
'25th' by another hand.

the Tower acknowledged before the Lords Commissioners.[1]

'23 9ber 1605.

'MY MOST HONOURABLE LORDS,

'Not out of hope to obtain pardon; for speaking of my temporal part, I may say, the fault is greater than can be forgiven; nor affecting hereby the title of a good subject; for I must redeem my country from as great a danger as I have hazarded the bringing of her into, before I can purchase any such opinion; only at your Honours' command I will briefly set down my own accusation, and how far I have proceeded in this business; which I shall the faithfuller do, since I see such courses are not pleasing to Almighty God, and that all, or the most material parts, have been already confessed.

'I remained with my Brother in the country from Allhallow's-tide [2] until the beginning of Lent in the year of Our Lord, 1603, the first year of the King's reign; about which time Mr. Catesby sent thither, entreating me to come to London, where he, and other my friends, would be glad to see me.   I desired him to excuse me; for I found myself not very well disposed; and, which had happened never to me before, returned the messenger without my company.   Shortly, I received another letter, in any wise to come.   At the second summons, I presently came up, and found him with Mr. John Wright, at Lambeth, where he broke with me how necessary it was not to forsake our country, for he knew I had a

[1] This heading is attached to the Hatfield copy.
[2] October 31st.

resolution to go over,[1] but to deliver her from the servitude in which she remained, or at least to assist her with my utmost endeavours. I answered, that I had often hazarded my life upon far lighter terms, and now would not refuse any good occasion, wherein I might do service to the Catholic Cause; but for myself I knew no mean probable to succeed. He said that he had bethought him of a way at one instant to deliver us from all our bonds, and without any foreign help to replant again the Catholic religion; and withal told me in a word, it was to blow up the Parliament-house with gunpowder; for said he, in that place have they done us all the mischief, and perchance God hath designed that place for their punishment. I wondered at the strangeness of the conceit, and told him that true it was, this struck at the root, and would breed a confusion fit to beget new alterations; but if it should not take effect, as most of this nature miscarried, the scandal would be so great which the Catholic religion might hereby sustain, as not only our enemies, but our friends also would with good reason condemn us. He told me, the nature of the disease required so sharp a remedy and asked me if I would give my consent. I told him Yes, in this or what else soever, if he resolved upon it, I would venture my life. But I proposed many difficulties, as want of an house, and of one to carry the mine, noise in the working, and such like. His answer was, Let us give an attempt, and where it faileth, pass no further. But first, quoth he, because we will leave no

[1] To the Netherlands.

peaceable and quiet way untried, you shall go over and inform the Constable [1] of the state of the Catholics here in England, entreating him to solicit his Majesty, at his coming hither, that the penal laws may be recalled, and we admitted into the rank of his other subjects; withal, you may bring over some confident gentleman, such as you shall understand best able for this business, and named unto me Mr. Faukes. Shortly after, I passed the sea, and found the Constable at Bergen, near Dunkirk, where by help of Mr. Owen, I delivered my message; whose answer was that he had strict command from his master, to do all good offices for the Catholics, and for his own part, he thought himself bound in conscience so to do, and that no good occasion should be omitted, but spoke to him nothing of the matter.

'Returning to Dunkirk with Mr. Owen,[2] we had speech, whether he thought the Constable would faithfully help us, or no. He said he believed nothing else, and that they sought only their own ends, holding small account of Catholics. I told him that there were many gentlemen in England, who would not forsake their country, until they had tried the uttermost, and rather venture their lives than forsake her in this misery. And to add one more to our number, as a fit man both for counsel and execution of whatsoever we should resolve, wished for Mr. Faukes, whom I had heard good commendations of; he told me the gentleman deserved no less, but was at

[1] The Constable of Castile (Juan de Velasco).
[2] Captain Hugh Owen.

Brussels, and that if he came not, as happily he might, before my departure, he would send him shortly after into England. I went soon after to Ostend, where Sir William Stanley,[1] as then, was not, but came two days after. I remained with him three or four days, in which time I asked him, if the Catholics in England should do anything to help themselves, whether he thought the Archduke would second them ? He answered, No, for all those parts were so desirous of peace with England, as they would endure no speech of other enterprise, neither were it fit, said he, to set any project a-foot, now that peace is upon concluding. I told him there was no such resolution, and so fell to discourse of other matters, until I came to speak of Mr. Faukes, whose company I wished over in England; I asked of his sufficiency in the wars, and told him we should need such as he, if occasion required ; he gave very good commendations of him. And as we were thus discoursing and ready to depart for Newport,[2] and taking my leave of Sir William, Mr. Faukes came into our company, newly returned, and saluted us. This is the gentleman, said Sir William, that you wished for, and so we embraced again. I told him, some good friends of his wished his company in England, and that if he pleased to come to Dunkirk, we would have further conference, whither I was then going : so taking my leave of them both, I departed. About two days after, came Mr. Faukes to Dunkirk, where I told him that we were upon a resolution to do

[1] A brilliant soldier, who had (after betraying his trust) deserted into the Spanish service.
[2] Nieuport.

somewhat in England, if the peace with Spain helped us not, but as yet resolved upon nothing; such or the like talk we passed at Graveling,[1] where I lay for a wind, and when it served came both in one passage to Greenwich, near which place we took a pair of oars, and so came up to London, and came to Mr. Catesby, whom we found in his lodging; he welcomed us into England, and asked me what news from the Constable. I told him "Good Words," but I fear the deeds would not answer. This was the beginning of Easter term, and about the midst of the same term,[2] whether sent for by Mr. Catesby or upon some business of his own, up came Mr. Thomas Percy. The first word he spoke after he came into our company, was "Shall we always, gentlemen, talk, and never do anything?" Mr. Catesby took him aside, and had speech about somwhat to be done, so as we might first all take an oath of secrecy, which we resolved within two or three days to do; so as there we met behind Saint Clement's, Mr. Catesby, Mr. Percy, Mr. Wright, Mr. Guy Faukes, and myself; and having upon a Primer given each other the oath of secrecy, in a chamber where no other body was, we went after into the next room and heard Mass,[3] and received the Blessed Sacrament upon the same. Then did Mr. Catesby disclose to Mr. Percy, and I, together with Jack Wright, tell to Mr. Faukes, the business for which we took this oath, which they both approved. And then Mr. Percy sent to take the house which Mr.

[1] Gravelines.
[2] Probably about May 10 (1604).
[3] Said by Father Gerard, S.J.

Catesby, in my absence, had learned did belong
to one Ferris, which with some difficulty in the
end he obtained, and became, as Ferris before
was, tenant to Whynniard.   Mr. Faukes underwent the name of Mr. Percy's man, calling himself
Johnson, because his face was the most unknown,
and received the keys of the house, until we
heard that the Parliament was adjourned to the
7 of February.   At which time we all departed
several ways into the country, to meet again at
the beginning of Michaelmas term.[1]   Before this
time also it was thought convenient to have a
house that might answer to Mr. Percy's, where
we might make provision of powder and wood
for the mine which, being there made ready,
should in a night be conveyed by boat to the
house by the Parliament because we were both to
foil that with often going in and out.   There was
none we could devise so fit as Lambeth where
Mr. Catesby often lay, and to be keeper thereof,
by Mr. Catesby's choice, we received into the
number Keyes,[2] as a trusty honest man.

'Some fortnight after, towards the beginning
of the term, Mr. Faukes and I came to Mr.
Catesby at Moorcrofts, where we agreed that
now was time to begin and set things in order
for the mine.   So as Mr. Faukes went to London
and the next day sent for me to come over to

[1] About the second week in October.

[2] A note in the margin of the Record Office copy states 'this
was abought a month before Michaelmas.'   In the Hatfield
copy the note says, 'abought a month before michelmas.'   The
Hatfield copy and Winter's examinations of January 9 and 17,
are on paper of the same watermark, different from that of the
Record Office copy.

him.   When I came, the cause was for that the
Scottish Lords were appointed to sit in conference
on the Union in Mr. Percy's house.   This hindered
our beginning until a fortnight before Christmas,
by which time both Mr. Percy and Mr. Wright
were come to London, and we against their
coming had provided a good part of the powder,
so as we all five entered with tools fit to begin
our work, having provided ourselves of baked-
meats, the less to need sending abroad.   We
entered late in the night, and were never seen,
save only Mr. Percy's man, until Christmas-eve,
in which time we wrought under a little entry to
the wall of the Parliament House, and under-
propped it as we went with wood.

'Whilst we were together we began to fashion
our business, and discourse what we should do
after this deed were done.   The first question
was how we might surprise the next heir; the
Prince[1] haply would be at the Parliament with
the King his father: how should we then be able
to seize on the Duke?[2]   This burden Mr. Percy
undertook; that by his acquaintance he with
another gentleman would enter the chamber
without suspicion, and having some dozen others
at several doors to expect his coming, and two or
three on horseback at the Court gate to receive
him, he would undertake (the blow being given,
until which he would attend in the Duke's
chamber) to carry him safe away, for he supposed
most of the Court would be absent, and such as
were there not suspecting, or unprovided for any

[1] Henry, Prince of Wales.
[2] Charles, Duke of York, afterwards King

such matter. For the Lady Elizabeth,[1] it were easy to surprise her in the country by drawing friends together at a hunting near the Lord Harrington's, and Ashby, Mr. Catesby's house, being not far off was a fit place for preparation.

'The next was for money and horses, which if we could provide in any reasonable measure, having the heir apparent and the first knowledge by 4 or 5 days was odds sufficient. Then, what Lords we should save from the Parliament, which was agreed in general as many as we could that were Catholics or so disposed. Next, what foreign princes we should acquaint with this before, or join with after. For this point we agreed that first we would not enjoin princes to that secrecy nor oblige them by oath so to be secure of their promise; besides, we knew not whether they will approve the project or dislike it, and if they do allow thereof, to prepare before might beget suspicion and not to provide until the business were acted; the same letter that carried news of the thing done might as well entreat their help and furtherance. Spain is too slow in his preparations to hope any good from in the first extremities, and France too near and too dangerous, who with the shipping of Holland we feared of all the world might make away with us. But while we were in the middle of these discourses, we heard that the Parliament should be anew adjourned until after Michaelmas, upon which tidings we broke off both discourse and working until after Christmas. About Candlemas,[2]

[1] Afterwards Queen of Bohemia.
[2] February 2.

we brought over in a boat the powder which we had provided at Lambeth and laid it in Mr. Percy's house because we were willing to have all our danger in one place. We wrought also another fortnight in the mine against the stone wall, which was very hard to beat through, at which time we called in Kit Wright, and near to Easter, as we wrought the third time, opportunity was given to hire the cellar, in which we resolved to lay the powder and leave the mine.

'Now, by reason that the charge of maintaining us all so long together, besides the number of several houses which for several uses had been hired, and buying of powder, etc., had lain heavy on Mr. Catesby alone to support, it was necessary for to call in some others to ease his charge, and to that end desired leave that he with Mr. Percy, and a third whom they should call, might acquaint whom they thought fit and willing to the business, for many, said he, may be content that I should know, who would not, therefore, that all the company should be acquainted with their names; to this we all agreed.

'After this, Mr. Faukes laid in the cellar, which he had newly taken, a thousand of billets and five hundred of faggots, and with that covered the powder, because we might have the house free to suffer anyone to enter that would. Mr. Catesby wished us to consider, whether it were not now necessary to send Mr. Faukes over, both to absent himself for a time, as also to acquaint Sir William Stanley and Mr. Owen with this matter. We agreed that he should (provided that he gave it to them with the same oath that we had taken before) viz. To keep it secret from all the world. The reason, why we desired Sir William Stanley should be acquainted herewith, was, to have him with us as soon as he could : and for Mr. Owen, he might hold good correspondency after with foreign princes. So Mr. Faukes departed, about Easter, for Flanders, and returned, the latter end of August. He told me that, when he arrived at Brussels, Sir William Stanley was not returned from Spain, so as he uttered the matter only to Owen, who seemed well pleased with the business, but told him, that surely Sir William would not be acquainted with any plot, as having business now a foot in the Court of England[1]; but he himself would always be ready to tell it him, and send him away as soon as it were done.

'About this time did Mr. Percy and Mr. Catesby meet at the bath,[2] where they agreed, that the company being yet but few, Mr. Catesby should have the others' authority to call in whom he thought best, by which authority he called in after Sir Everard Digby, though at what time I know not, and last of all Mr. Francis Tresham. The first promised, as I heard Mr. Catesby say, fifteen hundred pounds, Mr. Percy himself promised all that he could get out of the Earl of Northumberland's rent,[3] and to provide many

---

[1] Stanley, at that date, seems to have had some idea of seeking pardon from the British Government.

[2] The town of Bath.

[3] *i.e.* all that he could steal. According to a note in the King's handwriting, in the Record Office copy, this was 'about four thousand pounds.'

galloping horses, his number was ten.[1]   Meanwhile, Mr. Faukes and myself alone bought some
new powder, as suspecting the first to be dank,
and conveyed it into the cellar, and set it in
order, as we resolved it should stand.   Then was
the Parliament anew prorogued until the 5 of
November ; so as we all went down until some
ten days before, when Mr. Catesby came up with
Mr. Faukes to a house by Enfield Chace, called
White Webbes, whither I came to them, and
Mr. Catesby willed me to enquire whether the
young Prince came to Parliament.   I told him
that his Grace thought not to be there.   Then
must we have our horses, said Mr. Catesby,
beyond the water, and provision of more company
to surprise the Prince, and leave the Duke alone.
Two days after, being Sunday at night, in came
one[2] to my chamber, and told me that a letter
had been given to my lord Monteagle to, to this
effect, that he wished his lordship's absence from
the Parliament because a blow would there be
given, which letter he presently carried to my
lord of Salisbury.   On the morrow[3] I went to
White Webbs and told it to Mr. Catesby,
assuring him withal that the matter was disclosed,

[1] 'An unclear phrase,' writes the King.

[2] It is astonishing that Winter should not have been forced to
mention this person's name.   The anonymous 'one' was, however,
Warde, which fact strengthens my contention that the Government
did their utmost to shield both him and Mounteagle.   Had not this
'one' been under Government protection, the Privy Council would
have insisted on his name being divulged, because he, by giving
notice to Winter, was thereby committing misprision of treason.
It seems extraordinary that previous writers on the plot should
have omitted all reference to this incident.

[3] October 28, 1605.

and wishing him in any wise to forsake his country. He told me he would see further as yet, and resolved to send Mr. Faukes to try the uttermost, protesting, if the part belonged to himself, he would try the same adventure. On Wednesday, Master Faukes went, and returned at night, of which we were very glad. Thursday, I came to London ; and Friday, Mr. Catesby, Mr. Tresham, and I met at Barnet, where we questioned how this letter should be sent to my lord Mounteagle, but could not conceive, for Master Tresham forswore it, whom we only suspected. On Saturday night,[1] I met Mr. Tresham again in Lincoln's-Inn Walks ; wherein he told such speeches, that my lord of Salisbury should use to the King, as I gave it lost the second time, and repeated the same to Mr. Catesby, who hereupon was resolved to be gone, but staid to have Master Percy come up, whose consent herein we wanted. On Sunday, Mr. Percy, and no "Nay," but would abide the uttermost trial.

'The suspicion of all hands put us in such confusion, as Mr. Catesby resolved to go down into the country the Monday that Master Percy went to Sion, and Mr. Percy resolved to follow the same night or early the next morning. About five of the clock, being Tuesday,[2] came the younger Wright to my chamber, and told me that a nobleman called the lord Monteagle,[3] saying,

[1] November 2.

[2] November 5, a.m.

[3] This reference to Lord Mounteagle is very vague, and bears the impression of having been ' corrected ' by those who witnessed Winter's confession.

"Rise, and come along to Essex House, for I am going to call up my lord of Northumberland," saying withal "The matter is discovered." "Go back, Mr. Wright," quoth I, "and learn what you can at Essex Gate." Shortly, he returned, and said, "Surely all is lost, for Leyton is got on horseback at Essex door, and as he parted, he asked if their Lordships would have any more with him, and being answered 'No,' is rode as fast up Fleet Street as he can ride." "Go you then," quoth I, "to Mr. Percy, for sure it is for him they seek, and bid him begone; I will stay, and see the uttermost." Then I went to the Court gates, and found them straitly guarded so as nobody could enter. From thence I went down towards the Parliament house, and in the middle of King's Street found the guard standing that would not let me pass, and as I returned, I heard one say, "There is a treason discovered, in which the King and the Lords shall have been blown up," so then I was fully satisfied that all was known, and went to the stable where my gelding stood, and rode into the country. Mr. Catesby had appointed our meeting at Dunchurch, but I could not overtake them until I came to my brother's, which was Wednesday night. On Thursday, we took the armour at my lord Windsor's,[1] and went that night to one Stephen Lyttleton's house, where the next day, being Friday, as I was early abroad to discover, my man came to me and said that a heavy mischance had severed all the company, for that Mr. Catesby, Mr. Rookewood, and Mr. Grant were

[1] Hewell Grange.

burned with gunpowder, upon which sight, the rest dispersed. Mr. Lyttleton wished me to fly, and so would he. I told him I would first see the body of my friend and bury him, whatsoever befel me. When I came, I found Mr. Catesby reasonable well, Mr. Percy, both the Wrights, Mr. Rookewood, and Mr. Grant. I asked them what they resolved to do. They answered " We mean here to die." I said again, I would take such part as they did. About eleven of the clock, came the company to beset the house, and as I walked into the Court was shot into the shoulder, which lost me the use of my arm. The next shot was the elder Wright, and fourthly, Ambrose Rookewood. Then said Mr. Catesby to me, (standing before the door they were to enter), "Stand by me, Tom, and we will die together." " Sir," quoth I, " I have lost the use of my right arm, and I fear that will cause me to be taken." So as we stood close together, Mr. Catesby, Mr. Percy, and myself,—they two were shot, as far as I could guess, with one bullet,—and then the company entered upon me, hurt me in the belly with a pike, and gave me other wounds, until one came behind, and caught hold of both my arms, and so, I remain, your, etc.'

Of this confession of Thomas Winter there are three versions extant, viz., that at Hatfield, that in the Public Record Office,[1] and that printed in what is termed the 'King's Book'

---

[1] In the *Gunpowder Plot Book*, vol. ii. There is a copy of this copy in the British Museum (Add MSS. 6178).

relating to the Plot. The version at Hatfield is the original, written by Winter himself. That in the Record Office is a copy made by Lord Salisbury's secretary, Monck, and corresponds very nearly with that published in the 'King's Book.' Between the three exists no really material difference except in matters of punctuation. The Hatfield copy is, of course, the only one signed by Winter himself. In the copy published in the 'King's Book' the marginal note, referred to above, is incorporated in the text. I have mainly followed, in the above transcription, the Record Office version, although accepting occasionally the punctuation and textual arrangement adopted in the 'King's Book.'

The holograph text at Hatfield is, beyond doubt, in Winter's handwriting, and even if the signature, 'Thomas Winter,' attached to it, should ever be proved to be a forgery, as is quite possible, it would not impugn in the least the veracity of the contents of the document. No forger could have known about many of the incidents described by Winter. No agent of the Government could have invented, or hit upon, the meeting in September (1605) at Bath. No other person but Winter himself could have related the true story of his adventures in the Low Countries. Such suggestions of error that the writer was chronologically wrong in stating in what sequence the various conspirators joined the Plot are worthless. In a matter about which

there had been, of necessity, so much mystery
and secrecy, it surely may be forgiven the poor
harassed writer if he makes a slip now and then
in the precise chronological order in which certain
of the plotters were quietly enrolled! Catesby,
probably, alone knew of the exact data when all
the various plotters took the required oath, and
Catesby, it need not be repeated, was dead!
But, even if Thomas Winter had never confessed
at all, the history of this great Treason, as
handed down to us, would not thereby have
been affected, for Winter's information merely
corroborates what has been ascertained from
other sources in verification of the traditional
story of the Gunpowder Plot.

This confession shows us into what a state of
desperation the English Roman Catholics had
been driven soon after the accession of James,
from whom they had expected so much, but
received nothing of what they had expected. It
was not until they found that no concession was
likely to be forthcoming from James, and (after
that) no aid was likely to be forthcoming from
Spain, that they set about the concoction of their
diabolical scheme.

There is one important item in Winter's
confession of which, perhaps, insufficient notice
has been taken by writers dealing with the Plot,
and this is his reference to the probable, if not
absolutely certain innocence of Sir William Stanley, as to whom the British Government would

have been as glad to prove a guilty connection
with the conspiracy as they were similarly to
implicate Captain Hugh Owen. 'Sir William
Stanley,' Winter states, 'was not returned from
Spain, so as he (Faukes) uttered the matter only to
Owen, who seemed well pleased with the business,
but told him that surely Sir William would not
be acquainted with any plot, as having business
now afoot in the Court of England, but he himself
would be always ready to tell it him and send
him away as soon as it were done.' It has not
transpired that Stanley became acquainted with
the Plot before news of its detection reached the
Continent. This Sir William Stanley passed a
career made up of such extraordinary vicissitudes
that some account of him is worthy of mention
here.

Sir William Stanley was the head of the
ancient family of the Stanleys, of which, until the
death of the last of Sir William's descendants
in the male line,[1] the noble house of Derby
formed only the junior branch. Born in 1549,
Stanley was brought up from childhood as a
devout Roman Catholic. From 1567 till 1570,
he fought under Alva in the Netherlands, and
then volunteered for service under Elizabeth in
Ireland, where he remained, on and off, for
fifteen years, greatly distinguishing himself by
his military genius and valour. Whilst in Ireland
his faith seems to have offered no scruples in

[1] Sir John Massey-Stanley-Errington (1893).

regard to his fighting faithfully for the Queen against his co-religionists. After quitting Ireland, Stanley was selected to hold a command under the Earl of Leicester in the Netherlands, but, before joining the Earl, returned on a brief visit to the Emerald Isle, where he raised a force of about thirteen hundred men to serve under Leicester. At this juncture, Stanley was evidently meditating treason, and was in constant but secret communication with certain Jesuit priests in England, and with the Spanish Ambassador in London.

Arrived in Holland, he fought by the side of Sir Philip Sidney at Zutphen,[1] and evidently won the complete confidence of Leicester, who entrusted to him and his Irishmen the care of the walled town of Deventer, which he was to hold against the Spaniards. But, on January 29, 1587, he threw open the gates of this city to the enemy, and he and most of his men entered the service of Spain, to the undisguised joy of the Jesuits,[2] and to the consternation of the English Government. Henceforth, Stanley's life was utterly changed. No man ever more completely destroyed all prospects of a brilliant career than had he by the surrender of Deventer. By the States-General, acting in concert with England, a price was put upon his head, and he went to

[1] September 22, 1586.
[2] They actually had the audacity to print a book, extolling his treachery.

Spain, there to advise King Philip in his plans
for the invasion of England.   Stanley's scheme,
as tendered to the Spanish King, was to land
an army in Ireland, and after conquering that
country, to disembark troops at Milford Haven.
Having done this, the Spanish fleet was to hold
the Irish Channel, so that more troops could be
brought over from Spain for the invasion of
England on the grand scale.   Even if this latter
item in the programme were not feasible for some
time yet, Stanley argued that Spain would be
able to garrison Milford just as England had
formerly occupied Calais.

That Stanley's schemes were far more wisely
conceived and more likely of success than those
adopted by Philip when despatching his great
Armada, there can be no doubt; but (happily for
England) the King refused to listen to his advice.
Sir William Stanley, thereupon, returned to the
Netherlands, to serve under Parma in the army
which was to co-operate with the Armada (of
1588).   After the failure of the Armada, he
returned again to Spain in order to endeavour
to obtain, once more, Philip's approval of his
original scheme for sending troops to Ireland and
Milford.   From 1590 to 1600 he was serving, off
and on, in the Netherlands, whilst making several
visits to Madrid, and to Rome, to keep alive his,
cherished idea of invading England.

The accession of James I. opened, at last
Stanley's eyes as to the hopelessness of the

success of such schemes, and, indeed, of his own position. He had hoped that the English Roman Catholics, aided by Philip, would rise and proclaim as Elizabeth's successor some one, such as Lady Arabella Stewart, who might prove to be a mere tool in the hands of the Roman party. He speedily recognized, however, the stability of the new King's Government, and seems vainly to have been trying to obtain a pardon from James at the very time when his old friends, Winter, Faukes, and Wright, were preparing the Gunpowder Plot.

After the discovery of the Plot, Sir William Stanley plainly recognized that the Roman Catholic cause had become completely discredited, and that no hope of help could be entertained any longer from Spain. He spent the rest of his life in wandering about the Continent, consoling himself with special devotion to his religion, after having again been refused a pardon by the British Government. With his fast friends, the Jesuits, he appears to have fallen out towards the last, and to have become somewhat disgusted with their politics. At the great age of eighty-one, Stanley died at Ghent (1630), and was buried at Mechlin. He was the father of two sons and three daughters. His grandson, William Stanley, recovered the family estate of Hooton, Cheshire, and was the father of Sir William Stanley, of Hooton, Baronet.

That an Englishman of such noble birth and

of such undoubted military genius as Sir William Stanley should have fallen so low as to become a mere pensioner of Spain, and the enemy of his fatherland, is sad in the extreme.   Devotion to his religion utterly blinded him, and prevented him from discerning how fatal and how foolish was the course he was pursuing.   Had he held instead of surrendering Deventer, he would undoubtedly have obtained high honours in England ; and it is said that, at the very moment when he was plotting to surrender this city to Spain, Elizabeth had just consented to his being appointed the next Viceroy of Ireland.

CHAPTER XXI

BEHIND THE SCENES

SIR WILLIAM WAAD, Lieutenant of the Tower at the period of the Gunpowder Plot, has left on record [1] a list of names [2] which he considers to have included all the persons concerned in hatching the famous conspiracy. This list mentions not only the thirteen conspirators universally allowed to have been engaged in the plot, but the following persons in addition, viz.—Henry Morgan, Sir Edward Baynham, Hugh Owen, Sir William Stanley, Thomas Abington, Henry Garnet, John Gerard, Oswald Tesond,[3] Hammond,[4] John Winter, and Baldwin.[5] From this list we can erase the names of Sir William Stanley and Thomas Abington, for, I think, the good and sufficient reason that their innocence has been satisfactorily established. Of the rest, I have already dealt with Hugh Owen, Garnet,

---

[1] In an inscription preserved in the Council Chamber of the King's House, Tower of London.

[2] *Conjuratorum nomina, ad perpetuam ipsorum infamiam et tantæ diritatis detestationem sempiternam.*

[3] Father Tesimond, S.J., *alias* ' Greenway.',

[4] Father Nicholas Hart, S.J.

[5] Father William Bawden, S.J.

and Baynham. We are, therefore, left with
Gerard, Baldwin, Morgan, Greenway, John
Winter, and Hammond, into whose cases (as
regards their complicity in the Gunpowder Plot)
I shall now inquire; whilst I propose also to
consider the question of the innocence, or guilt,
of Anne Vaux, and Nicholas Owen, nicknamed
' Little John.' Yielding precedence to the fair
sex, I will first take the case of

ANNE VAUX. — This lady was the third
daughter of William, Lord Vaux of Harrowden,
by his first wife, Elizabeth Beaumont. The date
of her birth has not come down to us, but for
several years prior to 1605, she had been living
entirely under the direction of the Jesuits, for
whom she ever expressed the warmest admiration.
She put herself under a vow of blind obedience [1]
to Father Garnet and his society, and followed
him about like a pet dog whenever she could
safely do so, going often, in these adventures,
under the *alias* of ' Mrs. Perkins.' This close
intimacy with Garnet caused considerable scandal.
At Garnet's execution, some one in the crowd
having taunted him with this, he protested in
reply that ' this honourable gentlewoman hath
great wrong by such false reports. And for my
own part, as I have always been free from such
crimes, so I may protest for her upon my conscience that I think her to be a perfect pure

---

[1] Vide *Gunpowder Plot Book*, ii., p. 245, at the Record Office.

virgin, if any other in England or otherwise alive. She is a virtuous good gentlewoman, and, therefore, to impute any such thing unto her cannot proceed but of malice' (Gerard's *Narrative*).

Anne Vaux, with her sister, Mrs. Brooksby, frequently entertained Garnet, as we have seen, at White Webbs,[1] a resort of several of the conspirators, such as (her relative) Tresham, Catesby, and Thomas Winter. She was, during the twelve months preceding the plot, on terms of great friendship with these persons, as well as being intimately acquainted with Digby, Gerard, Oldcorne, Greenway, Grant, Robert Winter, and Ambrose Rookewood. When Tresham, on his death-bed, had perjured himself by swearing that he had not met Garnet for sixteen years, Anne Vaux's subsequent confession (in the Tower), to the effect that from 1602 to 1605 she had constantly been in the company of Tresham and Garnet, met together at her own house, was produced at Garnet's trial in refutation.

According to her own account, Anne Vaux had often questioned Garnet concerning the preparations being made by certain of the conspirators for military service. She was, for instance, surprised at the large number of horses kept ready in some of their stables. Garnet, however, told her that these preparations had no connection with any plot in England, but were

---

[1] And at Stoke Poges, Bucks (the scene of Gray's *Elegy*).

destined to help the Spanish forces in the Netherlands.

Liberated from the Tower early in August, 1606, Anne Vaux, although little is known of her subsequent career,[1] maintained all her old devotion to her religion, and as late as the year 1635 we find her keeping a Jesuitical school in Derbyshire for Roman Catholic children, which was broken up by order of the Privy Council.

That Anne Vaux was a willing accessory before the fact to the Gunpowder Plot I refuse to believe.   She was so much under the influence of the Jesuits that she may have been desirous of aiding in any mild scheme for helping her co-religionists, but she was too honest to have joined in so sanguinary a business as the Gunpowder Treason.   According to her evidence in the Tower (where nothing material was proved against her), she professed to have been much shocked at Garnet's connection with the plotters. Most of her letters to Garnet in the Tower were intercepted by the gaoler, and her handwriting is, as I have hinted, by no means unlike that of the Lord Mounteagle's anonymous correspondent. She seems also to have known that 'a plot was hatching' some weeks before the 'Powder' Plot was discovered.

NICHOLAS OWEN, S.J.—This Jesuit lay-brother,

[1] Garnet formally released her from her vow of obedience before his death.   She probably renewed it, however, to his successor.

famous as the constructor of hiding-places, must not be confused with Captain Hugh Owen, the friend of the Jesuits, employed by the Spaniards in the Low Countries.   Particulars of his death in the Tower of London are terrible in the extreme.   Captured at Hendlip, he was conveyed to the Tower, and there, after being severely tortured, died on March 2, 1606.   His enemies gave out that he had committed suicide.   Owen, they have recorded, 'murthered himself in the Tower.'   With this theory Dr. Gardiner agrees,[1] when he declares that 'his (Owen's) fear lest the torture should be repeated worked upon his mind to such an extent that, on the following day, he committed suicide.'

In justice, however, to Owen's memory, it should be emphatically stated that there is nothing whatever to lead us to suppose that he destroyed himself.   The evidence, indeed, is all the other way.   He died, it appears, of internal injuries received during the tortures to which he was submitted.[2]

Before being put to the torture, Owen denied all knowledge of the Plot, and refused to say a word that would injure, or could be construed to injure, either Oldcorne or Garnet.[3]   It is probable, however, that he knew something about the Plot;

[1] As do David Jardine, and other notable writers.

[2] Or, as another account states, whilst in the very act of being racked.

[3] He even denied, at first, that he was acquainted with either Oldcorne or Garnet.

Q

for a man who was (more than any other in England) *au fait* with secrets affecting the Roman Catholic cause, and who was personally acquainted with all the conspirators, must have known pretty well what was going on.   He was implicitly trusted by the Jesuit faction among the English Romanists, and it is quite likely that Catesby went to him for advice as to the best means of concealing the powder at Westminster, and arranging the train for the explosion.   The operations of the conspirators beneath the Parliament House would have been thoroughly in keeping with the proceedings of one who had been for years past burrowing like a mole in scores of houses for the purpose of contriving hiding-places and secret passages.   If, at any rate, Owen did not sympathize with the aims of the plotters, we may, nevertheless, reasonably suspect that he was acquainted with the details of the conspiracy.

HENRY MORGAN AND JOHN WINTER.—These gentlemen joined the 'hunting-party' at Dunchurch, but were not connected with the Westminster part of the Plot.   Morgan is described in one of the State papers, relating to his arrest and examination, as 'Harry Morgan, gentleman, of Norbrook,[1] Warwickshire.'   He was a well-known Recusant, and had for some time been suspected of treasonable proceedings

---

[1] This was Grant's residence,

by the Government. He was instrumental, whilst with the conspirators marching to Holbeach, in breaking into Warwick Castle and stealing horses, on which occasion he was attired 'in coloured satin done with gold lace.' He was one of those 'grievously burnt with powder' by the explosion at Holbeach. Frequently examined, when in the Tower, he succeeded in showing[1] that he was not privy to the Gunpowder Treason, but only joined the 'hunting-party' in order to strike a blow, if necessary, for the good of the cause.

John Winter, half-brother to Thomas and Robert, 'knew nothing of the treason intended, left the party at Holbeach, and surrendered at his brother's house' (Huddington). He was executed, with Oldcorne,[2] at Redhill, outside Worcester, April 7, 1606.

Neither of these gentlemen, therefore, was proved guilty of being an accessory to the Gunpowder Plot, of which they knew nothing when they joined Digby's 'hunting-party.' They merely thought there had been, under Catesby, an attempt made at an armed rising in London, which had failed, and to which the march to Holbeach was a sequel. Catesby, beyond doubt, grossly deceived them as to what had really taken place in London, and they foolishly believed what he said.

[1] Dom. S.P., vol. xvi., November 12, 1605.
[2] H. Lyttleton, R. Ashley, and two malefactors were also executed with Winter.

FATHER BALDWIN, S.J.—The career of this Jesuit [1] was peculiarly romantic, and he was more than once imprisoned in the Tower of London. Born in Cornwall (1563), he was educated at Exeter College, Oxford, and was then presumably a Protestant. Like his Superior, Parsons, he seems to have become a Roman Catholic on leaving the University. Studying next at Douai, he eventually entered the Society of Jesus in 1590. Five years later he was captured by an English ship off Dunkirk, when sailing for Spain, and taken to London, where he was thrown into the Tower. Nothing, however, being proved against him, he was released, and went in the course of a few months to reside at the English College at Rome. From 1599 to 1609 he was at Brussels, when he met Faukes and Winter, and his intimacy with them caused the British Government to accuse him of complicity in the Gunpowder Plot. His extradition was demanded by Salisbury, but refused. In 1610, however, whilst travelling through the Palatinate, he was arrested by the Elector, and sent a prisoner to England. He was submitted to great indignities and hardships, *en route*, and is said to have been bound with a chaine more than long enough to secure 'an African lion.' Arrived in London, nothing again could he proved definitely against him, yet he was kept in the Tower till 1618. On

---

[1] His real name seems to have been ' Bawden,' but he has been generally called Baldwin.

his release, he proceeded to Louvain. He died, as Rector of St. Omer's, in September, 1632.

Sir William Waad's charge against Baldwin as being an accessory before the fact to the Gunpowder Plot does not appear to have had any real foundation, or he would not have got off with only ten years' imprisonment. Although apparently innocent of actual complicity in the Gunpowder Treason, he was hand-in-glove with several of the conspirators in their attempts to induce Spain to invade England, and when living at Brussels, he maintained an active correspondence with men like Stanley, Hugh Owen, and Garnet, to such an extent that he and Owen were denounced by Cecil as having been accessories to the Gunpowder Plot from the beginning. Baldwin was a mere tool in the hands of the notorious Father Parsons, and was of a crafty and double-dealing character.

FATHER HAMMOND, S.J.—Although generally called Hammond, the real name of this Jesuit was Nicholas Hart. He seems to have used 'Hammond' as an *alias*. It was he who heard the confessions of the conspirators at Huddington, on November 7, 1605. Robert Winter (whose chaplain Hart had been) confessed (January 17, 1606) that Hart had absolved all those present at Huddington on November 7, and had given them the Sacrament at Low Mass. On the same day (January 17), Stephen Lyttleton also acknowledged

that he had received the Sacrament from Hart at
Huddington, but refused resolutely to reveal
what had passed between him and this priest in
confession. On January 21 (1606), Henry Morgan
admitted that he also had confessed to Hart at
Huddington,[1] and that Hart encouraged him to
act under Catesby's orders.

Hart was born at Kennington, 1577, and was
educated (as a Protestant) at Westminster School.
When one and twenty years of age, he was
received into the Roman Church by a Franciscan
friar imprisoned in the Marshalsea. He entered
the English College at Rome, 1599, and the
Society of Jesus five years later. In 1611 he
was arrested, at Harrowden, but released, and
banished, after a year's imprisonment in the
Gatehouse, Westminster. He had, however, the
temerity to return, and in 1646 was again
imprisoned for a short period. On his release he
was employed by his Society in South Wales,
where he died in 1650. The fact of his not
having been imprisoned more than a year under
James I. tends to show that he must have
succeeded in proving that he had not been an

---

[1] 'On the following morning (Nov. 7), the whole company, now
reduced to thirty-six persons, were present at Mass. After its
conclusion, they all confessed to the priest, who was a Father
Hammond. He was aware of their late proceedings, but does
not seem to have considered that there was anything in them
which needed absolution. At least, Bates naïvely stated that
when he confessed on this occasion it was only for his sins, and
not for any other particular cause' (Dr. S. R. Gardiner).

accessory before the fact to the Gunpowder Plot.
Considering, however, that he had absolved the
conspirators at Huddington, when they were
actually engaged in levying open war against the
State, it must surely be allowed that the Government treated him very leniently. Certainly, he
was far more guilty of misprision of treason than
had been Father Oldcorne, who was tortured
and hanged, and whose name is not even included
in Sir William Waad's black-list.

FATHER GREENWAY, S.J.—As Garnet confided
to Oldcorne in the Tower, it was (for several
reasons) a fortunate thing for the Roman Catholic
cause that Greenway, or Tesimond, successfully
escaped abroad. Had he been captured (and
tortured), he would probably have been made to
reveal information of a damning nature both as
regards his own and his Superior's knowledge of
the Plot. He would, moreover, if captured, most
certainly have shared Father Garnet's fate.

Although generally known in history by the
name of Greenway, this Jesuit's real name was
Oswald Tesimond, and Greenway, like Beaumont,
was only one of his *aliases*. Born in 1563, he
entered the English College at Rome in 1580,
and became a Jesuit four years later. He studied
for some time at Madrid, and then entered
England in the spring of 1598. In 1603 he
became 'professed' of the four vows of his
Society. The day after the fatal Fifth of November

(1605), he was entertained, as we have seen, by the conspirators at Huddington, where he said Mass. After failing to get other Roman Catholics to join the insurgents, Tesimond had to flee to save his own life, and with considerable cleverness as well as audacity, proceeded to London, instead of shutting himself up like a rat in trap, as did Oldcorne and Garnet, in a country house. Whilst in London, he amused himself on one occasion by reading a printed proclamation for his own capture. A man in the street, however, struck by Tesimond's resemblance to the official description [1] openly accused of him being the fugitive priest, seized him, and led him away with the object of giving him up to justice. For a few yards Tesimond proceeded quietly with his captor, when he suddenly made a desperate attempt to get free, and being stronger and quicker than his antagonist, found safety in flight. He then hid himself at a Roman Catholic gentleman's house in Essex, whence he was eventually smuggled in safety to the coast, and there procured a passage in a cargo-boat to Calais. With the exception of a short time passed by him in the seminary of his Society at Valladolid, the remainder of his life was passed in Italy. Formally called upon by the Pope to prove his innocence of complicity in the 'Gunpowder Plot' he wrote, in Italian, a brief *Autobiography*, which is not to be trusted, so far

---

[1] 'Of mean stature, somewhat gross : his hair black ; his beard bushy and brown, something long : a broad forehead, and about 40 years of age.'

as the account of his share in the Plot is to be concerned. It is not known that he ever ventured to return to England, and he died in 1635, at Naples.

That Greenway knew of the Plot through the medium of the confessional was admitted by Garnet at the latter's trial.[1] It is clear beyond doubt also that Greenway knew of the Plot outside the confessional, and made not the very slightest attempt to deter the conspirators from proceeding with their plans. He was also a party to sending Sir Edward Baynham to Rome. His visit to the conspirators at Huddington, when he was welcomed by their leader with the exclamation, 'Here is a gentleman who will live and die with us!' demonstrates by what close ties of intimacy he was connected with Catesby. Garnet in the Tower confided to Hall (Oldcorne) that, as regards his being proved guilty of complicity in the Plot, 'There was no man living who could touch him but one!' There is every reason to believe that that 'one' was Father Greenway.

'With respect to Greenway,' says Lingard, 'it is certain that he knew of the secret in confession; but of this the Ministers were unacquainted at the time of the proclamation. The grounds of the charge against him were the following :—(1) According to the Attorney-General at the Trial, Bates had acknowledged that he mentioned the

---

[1] 'Greenway both knew of the plot and favoured its execution; whilst Garnet had been acquainted with it at least as early as in July by Greenway in confession' (Dr. Gardiner).

matter to Greenway, and received from him instructions to do whatever his master should order. On the other side, Greenway, in a paper which lies before me, declares on his salvation that Bates never spoke one word to him on the subject, either in or out of confession; and Bates himself, in a letter written before he suffered, asserts that he merely said it was his suspicion that Greenway might have known something of the plot. (2) On the 6th of November, Greenway rode to the conspirators at Huddington, and administered to them the Sacrament. He replies that, having learned from a letter written by Sir Everard to Lady Digby, the danger in which they were, he deemed it a duty to offer to them the aids of religion before they suffered that death which threatened them; that for this purpose he rode to Huddington, and then after a few hours, left them for the house of Mr. Abington at Henlip.'

But Lingard is, here, not very veracious. He never mentions that Greenway went to Hendlip with the express object of getting the household to join Catesby; nor does he mention that he afterwards designed to raise the Catholics of Lancashire. As for his going to Huddington merely to offer the Sacrament to the conspirators, he omits to state that he went thither with Garnet's leave, and at Catesby's express invitation. As to Greenway's oath that Bates lied, I can only say that I would sooner believe a humble serving-man, who had been seduced by his master into treason, than I would a prevaricator like Greenway, who was, with his Superior Garnet, an adept

in all the arts of equivocation employed by their
Society.   Greenway never seems to have spoken
of the Plot in terms of detestation (before its
discovery), but talked it over with Garnet in as
calm a manner as if the scheme in hand was in
no way cruel and wicked.   Even if it were true
that he only knew of the existence of the Plot
from Catesby, *sub sigillo*, there still existed every
facility for him to stop the proceedings without
breaking the seal of the confessional.   Moreover,
it need not be disputed that Greenway knew of
the Plot before July, 1605, when he passed on
the secret to Garnet.[1]

There exists, therefore, I consider, no reason
whatever why Father Oswald Tesimond's name
should not be allowed to remain among Sir
William Waad's *Conjuratorum nomina, ad perpetuam ipsorum infamiam et tantæ diritatis detestationem sempiternam!*   Moreover, if Garnet's
statement is to be accepted as correct, to the
effect that he only knew of the Plot from Greenway in confession, and that Greenway only
knew it from Catesby in confession, what right
had Greenway to mention the matter, at all,
to Garnet?   But, we may rest assured that
both Greenway and Garnet eventually knew of
the Plot from Catesby himself without being

---

[1] Hume, the historian, rashly asserts that 'Tesmond, a Jesuit,
and Garnet, Superior of that Order in England, removed these
scruples (of the wavering conspirators), and showed them how
the interests of religion required that the innocent should here be
sacrificed with the guilty.'

compromised by restrictions of the confessional-box.

FATHER JOHN GERARD, S.J.—Although I have, earlier in this volume, practically acquitted this Jesuit of the charge of having been an accessory before the fact to the Gunpowder Plot, it must not be forgotten that he was privy to sending Sir Edward Baynham to Rome. But he evidently was not fully acquainted with all the details relating to the instructions given to Baynham. He probably had some general inkling of the fact that something was being done, *sub rosâ*, for the good of the Catholic cause, but he knew nothing about the intended explosion at Westminster. At the period of the Plot, he was not a 'Professed' Jesuit, as were his notorious colleagues, Fathers Greenway and Garnet, and was not so deeply in the secrets of his Society as they were.

Born in 1564, Gerard was the son of a Lancashire knight, of ancient race, and a cousin of Sir William Stanley. He was a gentleman both by birth and behaviour, which his colleagues, Oldcorne, Garnet, and Greenway, certainly were not. He entered the Society of Jesus at Rome, in 1588, and was then sent upon the English Mission. Between the time of his arrival and the period of the Plot, he passed a most romantic existence. He was imprisoned and tortured in the Tower, whence he escaped (1597) by climbing down a rope swinging over the moat. On several occasions he had to take refuge in one of the priest-holes in some old country house,[1] and was often within an inch of recapture. In 1603 he (with Garnet) betrayed William Watson to the Government, but reaped no personal benefit by this action. After the failure of the Plot, he baffled all the efforts of the Government to discover his whereabouts,[2] and eventually, disguised as a footman in the service of the Spanish Ambassador, succeeded in crossing the channel on the very day of Father Garnet's execution. He never returned to England, and died at Rome, 1637.

The most pleasant feature in Gerard's English career was his friendship with Sir Everard Digby. Had Gerard known of the Plot, he might have prevented Digby from joining it. Digby, on the other hand, seems to have thought that Gerard both knew and approved of the Plot. Although an innocent man, had Gerard been captured he would, almost certainly, have shared the fate of Garnet, for the Government was determined to stop at nothing in order to implicate him in the conspiracy. The circumstance of his having given the Sacrament to some of the conspirators at the house behind Clement's Inn was magnified into a story that he had given them the Sacrament

---

[1] He had a wonderful escape when hidden (1594) at Braddocks, Essex, the seat of the Wiseman family.

[2] He was hidden, for some time, at Great Harrowden, the seat of the Vaux family.

after they had just taken the formal oath of the plotters in his presence, and with his approval. As a matter of fact, they had taken the oath privately by themselves, and had then entered another room to hear a priest (who happened to be Gerard) say Mass. Again, it was absurdly said that he had worked with the conspirators when they were digging their mine beneath the Parliament House.

Father John Gerard has been held by some to have been the author of the *Treatise on Equivocation*, found in Francis Tresham's desk and produced at Garnet's trial. Adequate proof in favour of this theory is, however, wanting. Gerard was very successful in persuading rich men to join the Society of Jesus.

CHAPTER XXII

THE LIEUTENANT OF THE TOWER

I

'THAT beast Waad,' as Sir Walter Ralegh called him, had been appointed Lieutenant[1] of the Tower about eleven weeks before the capture of Guy Faukes at Westminster. Prior to his appointment, however, he had held several very important diplomatic and political posts. He had faithfully served William Cecil, the great Lord Burghley,[2] and was destined, in the matter of the Powder Plot, to serve with equal fidelity his son, Robert Cecil, Earl of Salisbury. Sir William Waad, under Elizabeth, had been Secretary to Sir Francis Walsingham, and afterwards Clerk of the Privy Council. He had been sent on frequent diplomatic missions to Madrid, Paris, and the Low Countries. In 1588 he was elected a member of Parliament, and in 1601 represented Preston, where his Protestant zeal made him very

[1] Lord Ronald Gower, in his history of the Tower of London, aptly remarks that ' Ralegh's feelings towards the new Lieutenant appear to have resembled those of Napoleon to Sir Hudson Lowe.'

[2] Especially in regard to obtaining evidence against the Queen of Scots.

255

:he Roman Catholics of Lan-
er the accession of James I. he
1 in August, 1605, he was, at
request, appointed Lieutenant

ipopular as he was as a gaoler,
no means the sordid villain
Roman Catholic writers. He
culture and letters, a promoter
:xploration, and had done some
.ce as a diplomat. He was an
it, and his sincere hatred of Roman
:d him to stoop to low means to
nation from, or obtain evidence
ers Garnet and Oldcorne. Having
: ill-will of Lady Somerset, the
was removed[1] eventually from his
; (his patron, Salisbury, being dead),
e remainder of his life in Essex, and at
.. He died, 1623, at Manuden, Essex.
below extracts from certain letters
him and his rule in the Tower, which
atter of much interest and importance
. from Number 6178, in the Additional
3ritish Museum). From the letters,
below, written by Waad, ample evidence
oming of the strained relations existing
him and Sir Walter Ralegh, and of his

Somerset thought him too honest a man to approve of
ie for the murder of Sir Thomas Overbury; hence
al from the Tower. He gave evidence against her at

subservience to Lord Salisbury. I also quote
from other papers, derived from the same source,
regarding the capture of Lyttleton and Winter
at Hagley, the closing of the Ports, etc.

As an unraveller of plots, Sir William Waad
certainly seems to have enjoyed a unique career.
He had, in fact, been connected with the detection,
or attempted detection, of almost every conspiracy
hatched in England during the eventful twenty
years antecedent to the Gunpowder Plot.[1] He
had ransacked the belongings of Mary, Queen of
Scots, at the time of Babington's conspiracy ; he
had taken a prominent part in the discovery of
the mysterious Lopez affair; he had helped
to suppress the Essex rebellion; he had been
employed in the matter of the proceedings of
Lord Cobham and Sir Walter Ralegh, as regards
their connection with Father Watson's conspiracy.
He was, therefore, likely to prove, in the eyes of
the Government, an ideal gaoler for the
conspirators and Jesuits captured after the failure
of the Gunpowder Treason, as well as for Sir
Walter Ralegh.

II

Waad to Salisbury, August 17, 1605, relating
to his installation as Lieutenant of the Tower:—

'My Lord Treasurer and my Lord of
Devonshire met at the Tower on Monday at
three of the clock in the afternoon and gave me

[1] And they were by no means few in number.

R

my oath. . . . Before I did sign the indentures
for the receiving of the prisoners, I went to see
them all in their several lodgings . . .

' I have given order the next time the lions[1]
be abroad to see them myself, and then I will
advertise your Lordship what I observe in them.'

Waad to Salisbury, November 7, 1605:
relating to the demeanour of Guy Faukes
(Johnson) :—

' It may please your Lordship, this morning
when Johnson was ready (who hath taken such
rest this night as a man void of all trouble of
mind), I repaired unto him and told him if he
held his resolution of mind to be so silent, the
preresolution in the State was as constant to
proceed with that severity which was meet in a
case of that consequence . . . I asked him
whether his vow and oath was taken here, or
beyond the seas ? He answered here. I asked
him when ? He said a year and a half sithence.
. . . He added that the Priest[2] who gave him
the Sacrament knew nothing of it. . . . I am
confident, notwithstanding his resolute mind, he
will be more open in the end.'

Sir (then Mr.) Thomas Lawley to Salisbury,
November 14, 1605: relating to the capture of
Holbeach :—

' Upon the 8th day of this present month, I

[1] Lions, the property of the Crown, were then kept in the
Tower, and had been for centuries. The Tower menagerie was
abolished in the reign of William IV.

[2] Gerard. Yet Lord Salisbury afterwards caused it to be put
in evidence that Gerard did know of the plot.

with all the small powder I was able upon a sudden to make, did attend Mr. Sheriff of Worcestershire into a place called Holbeach, and there did my best endeavour for the suppressing and apprehending of the Traitors there assembled, one of my servants being the first man that entered upon them, and took Thomas Winter alive, and brought him unto me, whom I delivered to the said Sheriff, and thereupon hasted to revive Catesby, Percy, and the two Wrights, who lay deadly wounded on the ground, thinking by the recovery of them to have done unto his Majesty better service than by suffering them to die.[1] But such was the extreme disorder of the baser sort that, while I with my men took up one of the languishing traitors, the rude people stripped the rest naked ; their wounds being many and grievous, and no surgeon at hand, they became incurable, and so died.'

Captain Burton to the Privy Council, November —, 1605 : relating to the abortive closing of the ports, after the discovery of the Plot :—

' Notwithstanding the care in all the ports, yet out of remote and not noticed cricks [2] there are small boats that usually transport priests and messengers, as namely, one Henry Paris, who dwells near Colchester, in Essex, who is a continual transport, and employed often one Anthony Hukmote, who dwells in Crutchet

---

[1] This, again, proves the falsity of the Jesuit cock-and-bull story that Catesby and Percy were killed by order of Salisbury.

[2] Creaks.

Friars. And one Henry King, whose dwelling,'
etc.

Waad to Salisbury, November 21, 1605:
relating to Winter's convalescence, and ability to
write :—

'Thomas Winter doth find his hand so strong,
as after dinner he will settle himself to write that
he verbally declared to your Lordship, adding
what he shall further remember.'

Sir Thomas Lake to Salisbury, November 27,
1605 : relating to the receiver of the gunpowder :—

'His Majesty, this evening, after his return
from his sports, commanded me to put your
Lordship in mind of (a) thing in the examination
whereof he doth not remember that you are yet
cleared, that is, that where at Lambeth at the
house whither the powder was brought by the
porters there was a young man that received it,
which His Majesty and your Lordship conceived
at first to be Winter, but since, as His Majesty
judgeth, could not be so because the examinations
make mention that young man had no hair on his
face, which is otherwise in Winter. He would,
therefore, know whether your Lordship hath yet
found who was the receiver of the powder, or, if
it hath not been enquired of, by reason of the
multitude of other things, then your Lordship
would best to labour to discover it?'

'The copy of a letter cast into the Lord of
Salisbury's court, December 4th, 1605 :—

'My Lords, whereas the late unapprovable,
and most wicked design for the destroying
of his Majesty, the Prince, and Nobility, with

many others of worth and quality, through the
undertaking spirits of some more turbulent than
truly zealous and dispassionate Catholics hath
made the general estate of our Catholic cause so
scandalous in the eye of such, whose corrupted
judgment is not able to fan away and sever the
faults of such professions from the profession
itself, as whoso is found to be of that religion is
presumed at least in mind to allow, though God
knows, as much abhorring it as any Protestant
whatsoever, the said former most inhumane and
barbarous project. And, whereas some of His
Majesty's Council, but especially your Lordship,
is known to be (as the Philosophers term
it) *primus motor* of such uncharitable taking
advantage by so foul a scandal to root out all
memory of Catholics either by sudden massacre,
banishment, prisonment, and some other un-
supportable vexations, and oppression, or perhaps
by decreeing in this next Parliament some more
cruel and horrible law against Catholics than is
already made. In regards of the promises there
are some good men, who through their earnest
desire for continuing of Catholic religion, and for
saving of many souls, both at this time and of
future posterity are resolved to prevent so great
a mischief though full assurance aforehand of the
loss of their dearest lives.

'You are, therefore, hereby to be admonished
that, at this present, there are five who have
severally undertaken your death and have
vowed the performance thereof, by taking already
the Blessed Sacrament, if you continue your
daily plotting these tragical stratagems against
Recusants. . . ,

'It may be your Lordship will take this as some forged letter of some Puritan, thereby to incense you more against Recusants, but we protest upon our salvation it is not so, neither can anything (in human liklihood) prevent the effecting thereof but the change of your course against Recusants.'

'The Manner of the Discrying and Apprehension of Robert Winter and Stephen Lyttleton,' at Hagley :—

'Upon Thursday morning, the ninth of January, 1605,[1] about nine of the clock, one John Finwood, servant and cook to Mr. Lyttleton of Hagley, in the county of Worcester, came unto Thomas Haslewood, Gent., one of the said Mr. Lyttleton's chief servants, and told him that the said Robert Winter and Stephen Lyttleton were with him in the said Mr. Lyttleton's house at Hagley, and that they were got into the house in the night time, after the servants were in their beds.   Whereupon, instantly the said Mr. Haslewood went unto the stable, and made ready his gelding, and rode post into the village adjoining to raise a few to apprehend them; in the meanwhile that the said Mr. Haslewood so rode, the Constable of Hagley being required by the said Mr. Haslewood did make his repair to the said Mr. Lyttleton's house at Hagley, attended upon with the servants and tenants of the said Mr. Lyttleton of Hagley aforesaid to the number of ten or twelve persons, where they being assembled, one Humphrey Lyttleton, Gent.,

[1] 1606.

commonly called "Red Humphrey," asked them what they did there? who answered him that they came to apprehend the said Robert Winter and Stephen Lyttleton, and thereupon the said Humphrey said that they were not there, and bade them begone. . . . But the said Constable and others said they came to credit the house and to apprehend the traitors, and thereupon the said traitors got forth of the house at a back door, which being known to one Daniel Bate, a servant to Mr. Lyttleton, he called to the said Constable and told him that the said traitors were gotten forth at a back door.   And then the said Constable, and the servants, and tenants of the said Mr. Lyttleton did beset the house, and apprehended the said Robert Winter and Stephen Lyttleton in the court adjoining to the said house endeavouring to get away towards a wood.'[1]

III

I further reproduce below extracts from tne original documents in the Public Record Office, (*Gunpowder Plot Book*) relating *inter alia*, to the plans made by the King for interrogating Johnson (Faukes) in the Tower, and to Lord Northumberland's anxiety that Percy's life might be saved. From the nature of the King's interrogatories to be put to Faukes, we can discern

[1] The 'Worcestershire Men' were so proud of their feat, that they refused to yield their prisoners into the custody of the Sheriff of Staffordshire, and (despite all threats) took Winter and Lyttleton to Worcester. A similar 'fracas' had occurred between the men of these two counties after the capture of Holbeach.

with what clever foresight Catesby had calculated that Guy Faukes would not be recognized in London. When captured, nothing was at first discovered as to the identity of Faukes, Waad and the others resting under the delusion that he was merely Percy's servant, as Catesby had intended it to be thought. The idea that the Gunpowder Plot was originally imagined by the Londoners to have been a Spanish contrivance is corroborated by Waad's second letter to Salisbury, despatched on November 5, from the Tower.

Waad to Salisbury, November 5, 1605 : relating to the news of the discovery of the Plot :—

'As nothing is more strange unto me than that it should enter into the thought of any man living to attempt anything against a Sovereign Prince of so great goodness, so I thank God on the knees of my soul that this monstrous wickedness is discovered, and I beseech God all the particulars may be laid open.'

Waad to Salisbury, November 5, 1605 : relating to the reception of the news in East London :—

'It may please your Lordship, I thought it very fit your Lordship should know what the people in these parts do so murmur and exclaim against the Spaniards and the Ambassador; as may grow into further making of disorder, if some good order be not taken to prevent the same.'

A list of interrogatories, drawn up by the King, to be put to Johnson (Faukes), November 6, 1605 :—

'1. As to what he is ? for I can never hear yet of any man that knows him.

'2. Where was he born ; and when ?

'3. What were the names of his parents ?

'4. What is his age ?

'5. Where hath he lived ?

'6. How hath he lived, and by what trade ?

'7. How he received the wounds in his breast ?

'8. If he was ever in service with any other before Percy?

'9. How came he in Percy's service; and when ?

'10. When was this house (in Westminster) hired by Percy ?

'11. How soon after getting it, did he begin his devilish practices ?

'12. Where did he learn to speak French ?

'13. What gentlewoman's letter was it, that was found upon him ?

'14. Why does she in it call him by another name ?

'15. If he ever was a priest ?

'16. Where was he converted, and by whom ?'

(The original, in the King's hand, is written in broad Scotch).[1]

Declaration signed by Guy Faukes, November 16, 1605 :—

'He doth call to remembrance that speech being moved amongst themselves of the Catholic lords they wished might be exempted from this Parliament, that Robert Catesby told them he

[1] *Eg.* No. 4. 'Of quhat age he is '?

had spoken with my Lord Montague, who made suit to be absent from the Parliament, and said he had advised his Lordship so to do, because he could do no good there.

'He likewise said the Lord Mordaunt would not come until the middle of the Parliament, because at the former occasion when the King went to the ceremony, he was fain to sit in the Parliament House with his robes on whilst the King was at church.

'And it was further said amongst them that the Lord Stourton by accident would not come until the Friday following. He further said that he understood by Catesby and Winter that Francis Tresham and they had some conversation about the Lord Mounteagle. Tresham having been exceeding earnest to have his Lordship warned to be absent from the Parliament.

'They were desirous to have warned the Earl of Arundel to absent himself, but they understood —though he was under years—yet he made great suit to be there.

'He likewise saith it was considered and concluded amongst them that the best course and most convenient means to persuade the Catholic lords to be absent from the Parliament was, in letting them understand the straight laws against Catholics, and the little good they could do with their presence.

'He further saith that Christopher Wright had been at the Earl of Northumberland's house on the Sunday before the Parliament, and at his return told Percy that it was known in my Lord's house he was come up to London, whereupon Percy went thither.

' He confesseth Percy bought on Monday at night the watch that was found about him when taken, and sent it to him by Keyes at 10 of the clock in the night, because he should know how the time went away.

' He also said he did not intend to set fire to the train till the King was come into the house, and then he purposed to do it with a piece of touch-wood, and with a match also, that the powder might surely take fire one quarter of an hour after.'

The Earl of Northumberland to Lord Salisbury, November 10, 1605 : relating to the capture of Thomas Percy :—

" May it please your Lordship that what I have to say at this time is little, and few words will express my desire ; not that I am to direct your Lordship's will, but only to lay down my own entreaty if you like it, and that is this.

' I hear Mr. Percy is taken, if that I hear be true, but withal shot through the shoulder with a musket ; our surgeons in these countries are not over excellent for a shot, if heat take it, the patient with a fever will soon make an end ; none but he can shew me clear as the day, or dark as the night, therefore I hope it shall not offend you if I require haste, for now will he tell truly if ever, being ready to make his account to God Almighty. Thus, with my humble well wishes to your Lordship, I rest to do your Lordship services.

' NORTHUMBERLAND.

' Sunday, this present afternoon.'

Memorandum, by Secretary Conway, respecting the unrequited services of one Henry Wright, an informer :—

'If it may please your Majesty, can you remember that the Lord Chief Justice Popham, and Sir Thomas Challoner, Kt., had a hand in the discovery of the practices of the Jesuits in the Powder Plot, and did reveal the same to your Majesty, for two years' space almost before the said Treason burst forth by an obscure letter sent to the Lord Mounteagle, which your Majesty, like an angel of God, interpreted touching the House, then intended to be given by powder? The man who informed Sir Thomas Challoner and Lord Popham of the said Jesuitical practices, their meetings, and traitorous designs in that matter, whereof from time to time they informed your Majesty, was one Wright, who hath your Majesty's hand for his so doing, and never received any reward for his pains and charges laid out concerning the same.'

This Henry Wright, it should be remarked *en passant*, was not the only notable agent employed by the Government to discover 'the practices in the Powder Plot' of the Jesuits and others. Among those employed to procure information likely to incriminate the priests was no less a person than Ben Jonson, the poet, who was for some years a Papist. He totally failed, however, to procure any information against the priests, but expressed his opinion that the discovery of Catesby's conspiracy would cast so great an odium upon the Roman Church in England that a great number of the Roman Catholic gentry would become Protestants.

CHAPTER XXIII

THE MYSTERY OF THOMAS WARDE

To my mind, there still exists one mystery, at any rate, connected with the Gunpowder Plot, which not only has yet to be cleared up, but which previous writers have practically made no attempt to solve. I allude to the connection of Lord Mounteagle's 'gentleman,' Thomas Warde, with the conspirators. Was this Thomas Warde in their secrets, or was he not?

It is, as I have already pointed out, a most peculiar circumstance that this man, Warde, should never have been closely examined by the Privy Council as to his relations with Thomas Winter. In the latter's lengthy confession, he distinctly stated that 'one' came to him and told him that 'a letter had been given to my Lord Mounteagle.' In other words, the Privy Council knew that Warde had committed misprision of treason by giving Winter[1] warning, intending thereby to save all the conspirators from capture, but yet made no attempt to punish him for this crime, the penalty for which was, if convicted, death!

[1] Which he did more than once.

Why, indeed, may we ask, in our perplexity, was Warde permitted to go unpunished? Why, too, was he not asked if he knew who it was that delivered the letter at his patron's house? Why was he never cross-examined as to his supposed intimacy with certain of the Jesuit priests? These are questions which seem to me to bear considerably upon the complicity of Lord Mounteagle in the plot, and his secret understanding with Lord Salisbury.

Thomas Warde was a Roman Catholic, a gentleman of good family, and no mere 'page' or 'domestic,' as he has been described by certain writers. He evidently was very well posted up in his patron's plans; for when Mounteagle suddenly resolved to have supper at his house at Hoxton, he specially took Warde with him, which there was no necessity to do. That Warde, *before* the receipt of the letter, was fully cognizant of Catesby's proceedings cannot be doubted, when we read of his conferences with Winter *after* the receipt of the letter. In all probability he must have known who wrote the letter, if he did not even write it himself. He was, as we have seen, talked of at the time as having been privy to the Plot, yet he was not arrested. Evidently, he must have known as much as Lord Mounteagle knew. One was just as much as the other responsible for staging the Hoxton comedy. The pair drew up, certainly with Tresham, and, as we shall see, probably with another party also, the contents of

the celebrated letter. Some very powerful motive
latent in the background must have saved him
from punishment over the matter of his giving
warning to Winter, and that motive must have
originated from the Government's fear of 'showing
up' Lord Mounteagle. Master and man had
played their game together, and to punish Thomas
Warde would be to ruin Lord Mounteagle. But
that Warde was ever implicated so deeply in the
Plot as to have taken the binding oath of secrecy
as one of the conspirators is unlikely in the
extreme. His tongue would, in that event, have
been tied, so far as his communicating with
Mounteagle was concerned; and had he taken
the oath, and broken it, as Tresham did, then he
would have at once been suspected by Catesby
and Winter, and would not up to the last have
remained on friendly terms with the latter. He
must be included among that little list of people
who, though not enrolled among the working
conspirators, were aware of what was going on—
a list which included such persons as Garnet,
Greenway, Baynham, Mounteagle, and (perhaps)
Oldcorne.[1]

Warde, in giving warning to the conspirators,
first of the letter's arrival at Hoxton, secondly, of
its delivery to Lord Salisbury, and thirdly, of its
inspection by the King, naturally calculated that
the conspirators would take the 'tip' and seek
safety in flight. He could never have conjectured

[1] And, perhaps, the redoubtable Captain Hugh Owen, abroad.

that they would have rashly awaited hopeless ruin by staying on at their posts, as they did. Perhaps both he and Mounteagle were frightened at what Winter and Catesby might divulge, if caught; and, up to the date of Tresham's death, this astute pair must have spent many a *mauvais quart d'heure.* Tresham's boasts that, conspirator though he was, his neck was safe, must have borne reference to the fact that influential parties would suffer if he were injured, and those others must have included Mounteagle and Warde.

The identity of the nameless messenger who delivered the letter at Mounteagle's house is also an unsolved mystery. No effort seems to have been made to discover who he was. By whom was he sent ? Whence did he come ? What was he like ? 'A tall man, wrapped in a cloak,' is all we are told about him, and nothing more. He appears suddenly on the scene at night, presses a letter into the hands of Mounteagle's footman, and disappears again, and for ever, into the darkness ! This individual may, of course, merely have been an illiterate man, simply hired to deliver a letter to Lord Mounteagle, and ignorant all the while of the letter's contents ; or he may have been a trusted person in the service of Mounteagle, Warde, and Tresham. Had he been, however, a mere ordinary messenger, he would have come forward, after the discovery of the plot, and claimed a reward from the State for performing

so great a service, in which case he would have
had to divulge the source wherefrom he obtained
the letter.   It is more probable, therefore, that
even this mysterious messenger was a member of
Lord Mounteagle's talented company of players.
The more, indeed, that one examines into the
way in which this comedy at Hoxton was staged,
the more one is amazed at the skill with which
every item in the programme was carried out, down
to the last detail.   Tresham, Mounteagle, and
Warde were no ordinary actors !

Some general idea that a Plot was being concocted seems to have been known to a good many
Romanists besides those (like Mounteagle and
Garnet) immediately in touch with the active
conspirators themselves.   Amongst those who
must have had some inkling of what was going
on was Garnet's too faithful friend, the infatuated
Anne Vaux.   Before the middle of October, 1605,
she grew very anxious and uneasy as to the
curious behaviour of some of her relatives and
intimate friends.   In the Tower, even Garnet
went so far as to make the following admission
in relation to her fears :—

'Mrs. Vaux came to him (Garnet), either
to Harrowden, or to Sir Everard Digby's at
Gothurst, and told this examinant that she feared
that some trouble or disorder was towards, that
some of the gentlewomen had demanded of her
where they should bestow themselves till the
"burst" was past in the beginning of the

Parliament.   And this examinant asking her who told her so, she said she durst not tell who told her so : she was choked with sorrow.'

This admission by Father Garnet certainly does not tend to lead us to accept as true the protestations of Roman Catholic writers that Anne Vaux knew nothing whatever of what was going on either in the Midlands or at Westminster.   We may be sure that Garnet would not admit 'too much' about his friend's knowledge, and he probably could, if he chose, have revealed a great deal more.   Again, what did Garnet mean by his strange prayer (uttered in the presence of Anne Vaux and many others) delivered at the memorable service at Coughton on All Saints' Day?[1]   In it, he asked his congregation to pray for some great event, which—to the concern of the Catholic cause — might happen at the opening of the coming Session.   Anne Vaux must have joined in this prayer, and for whom, or for what purpose did she pray ?

When examining into the relations existing between Anne Vaux and the Jesuits, we must remember that she was absolutely under their influence, and that, therefore, she being a disciple of tutors expert in equivocation, would have felt no scruple in telling a lie if the necessities of the Society of Jesus required her.   That very close friendship existed between her and Father Garnet is proved by the nature of the correspondence

[1] November 1, 1605.

which took place between the pair after Garnet's incarceration in the Tower. One of the first questions asked by him, in a letter, which Garnet hoped would be smuggled safely out of the Tower, was, 'Where is Mrs.[1] Anne?' In reply to Garnet, she signs herself, ' Yours, and not my own.'

I have said above that Francis Tresham and Company, when arranging for the delivery of the anonymous letter at Hoxton, were probably helped by some other party whose name has not come down to us. This person, as I have hinted, may have been a Jesuit priest. But there may also have been a woman in the case. That Mrs. Abington could have materially helped in the matter, I cannot—as I have already stated—believe. That she wrote the letter is a theory unsupported by proof or probability, and seems to have originated with some silly story told by one of her Worcestershire neighbours, after her death. If there was a woman in the case, it is almost certain to have been none other than Anne Vaux. From the curiosity displayed by her a few weeks before the fatal Fifth, it is clear that she was anxious to know what was going on, and evidently did get eventually to know, for she arranged where to ' bestow herself till the burst was past in the beginning of the Parliament.'

This leads us back again to the question, Could Anne Vaux have written the letter to Lord Mounteagle? To this query I will now tack on

[1] *I.e.* Mistress.

another, Could she have written to Mounteagle with the knowledge, or the tacit approval of Father Garnet ?

It is quite possible that Anne Vaux, terrified by her discovery of what was intended to be done at Westminster sought advice from Garnet. It is also most likely that she interviewed Tresham on the subject. Tresham may then have recommended her as a fitting person to write the epistle; for her handwriting, disguised, would not be familiar to the Lords of the Council. That there is something to be said in favour of the theory of her penmanship is forthcoming in the fact that hers is the only handwriting of which specimens are preserved in the Record Office, that can be claimed in any respect to resemble the caligraphy of Mounteagle's mysterious correspondent.

As to the further question whether Father Garnet advised her, *sub rosâ*, to communicate with Mounteagle, the supposition that he may have done so does not appear so improbable, when we consider the terrible position in which Garnet found himself during the six weeks prior to the date fixed for the explosion. To the difficulties of his position full justice has not been done by Protestant writers.

For him, the Superior of his Order in England, and the recipient of a most terrible secret, the outlook was by no means pleasant. If the Plot failed, he knew that the Jesuits would be the first persons to be suspected of having contrived it, and that the work of his Society in England would be ruined.   If it succeeded, he had sense enough to see that its success could only be transitory, and that not only all the Protestants in England would rise up in arms against the conspirators, but even a great number of the English Romanists would refuse to join with men who had committed murder on such a terrible scale.   Garnet's distress was acute in the extreme. As he himself has recorded, ' I remained in the greatest perplexity that ever I was in my life, and could not sleep at nights. . . . Good Lord, if this matter go forward, the Pope will send me to the galleys, for he will assuredly think I was privy to it.'   This reference to the Pope proves how fearful he was lest, even in the case of the Plot's success, the whole business would be denounced and condemned by the Holy See.   Moreover, some inkling of the fact that a plot was in process of manufacture seems even to have reached Rome, for during July, August, and September, 1605, Garnet received letters from Parsons, asking what was going on.   During, so far as we can tell, the whole of September and October, 1605, Garnet remained near or in the company[1] of Anne Vaux, and we may be sure that she must have noticed his perplexity of mind.

[1] Early in September, they went on the famous pilgrimage to St. Winifrid's Well. After that, they visited Harrowden, Gothurst, White Webbs, and Coughton (October 30).

I venture, therefore, to offer the following explanation of the proceedings that led up to the delivery of the letter at Hoxton. Garnet, recognizing that in any event, successful or unsuccessful, the Gunpowder Plot would bring forth the most disastrous consequences upon the Jesuit mission in England, the reputation of the whole of the English Roman Catholics, and the position of the Holy See itself, determined finally to prevent the Plot taking place. In arranging his plans to stop the Plot, he knew that he had no power to get such men as Catesby, Faukes, and Winter to withdraw. They would not listen to him, and if suspected by Catesby of being likely to betray the Plot, Garnet's very life might be in danger. He was dealing with desperate men, who would hesitate at nothing, when the safety of their scheme was concerned. Moreover, in the event of his giving warning to the Government, he would be at once accused of having been in the Plot itself; and, not only that, —what was (to him) far worse—he would be regarded by Roman Catholics throughout Europe as one who had not merely betrayed his friends, but as one who had broken the seal of confession.

His only chance, consequently, lay in contriving some scheme which would frighten the conspirators into abandoning their plan and taking refuge in flight. The scheme selected, *i.e.* that of sending an anonymous letter, was admirable, as was its sequel, *i.e.* the opportunity given to

Warde to warn Winter and advise him to escape, for all was discovered.

To arrange for the writing of the letter, Garnet needed an agent on whom he could thoroughly rely. He had one, and one only, close at hand, in the person of a woman, who was not only devoted to him personally, but who was to all intents and purposes, by virtue of her vow of obedience, a Jesuit herself. This person was Anne Vaux. Afraid to trust, in the first instance, the weak and crafty Tresham, Garnet probably sent Anne Vaux to Mounteagle and Warde, with the deliberate aim of devising means to stop the Plot. When I say that Garnet 'sent' Anne Vaux, he may have done it in such a way as not even to let her think that he was willingly betraying the conspiracy. She went to him for information as to what was going on, and he in return probably expressed himself shocked at hearing the rumours which she repeated to him, and advised her secretly to get certain of her friends to try and interfere. These friends must have been Mounteagle, Tresham, and Warde. With Mounteagle, Garnet was, possibly, in communication. They understood one another. Mounteagle comprehended the difficulties of Garnet's position, and what his views on the subject of the conspiracy really were. Garnet knew that Mounteagle was a traitor, who was also longing to stop the Plot, if he could find some way of doing so without incurring the anger of their co-religionists for delivering Catesby and his little band of Roman Catholic gentlemen into the hands of the heretics.

But, supposing that Garnet was either directly or indirectly the cause of getting written the famous letter to Mounteagle, we have to ask ourselves the question Why was his life not spared ? Why, also, did he afterwards pray at Coughton (November 1, 1605), for the success of something which was to happen at the opening of the Parliament ?

The answer to these queries is not so difficult to seek. His life was not spared, because he dared not, in the Tower, reveal his share in giving warning for the reasons already mentioned, namely, he would then be accused by the Privy Council, since he had known so much, of having been a conspirator himself; and he would then be regarded as a traitor and as a sacrilegious priest by his fellow-Papists. With regard to his prayer at Coughton, I take it that this prayer was a cry of despair. He invoked the aid of Heaven to save the Roman Catholic cause in England. The plotters foolishly had not fled, the Parliament House might or might not be blown up, and he and his helpless friends were left face to face with a most serious crisis. His anxiety, when in the Tower, to communicate with Anne Vaux strengthens the theory that there was something secret between them, upon which it was necessary for them to consult. He was afraid lest Anne should incriminate him in any way, or lower him in the eyes of their co-religionists. Concerning Lord Mounteagle, by keeping silent as to his knowledge of Mounteagle's treasons and treachery, Garnet thought that his lordship might intercede with Salisbury to save his life. That Mounteagle did intercede it is generally believed, but his intercession was of no use. Father Garnet was too valuable a prize to spare.

Garnet, in common with Tresham, Mounteagle, and Warde, evidently conjectured that so soon as the conspirators learnt that the letter delivered at Hoxton was in the hands of the Privy Council they would find refuge in flight to the Continent. The terrible disaster of the explosion would thereby be avoided, and the Papist cause in England left *in statu quo*. Garnet and the others must also have conjectured that the conspirators would be forced to escape, not merely because they knew that their secret was out, but because Cecil would also immediately announce the discovery of the Plot to the whole word, and consequently compel them to try to escape without delay. Instead of this, Cecil upset all calculations by displaying no sign that he held them in the hollow of his hand, and thus lulled them into a false security.

Father Garnet's behaviour during his imprisonment and trial directly favours the supposition that he had played an important part in the delivery of the letter. All the time that he was fighting the inquisitors he seems (to the very last) to have been buoyed up with some strange hope that he would not be put to death. All the time he seems to have been labouring like a man who possessed some great secret, which, if he could only divulge it, would demonstrate to the world that he was not quite so guilty as external evidences tended to indicate.

If Garnet induced Anne Vaux to communicate with Mounteagle and Tresham, we may be sure that he went about his work with sufficient craft to cover up his tracks, so that he could never be suspected by his co-religionists of having had a hand in the business. As soon as he discovered that Anne Vaux had obtained an insight into what was going on, he had wit enough to discern that, woman-like, she could not keep the secret to herself, and that, terrified at what she had heard, she would do her best to prevent the explosion, if only in order to save the innocent Roman Catholic peers in Parliament, such as the Lords Stourton, Mordaunt, Mounteagle, and Montague. That they were to be prevented from going to the Parliament by the conspirators she did not, of course, know, the final deliberations of the plotters to that end having only been taken at a very late date, and, of course, in secret. Garnet's task, therefore, in advising Anne Vaux to consult with Tresham or Mounteagle may have been a very easy one. Probably, if not almost certainly, Anne consulted him in confession

about her fears; and he, without in any way
implicating or identifying himself in the matter
at issue, contented himself with telling her to
seek any means possible to save the Roman
Catholic peers and gentlemen likely to be present
at Westminster, without at the same time delivering their own friends engaged in the conspiracy
into the hands of the Government.

In conclusion, then, I venture to submit that
the concoction and delivery of the famous anonymous letter was severally devised by Mounteagle,
Francis Tresham, Warde, and Anne Vaux; that
Father Garnet was Anne Vaux's adviser in communicating with Tresham and Mounteagle; that
Thomas Warde and Lord Mounteagle planned
together the delivery of the letter; that Salisbury
knew nothing of the subtle part played by Father
Garnet in the affair; that the letter was actually
written by Anne Vaux at Tresham's dictation;
that Mounteagle had, on behalf of Salisbury,
acted as a spy upon the conspirators for some
time previous to his going to Hoxton; and that
he had originally been enlisted by Robert Catesby
and Thomas Winter as a subordinate member
of the conspirators himself.

CHAPTER XXIV

THE OFFICIAL STORY OF THE PLOT

Not long after the execution of the conspirators, an official record of the discovery of the plot and its various ramifications was drawn up by order of the King. This account went by the title of *The King's Book*, and it was given out to the world that James I. was the actual author. That he was the author, however, is not correct, although he evidently perused the contents before going to press, and interpolated into the text several suggestions and alterations of his own, at Cecil's advice. The Book was eventually included in Bishop Montague's [1] collected edition of the King's works, whence I have transcribed that portion of the version rendered below.

The Book bears ample evidence of having been written under the direct supervision of Lord Salisbury, who saw the necessity of publishing an official account of the plot, which, whilst claiming recognition as the most accurate

[1] Richard Montague (1577–1641), Bishop of Chichester and Norwich. In Cobbett's *State Trials* he is erroneously called Bishop of Winchester.

KING JAMES THE FIRST.

and detailed story of the great conspiracy, would, at the same time, serve to conceal the secret negotiations that had taken place between him and Lord Mounteagle, prior to the arrest of Guy Faukes. Salisbury wished to make the public believe that the delivery of the famous letter at Hoxton was totally unexpected by Lord Mounteagle, and of course by himself.

The Book includes the two chief confessions made by Thomas Winter and Guy Faukes; but as these have already been printed above, I have omitted them from the following transcript, as I have, for the same reason, the text of the anonymous letter delivered to Lord Mounteagle, and the concluding three paragraphs, which contain no historical or otherwise important matter.

The publication of this Book afforded an additional impetus to the national rejoicings over the failure of the Plot. A special thanksgiving service was introduced into the Prayer-book, and was not withdrawn until the year 1859, whilst the anniversary of the famous 'fifth' came to be welcomed with scenes of extraordinary revelry and display in every town and village in England. Indeed, in many towns, until even recently, the 'fifth' was looked upon as one of the chief of the annual festivals, ranking second only to Christmas Day, and considerable sums were spent in the purchase of 'Guys' and ammunition for a bonfire. But, of late, the celebration of the 'fifth' has become a very tame affair, and Lewes and Bridgwater are probably almost the only places where the demonstrations approach anything like their pristine splendour. The last occasion on which the anniversary was welcomed with especial enthusiasm was in the year 1850, when the 'Papal Aggression'—as the restoration of the Roman Catholic hierarchy under Cardinal Wiseman was termed—gave rise to tumultuous proceedings throughout the country.[1]

The following, with the omission already noted, is the official account of the Plot :—

'While this land and whole monarchy flourished in a most happy and plentiful peace, as well at home as abroad; sustained and conducted by these two main good pillars of all good government, piety and justice, no foreign grudge, nor inward whispering of discontentment any way appearing : the King being upon his return from his hunting exercise at Royston,[2] upon occasion of the drawing near of the Parliament-time, which had been twice prorogued already, partly in regard of the season of the year, and partly of the term : as the winds are ever stillest immediately before a storm ; and as the sun bleaks often hottest to foretell a following shower ; so, at that time of greatest calm, did this secretly

[1] The fifth of November, however, it must not be forgotten, is famous for other events besides the Powder-Plot in our annals, for it was on this day in the year 1688, that William of Orange landed in Torbay ; and on this day in the year 1800, it was officially decided to abandon the style of ' King of France' as one of the titles of our Sovereigns.

[2] In Hertfordshire.

hatched thunder begin to cast forth the first flashes and flaming lightnings of the approaching tempest. For, the Saturday week immediately preceeding the King's return, which was upon a Thursday, being but ten days before the Parliament, the Lord Monteagle, son and heir to the Lord Morley, being in his own lodgings,[1] ready to go to supper, at seven of the clock at night, one of his footmen, whom he had sent of an errand over the street, was met by a man of a reasonable tall personage, who delivered him a letter, charging him to put it in my Lord his master's hands; which my Lord no sooner perceived, but that having broken it up, and perceiving the same to be of an unknown and somewhat unlegible hand, and without either date or superscription, did call one of his men unto him, for helping him to read it. But no sooner did he conceive the strange contents thereof, although he was somewhat perplexed what construction to make of it, as whether a matter of consequence, as indeed it was, or whether some foolish devised pasquil by some of his enemies to scare him from his attendance at the Parliament, yet did he, as a most dutiful and loyal subject, conclude not to conceal it, whatever might come of it.

'Whereupon, notwithstanding the lateness and darkness of the night in that season of the year,[2] he presently repaired to his Majesty's

---

[1] At Hoxton. Nothing is said of the curious circumstance that Lord Mounteagle had not visited these 'lodgings' for a long time, and that his sudden determination to go to Hoxton had only been arrived at the day before.

[2] October (late).

palace at Whitehall, and there delivered the same
to the Earl of Salisbury, his Majesty's principal
Secretary.

'Whereupon, the said Earl of Salisbury having
read the letter and having heard the manner of
the coming of it to his hands, did greatly encourage
and commend my Lord for his discretion, telling
him plainly that, whatsoever the purport of the
letter might prove hereafter, yet did this accident
put him in mind of divers advertisements he had
received from beyond the seas, wherewith he had
acquainted, as well as the King himself, as divers
of his privy-counsellors, concerning some business
the Papists were in, both at home and abroad,
making preparations for some combination
amongst them against this Parliament-time, for
enabling them to deliver at that time to the King
some petition for toleration of religion, which
should be delivered in some such order, and so
well backed, as the King should be loth to refuse
their requests; like the sturdy beggars, craving
alms with one open hand, but carrying a stone in
the other, in case of refusal.   And, therefore, did
the Earl of Salisbury conclude with the Lord
Mounteagle, that he would, in regard of the
King's absence, impart the same letter to some
more of his Majesty's Council, whereof my Lord
Monteagle liked well, only adding this request by
protestation.   That whatsoever the event hereof
might prove, it should not be imputed to him as
proceeding from too light and too sudden an
apprehension, that he delivered this letter; being
only moved thereunto for demonstration of his
ready devotion, and care for preservation of his
Majesty and the State.   And thus did the Earl

of Salisbury presently acquaint the Lord Chamberlain with the said letter.

'Whereupon they two, in presence of the Lord Monteagle, calling to mind the former intelligence already mentioned, which seemed to have some relation with this letter ; the tender care which they ever carried to the preservation of his Majesty's person, made them apprehend that some perilous attempt did thereby appear to be intended against the same, which did the more nearly concern the said Lord Chamberlain to have a care of, in regard that it doth belong to the charge of his office to oversee, as well as all places of assembly where his Majesty is to repair, as his Highness's own private houses. And, therefore, did the said two counsellors conclude that they should join unto themselves three more of the council to wit, the Lord Admiral, the Earls of Worcester and Northampton,[1] to be also particularly acquainted with this accident, who having all of them concurred together to the re-examination of the contents of the said letter, they did conclude, that, how slight a matter it might at the first appear to be, yet was it not absolutely to be contemned, in respect of the care which it behoved them to have of the preservation of his Majesty's person ; but, yet resolved for two reasons, first, to acquaint the King himself with the same before they proceeded to any further inquisition in the matter, as well for the expectation and experience they had of his Majesty's fortunate

---

[1] No mention is thus made of the fact that all these noblemen, including the Lord Chamberlain, had been on the premises when the letter arrived.

T

judgment, in clearing and solving obscure riddles and doubtful mysteries;[1] as also, because the more time would, in the meantime, be given for the practice to ripen, if any was, whereby the discovery might be more clear and evident, and the ground of proceeding thereupon more safe, just, and easy.   And so, according to their determination, did the said Earl of Salisbury repair to the King in his gallery upon Friday, being Allhallow's-day, in the afternoon, which was the day after his Majesty's arrival, and none but himself being present with his Highness at that time, where, without any other speech, or judgment given of the letter, but only relating simply the form of the delivery thereof, he presented it to his Majesty.[2]

'The King no sooner read the letter, but after a little pause, and then reading it once again, he delivered his judgment of it in such sort, as he thought it was not to be contemned, for that the style of it seemed to be more quick and pithy, than is usual to be in any pasquil or libel, the superfluities of idle brains. But the Earl of Salisbury, perceiving the King to apprehend it deeplier than he looked for, knowing his nature, told him, that he thought, by one sentence in it, that it was likely to be written by some fool or madman, reading to him this sentence in it: "For the danger is past, as soon as you have burnt the letter;" which, he said, was likely to be the saying of a fool; for, if the danger was passed, so soon as this letter was

---

[1] Referring, perhaps, to the strange conspiracy of the Gowries.
[2] The contents of the letter have been given already.

burnt, then the warning behoved to be of little
avail, when the burning of the letter might make
the danger to be eschewed.   But the King, on
the contrary, considering the former sentence in
the letter " That they should receive a terrible
blow, this Parliament," and yet should not see
who hurt them, joining it to the sentence
immediately following, already alleged, did
thereupon conjecture, that the danger mentioned,
should be some sudden danger by blowing up of
powder ; for no other insurrection, rebellion, or
whatsoever other private and desperate attempt
could be committed, or attempted in time of
Parliament, and the authors thereof unseen,
except only if it were by a blowing up of powder,
which might be performed by one base knave in
à dark corner.

'Whereupon, he was moved to interpret and
construe the latter sentence in the letter, alleged
by the Earl of Salisbury, against all ordinary
sense and construction in grammar, as if by these
words, " For the danger is past," etc., should be
closely understood the suddenness and quickness
of the danger, which should be as quickly
performed and at an end, as that paper should
be a blazing up in the fire ; turning that word of
"as soon " to the sense of " as quickly ; " and
therefore wished, that before his going to the
Parliament, the under-rooms of the Parliament-
house might be well and narrowly searched.

'But, the Earl of Salisbury wondering at this
his Majesty's commentary, which he knew to be
so far contrary to his ordinary and natural
disposition, who did rather ever sin upon the
other side, in not apprehending, nor trusting due

advertisements of practices and perils, when he was truly informed of them, whereby he had many times drawn himself into many desperate dangers; and interpreting rightly this extra-ordinary caution at this time to proceed from the vigilant care he had of the whole State, more than of his own person, which could not but have all perished together, if this designment had succeeded, he thought good to dissemble still unto the King, that there had been any just cause of such apprehension; and ending the purpose with some merry jest upon this subject, as his custom is, took his leave for that time.   But, though he seemed so to neglect it to his Majesty, yet his customable and watchful care of the King and the state still boiling within him, and having, with the Blessed Virgin Mary, laid up in his heart [1] the King's so strange judgment and construction of it, he could not be at rest, till he acquainted the foresaid lords what had passed between the King and him in private.   Whereupon they were all so earnest to renew again the memory of the same purpose to his Majesty, that it was agreed, that he should the next day, being Saturday, repair to his Highness; which he did in the same privy gallery, and renewed the memory thereof, the Lord Chamberlain then being present with the King.

'At which time it was determined, that the said Lord Chamberlain should, according to his custom and office, view all the Parliament-houses, both above and below, and consider what

---

[1] Luke ii. 51 : 'But his mother kept all these sayings in her heart.'

likelihood or appearance of any such danger might possibly be gathered by the sight of them. But, yet, as well for staying of idle rumours, as for being the more able to discern the mystery, the nearer that things were in readiness, his journey thither was ordained to be deferred till the afternoon before the sitting down of the Parliament, which was upon the Monday following. At which time he (according to this conclusion) went to the Parliament-house, accompanied with my Lord Monteagle, being in zeal to the King's service earnest and curious to see the event of that accident, whereof he had the fortune to be the first discoverer; where, having viewed all the lower rooms, he found in the vault, under the upper-house, great store and provision of billets, faggots, and coals; and, inquiring of Whyneard, keeper of the wardrobe, to what use he had put those lower rooms and cellars? He told him, that Thomas Percy had hired both the house, and part of the cellar, or vault, under the same; and that the wood and coal therein were the said gentleman's own provision. Whereupon, the Lord Chamberlain, casting his eye aside, perceived a fellow standing in a corner there, calling himself the said Percy's man, and keeper of the house for him, but indeed was Guido Faukes, the owner of that hand which should have acted that monstrous tragedy.

'The Lord Chamberlain, looking upon all things with a heedful indeed, yet in outful appearance, with but a careless and rackless eye, as became so wise and diligent a Minister, he presently addressed himself to the King in the said privy gallery; where, in the presence of the

Lord Treasurer, the Lord Admiral, the Earls of Worcester, Northampton, and Salisbury, he made his report what he had seen and observed there; noting that Monteagle had told him, that he no sooner heard Thomas Percy named to be the possessor of that house, but considering both his backwardness in religion, and the old dearness of friendship between him and the said Percy,[1] he did greatly suspect the matter, and that the letter should come from him. . The said Lord Chamberlain also told, that he did not wonder a little at the extraordinary great provision of wood and coal in that house, where Thomas Percy had so seldom occasion to remain; as likewise it gave him in his mind, that his man [2] looked a very tall and desperate fellow.

'This could not but increase the King's former apprehension and jealousy; whereupon, he insisted as before, that the house was narrowly to be searched, and that those billets and coals should be searched to the bottom, it being most suspicious that they were laid there only for covering of the powder. Of this same mind also were all the counsellors then present; but upon the fashion of making of the search was it long debated: For, upon the one side, they were all so jealous of the King's safety, that they all agreed that there could not be too much caution used for preventing his danger; and yet, upon the other part, they were all extreme loth and dainty, that in case this letter should prove to be nothing

[1] Monteagle, therefore, seems to have been on as intimate terms with Percy as he was with Catesby and Winter; on more intimate terms, indeed, than I have conjectured above.
[2] Guy Faukes.

but the evaporation of an idle brain, then a curious search being made, and nothing found, should not only turn to the general scandal of the King and the state, as being so suspicious of every light and frivolous toy, but likewise lay an ill-favoured imputation[1] upon the Earl of Northumberland, one of his Majesty's greatest subjects and counsellors, this Thomas Percy being his kinsman and most confident familiar. And the rather were they curious upon this point, knowing how far the King detested to be thought suspicious or jealous of any of his good subjects, though of the meanest degree; and therefore, though they all agreed upon the main ground, which was to provide for the security of the King's person, yet did they much differ in the circumstances, by which this action might be best carried with least din and occasion of slander. But, the King himself still persisting, that there were divers shrewd appearances, and that a narrow search of those places could prejudge no man that was innocent, he at last plainly resolved them, That either must all the parts of those rooms be narrowly searched, and no possibility of danger left unexamined, or else he and they all must resolve not to meddle in it at all, but plainly to go the next day to the Parliament, and leave the success to fortune; which he believed they would be loth to take upon their conscience; for in such a case as this, an half-doing was worse than no doing at all.

   'Whereupon it was at last concluded that

---

[1] This is absurd. So far from shielding Northumberland, it was Lord Salisbury's desire to incriminate him at all costs.

nothing should be left unsearched in those houses ; and yet for the better colour and stay of rumour, in case nothing were found, it was thought meet, that upon a pretence of Whyneard's missing some of the King's stuff, or hangings, which he had in keeping, all those rooms should be narrowly ripped for them. And to this purpose was Sir Thomas Knyvet (a gentleman of his Majesty's privy chamber) employed, being a justice of peace in Westminster, and one, of whose ancient fidelity both the late Queen and our now Sovereign have had large proof; who, according to the trust committed unto him, went about the midnight next after, to the Parliament-house, accompanied with such a small number as was fit for that errand ; but, before his entry in the house, finding Thomas Percy's alleged man [1] standing within the doors, his clothes and boots on, at so dead a time of the night, he resolved to apprehend him ; as he did, and thereafter went forward to the searching of the house, where, after he had caused to be overturned some of the billets and coals, he first found one of the small barrels of powder, and afterwards all the rest, to the number of thirty-six barrels, great and small ; and, thereafter, searching the fellow, whom he had taken, found three matches, and all other instruments fit for blowing up the powder, ready upon him ; which made him instantly confess his own guiltiness ; declaring also unto him, That, if he had happened to be within the house,[2] when he took him, as he was immediately before (at the ending of his work),

[1] Guy Faukes.

[2] This clearly proves that Faukes was *not* taken within the cellar, as generally stated.

he would not have failed to have blown him up, house and all.

'Thus, after Sir Thomas had caused the wretch to be surely bound, and well guarded by the company he had brought with him, he himself returned back to the King's palace, and gave warning of his success to the Lord Chamberlain, and Earl of Salisbury, who immediately warning the rest of the council that lay in the house; as soon as they could get themselves ready, came with their fellow counsellors to the King's bed-chamber, being at that time near four of the clock in the morning. And at the first entry of the King's Chamberlain, the Lord Chamberlain, being not any longer able to conceal his joy for the preventing of so great a danger, told the King in a confused haste that all was found and discovered, and the traitor in hands and fast bound.

'Then, order being first taken for sending for the rest of the Council that lay in the town, the prisoner himself was brought into the house, where in respect of the strangeness of the accident, no man was stayed from the sight, or speaking with him. And, within a while after, the Council did examine him; who seeming to put on a Roman resolution, did, both to the Council, and to every other person that spoke with him that day, appear so constant and settled upon his grounds, as we all thought we had found some new Mutius Scaevola[1] born

---

[1] Caius Mutius Scaevola, who attempted to assassinate King Porsenna.

in England.   For, notwithstanding the horror of
the fact, the guilt of his conscience, his sudden
surprizing, the terror which should have been
struck in him, by coming into the presence of so
grave a Council, and the restless and confused
questions, that every man all that day did vex
him with; yet was his countenance so far from
being dejected, as he often smiled in scornful
manner, not only avowing the fact, but repenting
only with the said Scaevola, his failing in the
execution thereof, whereof he said the devil, and
not God, was the discoverer; answering quickly
to every man's objection, scoffing at any idle
questions which were propounded unto him, and
jesting with such as he thought had no authority
to examine him.   All that day could the Council
get nothing out of him, touching his accomplices,
refusing to answer to any such questions which
he thought might discover the plot, and laying all
the blame upon himself; whereunto, he said, he
was moved, only for religion and conscience' sake,
denying the King to be his lawful sovereign, or
the Annointed of God, in respect he was an
heretic, and giving himself no other name than
John Johnson, servant to Thomas Percy.   But
the next morning being carried to the Tower, he
did not there remain above two or three days,
being twice or thrice, in that space, reexamined,
and the rack only offered and shewed unto him,[1]
when the mark of his Roman fortitude did visibly
begin to wear and slide off his face; and then

---

[1] This cannot be accepted as correct.   By it, we are asked
to believe that Faukes began to confess before being actually
tortured, whereas we know that he refused to utter a word until
constrained by the pain of the punishments of the torture-chamber.

did he begin to confess part of the truth, and, thereafter, to open the whole matter. . . .'

[Here follow the confessions of Faukes and Winter.]

'But here let us leave Faukes in a lodging fit for such a guest, and taking time to advise upon his conscience, and turn ourselves to that part of the history which concerns the fortune of the rest of their partakers in that abominable treason. The news was no sooner spread abroad that morning, which was upon a Tuesday, the fifth of November, and the first day designed for that session of Parliament ; the news, I say, of this so strange and unlooked-for accident was no sooner divulged, but some of those conspirators, namely Winter, and the two brothers of Wright's, thought it high time for them to hasten out of the town (for Catesby was gone the night before, and Percy at four of the clock in the morning the same day of the discovery) and all of them held their course, with more haste than good speed, to Warwickshire, toward Coventry, where the next day morning, being Wednesday, and about the same hour that Faukes was taken in Westminster, one Grant, a gentleman having associated unto him some others of his opinion, all violent Papists, and strong Recusants, came to a stable of one Benocke, a rider of great horses, and having violently broken up the same, carried along with them all the great horses that were therein, to the number of seven or eight, belonging to divers noblemen and gentlemen of that county, who had put them into the rider's hands to be made for their service. And so both that company of

them which fled out of London, as also Grant
and his accomplices, met all together at Dunchurch, at Sir Everard Digby's lodging, the
Tuesday at night, after the discovery of his
treacherous attempt; the which Digby had
likewise, for his part, appointed a match of
hunting, to have been hunted the next day, which
was Wednesday, though his mind was, Nimrod-
like, upon a far other manner of hunting, more
bent upon the blood of reasonable men than
brute beasts.

'This company, and hellish society, thus con-
vened, finding their purpose discovered, and their
treachery prevented, did resolve to run a desperate
course ; and since they could not prevail by so
private a blow, to practice by a public rebellion,
either to attain to their intents, or at least to
save themselves in the throng of others. And,
therefore, gathering all the company they could
unto them, and pretending the quarrel of religion,
having intercepted such provision of armour,
horses, and powder, as the time could permit,
thought, by running up and down the country,
both to augment piece and piece their numbers
(dreaming to themselves, that they had the virtue
of a snowball, which being little at the first, and
tumbling down from a great hill, groweth to a
great quantity, by increasing itself with the snow
that it meeteth by the way), and also, that they
beginning first this brave shew, in one part of the
country, should by their sympathy and example,
stir up and encourage the rest of their religion, in
other parts of England to rise, as they had done
there. But, when they had gathered their force
to the greatest, they came not to the number of

four score, and yet were they troubled, all the hours of the day, to keep and contain their own servants from stealing from them ; who, notwithstanding all their care, daily left them, being far inferior to Gideon's host in numbers, but far more, in faith or justice of quarrel.

'And so, after that this Catholic troop had wandered a while through Warwickshire to Worcestershire, and from thence to the edge and boarders of Staffordshire, this gallantly armed band had not the honour, at the last, to be beaten with a King's lieutenant, or extraordinary commissioner, sent down for that purpose, but only by the ordinary Sheriff of Worcestershire were they all beaten, killed, taken, or dispersed.

'Wherein, ye have to note this following circumstance so admirable, and so lively displaying the greatness of God's justice, as it could not be concealed, without betraying in a manner the glory due to the Almighty for the same.

'Although divers of the King's proclamations were posted down after these traitors with all the speed possible, declaring the odiousness of that bloody attempt, the necessity to have had Percy preserved alive, if it had been possible,[1] and the assembly together of that rightly damned crew, now no more darkened conspirators, but open and avowed rebels ; yet the far distance of the way, which was above 100 miles, together with the extreme deepness thereof, joined also with the shortness of the day, was the cause that the hearty and the loving affections of the King's good

---

[1] Here, again, we have absolute evidence of the absurdity of the Jesuit story that Percy was killed by order of Lord Salisbury.

subjects in those parts prevented the speed of his proclamations. For, upon the third day after the flying down of these rebels, which was upon the Friday next after the discovery of their plot, they were most of them all surprised by the Sheriff of Worcestershire, at Holbeach, about the noon of the day, and that in the manner following.

'Grant, of whom I have made mention before, for taking the great horses, who had not all the preceding time stirred from his own house till the next morning after the attempt should have been put in execution ; he then laying his accounts without his host, as the proverb is, that their plot had, without failing, received the day before their hoped-for success ; took, or rather stole, out those horses, as I said before, for enabling him, and so many of that foulest society, that had still remained in the country near about him, to make a sudden surprise upon the King's elder daughter, the Lady Elizabeth, having her residence near by that place, whom they thought to have used for the colour of their treacherous design, his Majesty, her father, her mother, and male children being all destroyed above, and to this purpose also had that Nimrod, Digby, provided his hunting-match against that same time, that numbers of people being flocked together, upon the pretence thereof, they might the easier have brought to pass the sudden surprise of the person.

'Now the violent taking away of those horses, long before day, did seem to be so great a riot in the eyes of the common people that knew of no greater mystery. And the bold attempting thereof did engender such a suspicion of some following rebellion in the hearts of the wiser sort,

as both great and small began to stir and arm
themselves upon this unlooked for accident. But,
before twelve or sixteen hours passed, Catesby,
Percy, the Winters, Wrights, Rookewood, and
the rest, bringing then the assurance that their
main plot was failed and bewrayed, whereupon
they had built the golden mountain of their
glorious hopes; they then took their last desperate resolution, to flock together in a troop, and
wander, as they did, for the reasons aforetold.
But, as upon the one part, the zealous duty to
their God, and their Sovereign, was so deeply
imprinted in the hearts of all the meanest and
poorest sort of the people, although then knowing
of no further mystery than such public mis-
behaviours, as their own eyes taught them, as
notwithstanding of their fair shews and pretences
of their Catholic cause, no creature, man, or
woman, through all the country would once so
much as give them, willingly, a cup of drink,
or any sort of comfort or support, but with
execrations detested them, so, on the other
part, the sheriffs of the shires, through which
they wandered, conveying their people with
all speed possible, hunted as hotly after them,
as the evilness of the way, and the unprovided-
ness of their people upon that sudden could
permit them. And so, at last, after Sir Richard
Verney, Sheriff of Warwickshire, had carefully
and straightly been in chase of them to the
confines of his county, part of the meaner sort
being also apprehended by him; Sir Richard
Walsh, Sheriff of Worcestershire, did likewise
dutifully and hotly pursue them through his
shire: and, having gotten sure trial of their

taking harbour at the house above-named, he did send trumpeters and messengers unto them, commanding them in the King's name, to render unto him his Majesty's Minister; and knowing no more at that time, of their guilt, than was publicly visible,[1] did promise, upon their dutiful and obedient rendering unto him, to intercede at the King's hands, for the sparing of their lives; who received only from them this scornful answer, they being better witnesses to themselves of their inward evil consciences, "That he had need of better assistance, than of those few numbers that were with him before he could be able to command or control them."

'But here fell the wondrous work of God's justice, that while this message passed between the Sheriff and them, the Sheriff's and his people's hearts being justly kindled and augmented by their arrogant answer; and so, they preparing themselves to give a furious assault, and the other party making themselves ready within the house to perform their promise by a defence as resolute; it pleased God that in the mending of the fire, in their chamber, one small spark should fly out, and light among less than two-pound weight of powder, which, was drying a little from the chimney; which, being thereby blown up, so maimed the faces of some of the principal rebels and the hands and sides of others of them, blowing up with it also a great bag of powder, which, notwithstanding, never took fire, as they were not only disabled and discouraged thereby from any

---

[1] The accuracy of this statement is, certainly, open to very grave doubt. Walsh must have known of what the conspirators were guilty.

further resistance, in respect Catesby himself, Rookewood, Grant, and divers others of greatest account among them were, thereby, made unable for defence, but also wonderfully struck with amazement in their guilty consciences, calling to memory how God had justly punished them with the same instrument, which they should have used for the effectuating of so great a sin, according to the old Latin saying, *In quo peccemus, in eodem plectimur;* as they presently (see the wonderful power of God's justice upon guilty consciences) did all fall down upon their knees, praying God to pardon them for their bloody enterprise; and, thereafter, giving over any further debate, opened[1] the gate, suffered the Sheriff's people to rush in furiously among them, and desperately sought their own present destruction: the three specials of them joining backs together, Catesby, Percy, and Winter, whereof two, with one shot, Catesby and Percy, were slain,[2] and the third, Winter,[3] taken and saved alive.'

[1] This is most unlikely to have been the case.

[2] Percy was not killed at Holbeach. He died of his wounds later.

[3] Thomas Winter.

U

INDEX

Abbott, Dr. Robert, on Garnet, 173
Abercromby, Father, tradition about, 19
Abington, Mrs. Mary, not the author of the Mounteagle letter, 204
    her connection with the Plot, 275
Abington, Thomas, history of, 142 *sq.*
    innocence of, 237
Ainsworth, 83
Alrington, Mrs., 73
Andrew, Sir Euseby, letter of, 89 *sq.*
Anne of Denmark, her religion, 19
Apologia of Father Greenway, 8
Ashby St. Legers, 30
Ashley, R., Death of, 243 *n.*
Aubrey on Sir E. Digby, 118 *n.*

Baldwin, Father, his knowledge of the Plot, 244
Barlow, Bishop T., 120 *n.*
Barnet, rebel meeting at, 78
Bates, Thomas, confession of, 9
    joins the Plot, 46
    why chosen, 58
    his desertion, 85, 92 *n.*
    examination of, 110
    answer of, 117
Bath, rebel meeting at, 69 *n*, 211
Baynham, Sir Edward, 166
Bibliographical Dictionary of English Catholics, 30 *n.*

Birkhead, George, action of, 199
Blackwell, Mr. George, conduct of, 131 *n.*
    advice of, 199, 202
Braddocks, escape from, 253 *n.*
Breves from Rome, 156
Bright, Dr. F., on Garnet's perjury, 180
Bromley, Sir Henry, at Hendlip, 100, 144 *sq.*
    letter of, to Salisbury, 147
Brooksby, Mrs., 155
Burnaby, Sir Thomas, letter of, 89 *sq.*
Burton, Captain, letter of, 259
'Bye Plot,' the, 24

Castleton, sale of, 30
Catesby, Robert, a rebel, 17
    social position of, 18, 23 *n.*
    originator of the Plot, 26
    character of, 27
    family of, 28
    estate of, 29
    bigotry of, 29
    is fined, 30
    motives of, 30
    influence of, 31
    flight of, 82
    his march to Wales, 83
    prayers of, 92
    death of, 93
Catesby, William, couplet about, 28
Cecil. *See* Salisbury
Chambers, George, 144 *n.*

Gardiner, Dr. S. R., on Holbeach explosion, 93 *n.*
  on Digby letters, 135
  on Garnet's perjury, 179
  on tricks of Government, 182
  on Tresham being author of letter, 206
  on Greenway's knowledge of the Plot, 249 *n.*

Garnet, Father Henry, his knowledge of the Plot, 6
  character of, 7
  letter of, 18 *n*
  aliases of, 22
  his complaint against Catesby, 27
  at Coughton, 84
  capture of, 99
  death of, 100
  equivocation of, 105
  peril of, 141
  goes to Hendlip, 141
  his story of his surrender, 148 *sq.*
  story of his journey, 151
  in prison in the Tower, 153
  drunkenness of, 153 *n.*
  examination of, 154 *sq.*
  confession of, 155 *sq.*
  perjury of, 157
  Government trick to obtain evidence from, 158
  letters of, 159
  his conversations with Oldcorne, 159 *sq.*
  trial of, 162 *sq.*
  indictment of, 163
  sentence on, 166
  death of, 167
  personal appearance of, 172
  history of, 173 *sq.*
  was he guilty ? 176 *sq.*
  his lying, 178
  criticisms of, 179 *sq.*
  charges against, 183
  on fears of Anne Vaux, 273 *sq.*
  his connection with the letter of warning, 276 *sq.*

Gerard, Father John, character of, 21
  aliases of, 22
  on Faukes, 39
  on Percy, 40
  on C. Wright, 46
  he did not know of the Plot, 102
  on Digby, 140
  his connection with the Plot, 252 *sq.*
  on Grant, 17
  on N. Owen, 142
  on Sir H. Bromley, 145

Gillow, 30

Goodman on authorship of warning letter, 206 *n.*

Gotch, Mr. A., 56

Gower, Lord Ronald, on Ralegh, 255 *n.*

Grant, John, conduct of, 17
  character of, 47
  why chosen, 57
  taken to the Tower, 94
  answer of, 117

Great Harrowden, a hiding-place, 253 *n.*

Green, J. R., on Garnet's perjury, 179

Greenway, Father Oswald, his knowledge of the Plot, 7
  Apologia of, 8
  aliases of, 23
  on Percy, 42 *n.*
  at Huddington, 84
  treason of, 111
  his connection with the Plot, 247

Groome, Christiana, 45

Groome, Thomas, 45

Gunpowder Treason, 120 *n.*

Guy Fawkes, 83 *n.*

HAGLEY HOUSE, rebels at, 98, 262

Hallam, on capture of Garnet, 100 *n.*
  on perjury of Garnet, 180

THE END

PRINTED BY WILLIAM CLOWES AND SONS, LIMITED, LONDON AND BECCLES.

The Anti-Papal Library.

ROADS FROM ROME. A Series of Personal Narratives.

Compiled by Rev. CHARLES S. ISAACSON, M.A., Rector of Hardingham, Norfolk. With a Preface by the Right Rev. HANDLEY C. G. MOULE, D.D., Bishop of Durham. Crown 8vo, cloth gilt, 2s. 6d.

The English Churchman says :—"It is a timely volume—a counter-blast to the somewhat boastful advertisement of perverts to Rome, issued about a year ago under the auspices of Cardinal Vaughan, entitled 'Roads to Rome.'"

The Protestant Observer says :—"We cordially recommend this intensely interesting and most useful volume."

The Church of Ireland Gazette says :—"It is very effective for our controversy with Rome."

The Record says :—"This is indeed an informing book."

The Protestant Churchman says :—"We heartily recommend the volume. It is one which might be left on drawing-room or parlour tables to be perused by visitors."

The Life of Faith says :—"Many a bewildered soul will be mercifully guided and assisted by these testimonies."

The Church Family Newspaper says :—"We commend a study of this volume to those who have been captivated by extreme ritual."

ROME IN MANY LANDS. A Survey of the Roman Catholic Church, with an account of some modern Roman developments.

Compiled and Edited by the Rev. CHARLES S. ISAACSON, M.A., Editor of "Roads from Rome." Crown 8vo, cloth gilt, 2s. 6d.

The Times says :—"It undertakes to give an account of Rome's distortions of Christian doctrine due to hallucinations or over-subtlety."

The British Weekly says :—"The book is rich in facts, and is written from the standpoint of an impartial inquirer."

The Record says :—"No more startling revelations of the present-day position of Rome in many lands has yet appeared."

The Athenæum says :—"Its information is free from that inaccuracy which is often the mark of controversial works on religion."

The Methodist Recorder says :—"It is a powerful indictment of Papal Policy."

The Protestant Standard says :—"It is most ably written and deeply interesting."

EVANGELICAL BELIEF: Its Conflict with Rome.

By JOHN BROADHURST NICHOLS. Second and Cheaper Edition, Revised, with Preface by R. F. HORTON, M.A., D.D. Crown 8vo, cloth gilt, 2s. 6d.

The Expository Times says :—"It is the work of a scholar and a writer. Its subject has been hotly contested and thoroughly sifted of late ; and yet Mr. Nichols is neither partisan nor stale. His exposition of 'Justification by Faith' is a theological contribution of striking value. His faith in the Evangelical religion is as strong as his grasp of its meaning. For our part this is the book we recommend—not the polemical, but the expository—in the present crisis."

THE HOMES AND HAUNTS OF LUTHER.

By JOHN STOUGHTON, D.D. Third Edition, Thoroughly Revised by C. H. IRWIN, M.A. With Eleven Illustrations. Crown 8vo, cloth gilt, 2s. 6d.

Several new Illustrations are included in this Third Edition, including a reproduction of a very rare portrait of Luther by Cranach. The Reviser's notes contain a considerable amount of new material, especially in regard to Wittenberg and its historic Castle and Church.

A Striking Series of Personal Narratives.

ROADS TO CHRIST.

Compiled and Edited by Rev. CHARLES S. ISAACSON, M.A., compiler of "Roads from Rome," etc. With contributions by the BISHOP OF DURHAM, Canon HAY AITKEN, the Rev. F. S. WEBSTER, Preb. FOX, Dr. TORREY, and others. Large crown 8vo, cloth gilt, 3s. 6d.

In this volume, Mr. Isaacson has brought together a striking series of narratives detailing the conversion and spiritual history of men of various nations, in many ranks of society, and of strongly contrasted character. **Some of these, like the Bishop of Durham, Prebendary Webb-Peploe, Sir Robert Anderson, and the Rev. F. S. Webster, tell their own stories.** The spiritual histories of a group which includes men so varied as the Seventh Earl of Shaftesbury, Sir Arthur Blackwood, Sir Henry Havelock, Bishop Daniel Wilson, the Rev. C. H. Spurgeon, and Mr. D. L. Moody, form the contents of Part II. In Part III. we have set before us the varied paths by which men were led out of the Church of Rome, from Non-Christian religions, and from Atheism, into the faith of Jesus Christ.

The Record says :—" Mr. Isaacson has done his work well, and merits our gratitude for so truly valuable and attractive a book. We would say to all Christian workers, Get it, read it, lend it, and use it in your own work. ' A blessing is in it,' and we should not be surprised if it proves to be one of the most fruitful of all the fruitful publications issued by the Religious Tract Society."

"Champions of the Truth" Series.

1. CHAMPIONS OF THE TRUTH. Short Lives of Christian Leaders in Thought and Action by various Writers.

Edited by A. R. BUCKLAND, M.A. With Portraits. Crown 8vo, cloth gilt, **3s. 6d.**

The Academy says:—"Here are pen portraits of eighteen Evangelical teachers, beginning with Wycliffe and ending with Spurgeon. It need hardly be said, perhaps, that their eighteen biographers treat them from about the same point of view. The admirable thing is that, though that point of view is one with which a given reader may not be so fortunate as to find himself in sympathy, it is one which has the advantage of showing the subject of the biography at his best. A very pleasant volume, and the more to be valued for the sake of its fifteen portraits."

2. HUGH LATIMER.

By ROBERT DEMAUS, M.A., Author of "William Tindale," etc. Popular Edition. With a Portrait. Large crown 8vo, cloth gilt, **3s. 6d.**

The First Edition of this work was published by the Society in 1869, but so careful was the Author in his method and research that it still ranks as the **standard life of the Great Reformer.**

3. WILLIAM TINDALE.

A Biography. By ROBERT DEMAUS, M.A. Popular Edition. Revised by RICHARD LOVETT, M.A. With 11 Illustrations. Large crown 8vo, cloth gilt, **3s. 6d.**

The high estimation in which Demaus's "William Tindale" is held by students of the history of the English Bible is a proof of the sterling value of the work. Demaus wrote out of a full knowledge, and his task was a labour of love. Hence it was but natural that the book should at once become the standard authority on the subject, which it is now admitted on all hands to be.

4. JOHN WYCLIFFE AND HIS ENGLISH PRECURSORS.

By Professor LECHLER, D.D. Translated by PETER LORIMER, D.D. Popular Edition, carefully revised. With 7 Portraits and Illustrations. Cloth gilt, **3s. 6d.**

The Times says:—"The importance of the biography cannot be over-estimated, especially as the author had the immense advantage of free and leisurely access to the valuable Wycliffe manuscripts of the Imperial Library of Vienna."

PROTESTANT PUBLICATIONS OF THE RELIGIOUS TRACT SOCIETY.

THE WRITINGS OF ST. PATRICK. The Apostle of Ireland.

A revised translation with notes, critical and historical. By Dr. C. H. H. WRIGHT. Fcap. 8vo, cloth, 2s. Cheap Edition Crown 8vo, paper covers, 3d.

ROMAN CLAIMS AND BIBLE WARRANTS; or, "Which Way."

By E. JANE WHATELY. Fcap. 8vo, cloth gilt, 1s. 6d.

Miss Whately's treatise, hitherto issued under the title of "Which Way?" deals with the claims made by Roman Catholicism, and shows how they conflict with the teaching of the Word of God.

THE PAPAL ATTEMPT TO RE-CONVERT ENGLAND.

By One born and nurtured in Roman Catholicism. Crown 8vo, cloth, 1s. 6d.

This book contrasts sharply the claims of the Roman Catholic Church to be the only true and infallible Church with its past history and teaching. It shows that judged by its fruits in the ages that are gone these claims are audacious and untrue; and that the Catholic Truth Society of to-day seeks to win over the English people by discreetly ignoring the past.

A PRIMER OF ROMAN CATHOLICISM: or, The Doctrines of the Church of Rome Briefly Examined in the Light of Scripture.

By the Rev. CHARLES H. H. WRIGHT, D.D. With Illustrations and a Facsimile of a Tetzel Indulgence. Fcap. 8vo, cloth, 1s.

The British Weekly says :—"This is a remarkably useful book."

The Saturday Review says :—"Dr. Wright puts the extreme Protestant views with less than the usual malice, and more than the usual knowledge."

The Christian World says :—"It is the best text-book for Protestant classes that we have seen."

THE MASS IN THE GREEK & ROMAN CHURCHES.

By the Rev. C. H. H. WRIGHT, D.D. With Illustrations. Crown 8vo, limp cloth, 1s., or in paper covers, 8d.

Dr. Wright gives in a compact form a full and clear account of the ceremony of the Mass in the Greek and Roman Churches. He shows what the different parts of the service are intended to symbolise. He contrasts it with the simple words of the New Testament, and shows how far both Churches have wandered from the true observance and meaning of the Lord's Supper.

INTERESTING STORIES

Illustrating the Evils of Romanism.

BY DEBORAH ALCOCK.

DR. ADRIAN. A Story of Old Holland.

By DEBORAH ALCOCK. With many Illustrations. Large crown 8vo, cloth gilt, 6s.

The Guardian says:—"It is a thoroughly well-written and interesting story, true to history, and well studied in the details. The book is a really good illustration of history."

The Christian World says:—"From beginning to end the story is vividly interesting."

UNDER CALVIN'S SPELL.

By DEBORAH ALCOCK. With Fifteen Illustrations by J. SCHONBERG. Large crown 8vo, cloth gilt, 3s. 6d.

The St. James's Gazette says:—"It is an interesting picture of the most successful attempt at theocracy since the days of Moses."

The Record says:—"It is a thrilling story."

THE KING'S SERVICE. A Story of the Thirty Years' War.

By DEBORAH ALCOCK. Illustrated. Crown 8vo, gilt edges, cloth, 3s. 6d.

THE FRIENDS OF PASCAL; or, The Children of Port Royal. A Story of Old France.

By DEBORAH ALCOCK. With Illustrations. Crown 8vo, cloth boards, 3s. 6d.

The Guardian says:—"It is an exceedingly well-studied tale. Well worth reading."

CRUSHED, YET CONQUERING. A Story of Constance and Bohemia.

By DEBORAH ALCOCK. New Edition. With Seven Illustrations. Crown 8vo, cloth gilt, 3s. 6d.

PRISONERS OF HOPE.

By DEBORAH ALCOCK. Illustrated. Crown 8vo, cloth gilt, 1s.

THE WELL IN THE ORCHARD.

By DEBORAH ALCOCK. Illustrated. Crown 8vo, cloth gilt, 1s.

"For Faith and Freedom" Series.

Illustrated. Large Crown 8vo. Cloth gilt, **2s.** *each.*

1. PETER THE APPRENTICE. A Tale of the Reformation in England.
   By EMMA LESLIE. 2s.

2. FOR THE SAKE OF A CROWN. A Tale of the Netherlands.
   By Mrs. FREDERICK WEST. 2s.

3. DEARER THAN LIFE. A Story of the Times of Wycliffe.
   By EMMA LESLIE. 2s.

4. HID IN THE CEVENNES; or, The Mountain Refuge.
   By BLANCHE M. MOGGRIDGE. 2s.

5. THE SHADOW ON THE HEARTH.
   By Rev. T. S. MILLINGTON. 2s.

6. UNDER THE INQUISITION.
   By E. H. WALSHE. 2s.

7. IN A JESUIT NET. A Story of the Time of Louis XIV.
   By H. C. COAPE. 2s.

8. THE ADVENTURES OF HANS MULLER.
   By ALICE LANG. 2s.

"Led to the Light" Series.

Crown 8vo, 192 *pages and upwards.* **1s. 6d.** *cloth gilt.*

1. NOT PEACE, BUT A SWORD.
   By G. ROBERT WYNNE, D.D., Archdeacon of Aghadoe.
   With Three Illustrations. 1s. 6d.

2. GLAUCIA, THE GREEK SLAVE.
   By EMMA LESLIE. 1s. 6d.

Lightning Source UK Ltd.
Milton Keynes UK
UKOW05n0608200117

292472UK00010B/84/P

9 781355 855125